6040764

FILM

An Introduction

FILM

An Introduction

John L. Fell

PRAEGER PUBLISHERS
New York

Published in the United States of America in 1975
by Praeger Publishers, Inc.
111 Fourth Avenue, New York, N.Y. 10003

Library of Congress Cataloging in Publication Data

Fell, John L   1927–
    Film: an introduction.

    Bibliography: p.
    Includes index.
    1. Moving pictures.   I. Title.
PN1994.F38   791.43   73-18865
ISBN 0-275-50950-8
ISBN 0-275-89110-0 pbk.

Printed in the United States of America

This Book Is Dedicated
To My Mother and
To the Memory of My Father

Acknowledgments

Special thanks are due here to those people who provided the family shelter while I typed, who sought out pictures, and who chased down little facts. In the first instance Eleanor, Herbert, and Marguerite Kirk graciously made available a handsome farmhouse overlooking Montana's beautiful Gallatin Valley. There is special pleasure in acknowledging the assistance of Terry Sheehy. She sought out elusive stills and, even more to the point, copied off significant frames from the films themselves when this was possible. Thanks also to artist Alex N. Niño and his agent Orvy Jundis; Will Eisner; John H. Door of the Academy of Motion Picture Arts and Sciences; and Tom Johnston, Gary Bush, and John Boundy of the National Film Board. For assistance in locating distributor credits, thanks to Vicki Loustalot. Finally, I am especially appreciative of the help of Denise Rathbun and Steven Frankel, editors extraordinary, who encountered my excesses with professional candor and my truculence with personal forbearance.

Contents

Introduction   ix

PART I. Understanding Film
  1. Film and Ourselves   3
  2. Film and Other Media   28
      Recommended Reading   52
      Notes   53

PART II. Film Elements
  3. Space and Time   57
  4. The Impact of Editing and Sound   82
  5. Color   98
  6. Point of View   103
  7. Genre   116
      Recommended Reading   122
      Notes   123

PART III. How Films Are Made
  8. Conceptualization   127
  9. Direction   134
  10. Visualization   142
  11. Performance   152
  12. Editing   161
  13. Special Effects   168

14. Production   173
    Recommended Reading   178
    Notes   179

PART IV. Film Theory and Criticism
15. Reviewers and Critics   183
16. Getting at the Film Experience   188
17. Theorists   193
18. *Auteur* Criticism   200
19. Structuralism and Semiology   216
    Recommended Reading   222
    Notes   223

PART V. Film and the Future
20. The Shape of Films to Come   227
    Recommended Reading   249
    Notes   250

Appendix A: A Selected List of American Film Reference Publications 251
Appendix B: A Selected List of English-Language Film Periodicals 253
Appendix C: Film Study in the United States   255
Appendix D: 16mm Film Distribution Sources   257
Appendix E: Distributors   259

Index of Film Titles   263
General Index   267

Introduction

Film history is just beginning to outdistance the life span of any man. As written records replace memory, there has developed a body of critical speculation and argument with regard to the traditions and achievements of the narrative (or "story") film. The questions of just what any particular film accomplished and how its effects were achieved increasingly become matters of general public interest.

Such speculations characterize what has usually been regarded as academically legitimate. They also create a certain tension by making us feel a contradiction between what we study and what we enjoy. This contrast is especially marked in film because movies debuted as a very light-hearted scientific curiosity, another of Thomas Edison's marvels. In the early period they vied for audience attention with singers, comedians, and conjurers in the music halls. When film finally drove out the live competition, the reflected, moving shadows in no way compromised their impulse to entertain. Rather, they triumphed because they entertained better than the competition. Whatever its other motives, commercial film has always tried above all to be "fun."

Somehow, whatever occupies the attention of large audiences is likely to appear eventually in the schools—a little late, a little polished up, and fitted out for pupil consumption. Our first problem, then, is one of reconciling the entertainment movie to this new setting without doing an injustice to either element. Since the 1960's, the study of movies has made impressive inroads in American high school and college curriculums, a mixed blessing for everyone, and for film too. Once viewed with suspicion by teachers of English, drama, and art, film has become instead their ally and sometimes has displaced earlier academic loyalties. Students of film—instructors included—nurse secret satisfaction at seeming to linger over something so pleasurable, but beneath the apparent joys of film study, a danger attends all this success: that with the acceptance of film as a legitimate field of study, film as a source of delight may be obscured by too much analysis and verbiage. Lusting for respectability, the teacher who uses film not as audio-visual aid but as primary source increasingly seems to run the risk of academic overkill by seeking to standardize responses with aesthetic yardsticks.

A further peril is the disposition of some people to miss through ignorance or naïveté what actually happens or fails to happen on the screen and instead to indulge in involuted analyses that, however self-satisfying, ignore the realities of film production. For example, pages of conjecture were devoted to explaining Lea Massari's disappearance in the early reels of Michelangelo Antonioni's *L'Avventura* (1959).* Naturally, her replacement by Monica Vitti in the affections of Gabriele Ferzetti was central to the story. At the same time, it was a matter of record that Ms. Massari had a very short-term contract with the production, which limited how and how much Antonioni could use her in the film.

Between the extremes of experiencing movies for enjoyment alone and studying them to death lie two other approaches. As film study has gained curricular autonomy, some teachers and writers have argued persuasively for considering movies as an altogether unique medium. This approach would have us develop a critical vocabulary exclusively for film and construct a body of criticism that enriches our responses to new films by drawing on the analyses of old ones, independent of other media and of the social and economic pressures of production and distribution.

The other approach—and this is the premise of this book—suggests that the character, design, and substance of movies can be understood more effectively in a broad context than in a narrow one. By "broad context" we refer to the several realms of experience (financial and social, but even more important, psychological and cultural) that overlap the movie image, however faintly.

Central to the dichotomy presented here is a distinction (often unexpressed) between the "good" and the "popular": Does a large audience add to a film's "importance," or does it keep a film from having any success greater than a large financial return? Clearly, one main thrust of film's heritage has been its relation to a base of popular (that is, mass) support and enthusiasm—in part because of its origins purely as mass entertain-

* Each film title noted in the text is given a release date on its first citation. The 16mm distribution sources have been compiled in the title index. The name of an actor will be used interchangeably with his or her script name while discussing performance, where such usage seems appropriate and not misleading.

ment, in part because the conception, production, and exploitation of any movie is so very expensive.

Nomenclature encapsulates the problem. The polysyllabic Greek and Latin words that were first used in creating names for projection and camera equipment at the turn of the century—for example, the Kinetograph and Vitascope—were replaced soon afterwards by practical American slang—the *moving picture* or *movies* (*motion pictures* for the more genteel). The *kine* (moving) part of the invention journeyed through Europe and returned as *cinema*. Even today, what some tastes savor as admirable, especially artful, or refined will be praised as *cinema* or *cinematic,* carrying with it a particular overtone of European sophistication. In any case, we shall stay with the more-or-less neutral term *film* (leaning sometimes toward *movies,* but shunning *flicks*) as much as possible, except where repetition becomes irksome.

Of course, film, like every medium, has qualities unique to itself, and many of its effects on an audience cannot be accomplished in any other medium. A duel or the simulation of sex on the stage is different when translated to film. A light show comes through more modified and "distanced" by film projection than it does "live." Seeing the movie version of *Slaughterhouse-Five* (1972) provides an experience that is quite different from Kurt Vonnegut, Jr.'s novel. The music we may hear from loudspeakers before the lights dim in a theater would not sound the same if we were also viewing filmed images.

Such special attributes of film, the uniquenesses both of the image itself and of the circumstances under which it is experienced, are rarely introspected by an audience. A shrewd filmmaker, however, will take advantage of this. Likely, he shares many of the viewers' predispositions, intuitively or else quite consciously. The conventions of narrative form provide the bases for communication between filmmaker and audience. These conventions also challenge the filmmaker's capacities to operate creatively within orthodoxies that contribute to film's popularity.

Among the lowest of common denominators are the inevitable shootouts along dusty Western streets on Hollywood backlots or at Cinecittà in Italy; these are noisy evidence of basic mental and emotional lethargy. The French director François Truffaut once said that he tried to construct his feature films like a baseball game or a circus so that the audience could take a seventh-inning stretch, even go to the bathroom or buy popcorn in the lobby, without missing the thread of his story. This reflects broad comprehension of an audience's capacities to concentrate, to sit still. Harry Cohn demonstrates the same understanding in his remark that, as president of Columbia Pictures, he measured the success of a new production by whether his fanny itched while he was watching it.

An artist of different inclination may put these dispositions to other use. He can, like Andy Warhol, experiment with the expectations of narrative progression by slowing down his exposition to a frustrating snail's pace, asking only half in jest that we watch a performer eat fruit while he stares at the camera, talk on and on about nothing, or even sleep, while we try to decide what it is we're supposed to be *seeing*. (See *Sleep* [1964].)

Somewhat more orthodox is the approach Antonioni undertook in the island scenes of *L'Avventura* and the last sequence of *L'Eclisse* (1962), in which he counterposed the "real time" of an event against our anticipations of a different "screen time," which is customarily either truncated for dramatic economy or elongated to stretch out the experienced moment. The resulting tension, between what we expect to "happen," and what really does (or doesn't) happen, served Antonioni's interest in showing human alienation as he manipulated our moment-to-moment feelings. But this is not a device unique to the movies. We find it in the theater, in prose, in much lyric poetry and jazz, and during the battles of superheroes in Marvel Comics.

The study of film, then, cannot be divorced from the culture in which film was nurtured, from the circumstances of its production, and from the requirements imposed by its audience. These are certain *givens*, just as we expand our sensitivities to the works of, say, nineteenth-century novelists by learning about the society from which they came, how they viewed the world, and whom they wrote for.

At the start, we ought to clarify the frames of reference that encompass this study and the meanings of certain terms that, because of their other usages, might be confusing—film, narrative, popular, and commercial.

Film. As a generic expression, *film* can legitimately cover everything from children's animation on Saturday morning television (a good way to study audience expectations, by the way) to Super-8 home movies, from after-the-fact news résumés to short productions by university film majors. The concept of film as a particular, physical medium—that is, cellulose acetate running through a motion picture camera and then a motion picture projector—has been broadened by television electronics and the advent of videotape equipment, including portable outfits. The present study proposes that there exists a particular vision to which we generally attach the name *film*, but which may apply equally to different physical media as diverse as tape, comics, and print. It is a particular way of seeing events transpire and of affecting the character of an audience's perceptions toward those events. This is not to say that other forms, television included, do not differ from the motion picture as well. But in any case, film cannot be defined adequately by way of technological description.

Here, what we mean by *film* is more exclusive: narrative—that is, story—features usually made for theatrical viewing. (This is not *always* the case. "Films for Television" are quite literally theatrical ventures given a different form of distribution.) Where reference is made to other film "forms," we will try to identify their intentions and to relate them to the story film.

Narrative. As used here this term refers to that mainstream of tradition dating back to a group of skin-clad men, women, and children gathered around a campfire, listening to one among them—the person who had learned to sustain the interest of his fellows by expanding the exciting parts of his tale, overlapping different portions so it would *move along,* and letting his audience know *why* each character felt an urge to act the way he did. In *Aspects of the Novel,* E. M. Forster said that the most basic, the primordial essence of *story* is that sense of "and then . . . and then . . ." with which listener confronts tale-teller, and which the tale-teller understands and uses to hold his group in anticipatory thrall. (Ambrose Bierce said that there was another singular figure squatting at that early campfire, sitting a little apart from the rest. When the story was over and after there had been an appreciative murmur of praise, this man turned to his neighbor and muttered, "This time he changed the part where the guy met the bear in the cave, and it didn't sound as exciting the new way because . . ." The first critic.)

Popular. Derived from a Latin word meaning "of the people," *popular* is embedded in the heritage of the story film. In one of the earliest documentations of the Nickelodeon operation, a storefront proprietor told a *Saturday Evening Post* writer that "the people want stories." He said audiences were no longer satisfied with fragmented clips of incidents. If there was a horse race, there should be someone in the stands whose future depended vitally on the running. If a baserunner slid into third, we should know enough about him to feel for or against the play. And so forth.

As film evaluation has itself established enough of its own popular base to warrant articles, periodicals, and books (like this one), the question of what films shall be thought praiseworthy may be at odds with what has proved successful in the marketplace. To put it another way, the critic at the primeval fire begins to distinguish his own sensibility from that of his peers. In doing so, he is required to explain himself.

The history of film criticism is young enough that well-regarded film-makers continue to teeter on the slippery precipice of reputation. At various times, those directors judged especially worthy of commendation have been men and women who drew most heavily on more secure traditions like drama and literature for their materials. In more recent years, the Europeans (and occasional Americans) who could be identified in terms of ideological contexts—religious or philosophical or artistic—have been much admired.

A countermovement heralds the popular for its popularity. The prospectus of the *Journal of Popular Film* advises its readers that "rather than stand in awe of the personal beliefs of Bergman, Antonioni, or Fellini, the *Journal* intends to explore the public visions of John Ford, Frank Capra, Arthur Penn and all of the many others. The purpose is to present material which treats films because of their popularity, not in spite of it." Such an approach is likely to consider movies not so much in terms of formal accomplishments or the individuality of their ideas, but rather as reflections of the cultural inclinations of their audience. The movies as mirror.

To admit to the popularity of a form and yet ignore the consequences of that popularity (what the audience sees of or learns about itself in the experience) would be foolish. However, a paramount interest of the present study is the consideration of film as an event that differs from the world "outside." In consequence, we are inclined to think of the culture as contributing to our understanding of the movie and not the reverse. Underlying such an approach is the premise that each film poses, at least potentially, its own particular problems—that is, it asks its own special questions of the world and of itself. This in turn means that what we regard as interesting about a film is, ultimately, how it resolves self-imposed challenges.

By this measure, we are neither in awe of Bergman, Antonioni, and Fellini (to whom the *Journal of Popular Film* awards one-name status like Raphael and Michelangelo, tongue-in-cheek), nor are we condescending toward Ford, Capra, or Penn. Each undertakes a common problem: proposing a set of ideas or concepts that externalize his individual vision, whether that vision is shared or private, about the nature of the world we inhabit, including its inner space. These propositions are made in the language of a public medium, the movies, and they are worked out with the resources of that form. (Such a critical posture is hardly original. Matthew Arnold, for example, proposed it as the way we ought to approach a poem.)

Commercial. A word that is neither pejorative nor flattering, it describes the conditions under which almost all story motion pictures are made. The fact that films cost extraordinary sums of money has much to do with the character they assume.

Now that our nomenclature has been established, we are in position to proceed. By the end of the book, each reader would do well to ask himself just how effectively the definitions operate, that is, how comfortably different movie approaches live together. We refer to such qualities as the crass and the cultivated, direct and oblique appeals; busy, complex pictures and slow, staid ones. All these impulses merge historically in the tradition of popular, commercial, narrative film, but they rarely attract a common audience with equal power.

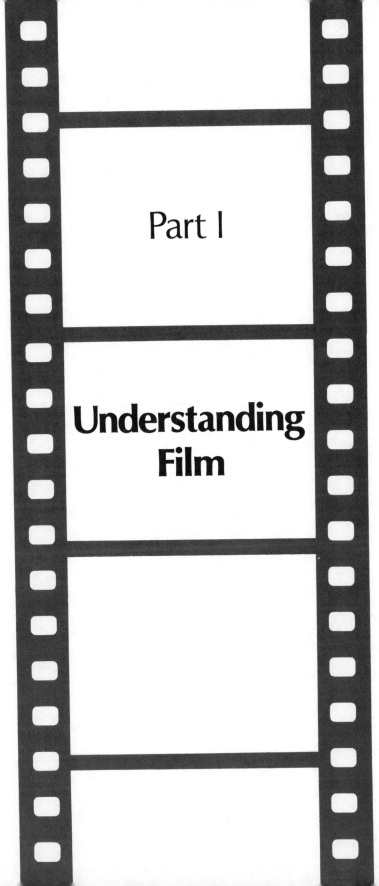

Part I

Understanding Film

1 ▪ Film and Ourselves

The first phase of our investigation will be pointed toward ourselves, toward the inclinations and expectations that each of us brings into the movie theater, whether we admit to them or not. In this respect, the movies may be found to constitute a sort of looking glass in which our own image (sometimes distorted and oftentimes hazy) mingles with the projector's pictures.

Many of us may have seen more movies on television than in theaters. Aside from television, we have also looked at movies on 8mm projectors in living rooms; we have squinted at 16mm films projected in classrooms where the venetian blinds failed to close and stripes of light stained the screen with glare while the grinding reels obscured half the soundtrack. We have seen movies in church basements, YMCA auditoriums, and basketball courts. If we have been in the army, we stood in line to view on film the depredations of venereal disease and the bite of the anopheles mosquito, perhaps even explanations of why we entered World War II: the U.S. Army's own horror films. If we went to summer camp, we sat on underbrush to watch the pursuits of Tom and Jerry projected on a bedsheet stretched between two trees, flicking away mosquitoes, hopefully not anopheles. Yet the quintessential film experience takes place in the movie theater. Whether it's a twenties "palace" designed to suggest Middle Eastern opulence or some modern shopping center's streamlined showcase with five projectors unwinding five features to five audiences, a neighborhood Rialto where boys throw spitballs from the first row balcony or a city grind house peopled with old men sleeping in the smell of disgorged milk shakes, the movie theater is the true home of the movies.

FILM AND THE DREAM

Since the movies' infancy, writers have likened the viewing of films in theaters to the experience of dreaming. The parallels warrant our consideration.

In a movie theater, we sit, quiet, attentive, on more-or-less comfortable furniture, facing forward, eyes directed toward a single, rectangular composition suspended in front of us. All is dark in the auditorium except for that one area suffused with light, and sometimes it is only with conscious effort that we pull back momentarily from what is happening on the screen and move our eyes to another spot.

The source of the image is behind us, although its consequence, sound included, is in front of us. Thus, were we to equate the model of the theater itself to our own apparatus for seeing and hearing—head–auditorium, eye–projector lens, film–cerebral cortex—we would see that the screen image remains a factor common to both systems. (In essence, motion picture camera and projector are the same piece of technology. The light source is simply relocated.) Indeed, from the turn of the century, when motion picture technology still boasted Greek and Latin nomenclature (*kine* for movement, *vita* for life), its machines were often equated with the human perceptual organs.

As early as 1903, in a series of lectures later published under the title *Creative Evolution,* the French philosopher Henri Bergson used the "Cinématographe" as a paradigm for human vision and memory: The process whereby a physical medium (cellulose) defines the dimension of time by accumulating linear sequences of separate still images certainly resembles somewhat the human physiological apparatus. Once recorded in the brain, mental images seem to be stored somewhere, latent, until a time when we choose to rerun them, or perhaps a moment of unsolicited, even unwanted, return. Similarly, Marcel Proust wrote of memories that are recalled only when activated by a seemingly insignificant detail, a chance vision or gesture. He was haunted too by childhood memories of pictures projected on his bedroom wall by a toy magic lantern. Another French author, Christian Metz, in the Parisian journal *Cahiers du Cinéma,* described the experience of looking at photographs as combining, in perpetual tension, the "now" and the "then": time past, image present. The American writer William Burroughs has compared many of his literary images to old, scratched film.

In one sense, the progression of any film is inexorable, and this is because, like music and the theater, it is an art based on cumulative time. Unless we arrive late to a performance, we experience a film from beginning to end at a constant rate of clock-measurable progress. We do not have the freedom afforded by reading a book; we cannot stop, mark our place, rub our eyes, or walk the dog while reflecting on what we have just assimilated. Unlike commercial television, there are no built-in station breaks for visits to the bathroom (with the exception of Truffaut's seventh-inning stretch). This aspect of film time seems especially to parallel the experience of dreaming—the sense of being involved in an adventure that we can neither escape nor affect, that must be followed through to its conclusion, regardless of the consequences.

The tension between our sense of participation in the event and the running awareness that we stand apart from that experience, powerless to affect its outcome, is explored in *Peter Ibbetson*, a novel by the Edwardian writer George du Maurier. Du Maurier evokes these sensations in describing the situation of two lovers who simultaneously dream the same dream. Ibbetson's sense of this dream is similar to what he felt when watching silent figures moving on a wall within an amusement park *camera obscura*.* He felt a part of the projected and dreamed images, while at the same time he was conscious of himself, older, changed, the dreamer dreaming the dream.

Dream images are not limited to the usual kinds of experience possible in the waking state. In the dream, we move from place to place, from time to time, from event to event, free of the restrictions that gravity and circumstance place on us in our daily lives. We dream our dreams with the freedom of film. Images shift, dissolve into other images, stand steady against changing backgrounds, behave with curious disregard for earthbound realities. That sense of flow, of being both in—sometimes excitedly or frighteningly in—the experience, while yet observing it all, is also like a dream or a movie, as is the capacity to cut across space and time. In this way, dreams and movies tend to be laconic, tend toward condensation and a brief succession of significant moments.

In our dreams, we have boundless energy for exploring and a chance to escape our customary inhibitions. We appear to live on an elemental, even primordial level that draws on impulses less accessible in daily human interchange or in the classroom. If the feelings are not actually antisocial (and some may be antisocial indeed), they seem at times to encompass something earlier than the social, a time, perhaps at the genesis of the species, perhaps in the earliest moments of our lives, buried now from conscious memory, hinting at another sort of closeness to the wellsprings of life.

This is what art is about, if one believes that it is the purpose of art to put people more in touch with themselves. The world of images can elicit, as from a great depth, very early and strongly felt sensations. The disposition to conceptualize in terms of images seems to amount almost to a kind of thinking, for it orders, organizes, and strikes attitudes toward experience quickly and efficiently. Neither is the inclination to think with pictures, exclusive of words perhaps, necessarily restricted to the "concrete." A feeling or idea can, too, be embodied in images, even shifted

* The *camera obscura* projects outside images through a lens system onto the surface of a darkened room, which acts like the interior of a camera.

from one form to another. For example, an image in Picasso's *Guernica* may invoke anguish or holocaust or despair. The emotionality of an image is transferable. Yet should we do no more than equate just the elemental, the atavistic, and the strongly felt with art, we miss the point, or else limit ourselves to high-amp rock music and gladiator contests. Art is not simple.

FILM AND PERCEPTION

Attending the movies is an event that combines the personal and the social, private experience and shared experience. On most occasions, it is a shared commitment, whether with people we know or with strangers. (If one has ever sat alone in a large, empty theater while watching a feature, particularly a comedy paced to audience laughter, the experience is peculiar and sometimes unnerving.) Even if our companions are strangers, we still share with them a collective sensibility that affects our reaction to the film. This sensation reaches consciousness at times when we laugh, or draw in our breath in impotent shock—as when Janet Leigh is attacked in the shower in Hitchcock's *Psycho* (1960). On a lesser scale, there is a broad continuum of audience rustles, murmurs, head movements, and pin-drop quiet which measures everything from inattention to the most concentrated, vicarious pleasure-taking. Listen, for example, for the sudden nervous silence of an audience the moment a known movie star first appears nude on the screen.

The vicarious pleasure marks differences in media as well. French theoretician André Bazin wrote in *What Is Cinema?* that a male spectator's attitude toward a performing heroine is quite distinguishable between film and stage. When one watches an attractive woman on the stage, Bazin said, he is jealous of the leading man who will more literally enjoy her favors. In the movie theater, jealousy is abated, for one can *become* the leading man. One may enjoy the actress himself.

In literature, our sensations parallel those of the film spectator, but to a different degree. Compare, for example, a story we may know both as novel and film, *The Maltese Falcon* (1941). Reading the novel, working only with the information Dashiell Hammett, the author, has provided, each of us will create a more personalized Sam Spade, who will probably resemble something of ourselves, even though we must stay within the descriptive boundaries set forth by the book. ("Samuel Spade's jaw was long and bony, his chin a jutting v under the more flexible v of his mouth. His nostrils curved back to make another small v. His yellow-grey eyes were horizontal.")[1] We will have to stick to the dialogue supplied, but even so, there is freedom to organize the reality of all the characters according to one's own personal vision.

To see *The Maltese Falcon* is to see Humphrey Bogart, after which one

A revealing piece of body language that communicates Humphrey Bogart's characterization of Sam Spade in *The Maltese Falcon*.

will never again think of the book without recalling the tick in Bogart's cheek or the upper lip drawn back across the teeth or his gestures—rubbing his hands as he walks down a hotel corridor or leaning back, elbows bent against a fireplace mantel, as he says to Mary Astor, "You're good. You're very good. I think it's mainly the voice."

When a psychologist is interested in eliciting nonindividualized, like responses from a group, he provides it with a stimulus which is specific and uncluttered by multiple alternatives. If, on the other hand, a psychologist is interested in maximizing differences, in tapping the most individualized responses from among his subjects, he will present them with ambiguous material—with Rorschach ink blots or Thematic Apperception Tests in which age and sexuality and motive are only sketchily implied, in which a boy can be climbing up or down a rope, a girl may be turning toward or away from her mother.

It would be unrealistic to ignore the possibilities of difference in multiple perceptions of a common film. Adolfas Mekas made a movie he called *Hallelujah the Hills* (1963). During one sequence, two young men are sitting under a tree, looking across the New England hillside. One says to the other, "My movie is better than your movie." To be sure, they are watching not movies but the countryside. They could as well have been in a theater, and as a matter of fact, *Hallelujah the Hills* is a case in point, for identical passages in it were praised and damned by different critics at the time of its release.

Like Hermann Rorschach, a filmmaker can, of course, design particular ambiguities into his production. This is not uncommon, for the modern sensibility delights in ambiguity. In *Styles of Radical Will*, Susan Sontag, who makes films, criticizes them, writes novels, and criticizes *them*, says, "Good and bad have become useless concepts—the most valid forms—in art—in philosophy—are those which accommodate the greatest ambiguity; they are profoundly disturbing but they are psychologically appropri-

Adolfas Mekas (right) directing the "my movie is better than your movie" sequence in *Hallelujah the Hills.* *(Credit: Adolfas Mekas)*

ate to our condition. Bergman's *Persona* (1966) and the films of Godard are exemplary esthetic models."[2] Ambiguities can also result from inadequacies in a production or performance—that is, they can be completely unintentional. More often, however, we seem to perceive ambiguity because of the inescapable differences that each of us brings to what *seems* to constitute a common experience.

We have to account, too, for substantial differences in individual perceptions, particularly the charged perceptions in a movie theater. After watching a film, we may consult our memory to recreate and to verify what happened in the film, but memory is not entirely reliable. Taking notes in the dark is never quite satisfactory even if one has a clipboard and an illuminated pencil, although these are recommended. To accomplish this, we must try to see and hear everything, decide what is worth noting and how to represent it accurately and appropriately, and then get it down—and at the same time remain altogether in touch with what is happening on the screen. On leaving the theater, I often find my notes incomprehensible: Phrases and dialogue that are legible seem to have nothing remotely to do with what I remember from the film; or sketches of what struck me as interesting camera work have turned into childlike rectangles leaning nowhere at erratic angles, peopled with obscure arrows and stick figures whose significance is as cloudy as last night's dream.

Along this line, I have experimented with classes in film theory and criticism attended by students who boast some familiarity with movie techniques, movie viewing, and movie discussion. I usually show, unannounced, a very short, somewhat concentrated bit of film. Most recently it has been a 50-foot clip from *Intermezzo, a Love Story* (1939), an old weepie with Ingrid Bergman and Leslie Howard, in which various events of a love affair and musical concert tour are compacted into a succession of shots and special effects, unified by theme music. (Fifty feet of 16mm film runs about a minute and a half.) When it is over, the lights are turned up, and I give the class a short quiz, allowing them to draw on whatever notes they took as viewers. The questions seem simple, even matter of fact: Identify the characters you saw. Write down any dialogue you remember. What sound effects were used? How many shots were in the clip? What special optical effects appeared? Was there music? Was it constant or intermittent? What, if any, overall design underlay the sequence?

Answers vary extremely. Characters disappear. Dialogue seems not so much forgotten as simply not heard. Railroad whistles and the rush of steam are unnoticed. No one mentions the dissolves, complicated optical flips, or multiple-overlays. Estimation of the number of shots varies from eight to forty-five. (There were twenty-one, although arguably you could count them different ways.) Rarely, if ever, does anyone perceive an overriding structure to the little sequence. No grades are assigned the sophisticated film students.

It is interesting that on second viewing of the same film clip, they still give answers that vary widely, even after being alerted to "what to look for." Arguments develop (film students are a bellicose lot) about the quantifications and identifications, and a third viewing is necessary to resolve the differences if, indeed, that is ever possible.

There are other reasons for our perceiving the same movies differently. To some audiences, *The Maltese Falcon* is an escapist whodunit, slightly campy because of its age and the extent to which both plot and dialogue have become clichéd. (Sam to Gutman as he hands over Wilmer's two automatics, "A crippled newsie took them away from him, but I made him give them back." Sam to Brigid, "The chances are you'll get off with life. That means you'll be out again in twenty years. You're an angel. I'll wait for you. If they hang you I'll always remember you.") To others, the movie is offensive, a brutalized caricature of greedy, inhumane, cosmopolitan types who live for money, sex, and the kicks of danger, a cynical picture of a cynical world. Yet another group finds in *The Maltese Falcon* a tough, biting exposé of the ugliness of modern life. There is also a Marxist interpretation, which views Hammett first as unearthing the virulence of the capitalist system, including its individual entrepreneur private eye, then calling for some collective sense of social responsibility at the end, when Sam Spade sends Brigid over because otherwise, "It's bad all around —bad for that one organization and for every detective everywhere."

In this as in other cases, every spectator brings to each film his biases of personal pleasure and need, even more to the point, his impulse to locate a meaning useful to himself in every vicarious adventure. One common teaching tool in film classes is a short called *Interpretations and Values,* prepared by the American Cinema Editors to publicize their craft. The film consists of all the takes shot and printed for a particular sequence in the "Gunsmoke" series, followed by three different final versions of the sequence—assembled "as I see it"—by three Hollywood editors. The last version includes music and sound effects as the episode was screened on TV.

One moment of action in the sequence involves an instant in a fight between Matt Dillon and the heavy of the week, Seippel. The villain has drawn a hunting knife, but the unarmed Matt disarms him and knocks him to the ground. Seippel rolls and reaches for his weapon, and at that moment Dillon lunges forward and kicks the knife out of his enemy's hand. This last "bit" is shown by a long shot of the two men, a close-up on the knife lying in the dirt, and, finally, a shot of Dillon as he lunges forward to kick it aside. Variations of the shots are covered more than once, as is often the case in trying to capture moments of violence, which must be made to look as authentic as possible.

Students were asked, "Why did Matt Dillon kick at Seippel while Seippel was lying on the ground?" A surprising number of students replied with answers such as: "To keep him from getting up again," "To knock him out," "To break his spirit." Most depressing was the answer, "To make sure that he is dead."

Other elements of the theater experience ought to be noted—first of all,

Two differently angled shots of Marshal Dillon kicking away Seippel's knife.

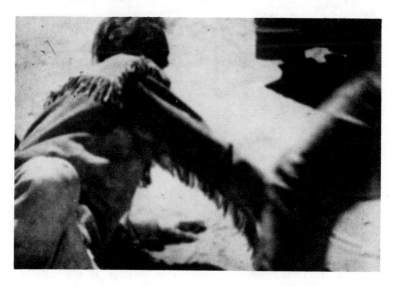

the awareness that we are, in fact, sitting there, removed from the events on the screen, not really party to them. As in our ordinary pursuance of routine matters, we do not always pull our conscious selves back into the cognizance of a dual role. The psychologist and film theoretician Rudolf Arnheim terms this duality "oscillation between witting and unwitting behavior." A surprising number of our mental processes, including cognition, memory, reaction, and even some forms of reasoning, manage to take place independent of any sense of arbitration on the part of our conscious selves. (We are not always in charge of what we do.) This duality plays a special role in the activities of the creative artist, for he must so attune these behaviors toward a common goal that none singly dominates his behavior.

Dreaming a film may be at odds with evaluating it. Both sides of the Arnheim duality are equally important to consider in responding attentively to motion pictures or, for that matter, to any other demanding form of audience experience. We have to maintain a special degree of cognitive alertness while viewing films, and this at times seems painfully at odds with a will to bathe ourselves in the moment, unthinking. Additionally, we need to understand *how* we are experiencing the film as it progresses —a kind of self-questioning to accompany inquiries we raise toward the screen.

FILM AND THE WORLD

"Film," Orson Welles once said, "is a ribbon of dreams." He continued, "some of us dream in Technicolor but nobody dreams in CinemaScope." This raises some other matters, most particularly the issue of film's reality in relation to "reality."

All media simulate and attenuate aspects of the human senses. The telephone and its mass media extension, radio, for example, isolated our capacities for making and listening to sounds and projected them great distances—an accomplishment which has produced untold accumulations of money, a great boon to family interchange, marked alterations in politics because of the dissemination of knowledge, and a large number of phonograph records. The relation of radio and the telephone to anything which presumed to the character of art has been minimal, submerged in communicative functions of transmission. (Radio, like television, *brings us* things that originate elsewhere, ballgames, music, drama and so forth, which have their own form independent of the transmission.) No one has seriously broached the likelihood of sound being accompanied by smell or touch: feelie radio. The combination of transmitted voice with image resulted in another medium.

The motion picture evolved in different fashion. It was initially conceived by Mr. Edison to be used in conjunction with his phonograph as portable office machinery, for private viewing; hence the tininess of the printed photographs in his earliest ventures. The first marketable version, in 1893, was the coin-in-the-slot, penny arcade Kinetograph.

Early experiments with combining sound and pictures were not successful, partly because of the difficulties of achieving dependable synchronization, partly because, even after the movies had become a large-audience medium, sound magnification was for a number of years inadequate for large auditoriums. It was not until two decades after the development of the audion tube by Lee De Forest in 1906 that speech and music could be sufficiently amplified, making possible the sound film as we know it.

In its earliest stages, the motion picture seemed to astonish viewers with its evocations of "exterior" reality at the same time that it displayed obvious differences between itself and what it purported to represent: What occupied three dimensions in the real world was flattened out into two. What had originally been "living color" was translated along a black-to-white continuum, showing up on the screen primarily as intermediate shades of gray. The size of photographed objects contrasted, sometimes markedly, with the magnified or diminished proportions of their photographic images. The circumstances of seeing these new images partook not of ordinary life but of the theater, as several of our senses remained dormant while we concentrated with the others. The developing syntax of transition and continuity bore less resemblance to life experience than to the dream.

Subordination of the other senses—hearing, smell, taste, touch—to the sense of sight gave additional intensity to the experience of seeing filmed images. What was often most remarked upon by critics of early moving pictures was the power of film to suggest through vision alone sensations normally experienced through the other senses—as when the sudden flight of birds seen in long shot swooping out of a forest might advise us that a rifle had been fired. The outstanding moments were often those that communicated with minimal means. A kind of aesthetic law of parsimony found itself in operation, and the very limitations of the flickering images became a source of potential artistry, based on the imaginations of filmmakers. An actor like Charlie Chaplin, trained in mime on the English stage, found himself extremely successful on the screen because his skills managed to express universally shared joys and anxieties with the "merest" gestures.

In some minds even today, the "Golden Age" of silent film marked the movies' highest achievement for these reasons—notwithstanding the banal stories or second-rate acting performances. At its best, the position is not grounded in nostalgia, but based on sensitive response to a departed form, to the principle that less is more, that the minimal transmission of information and most especially of emotion is superior to any bombardment of our senses. It is the reason why someone might prefer Saul Bellow to Norman Mailer, the harpsichord to the pianoforte, the Greeks to the Romans, William Carlos Williams to Allen Ginsberg. Unfortunately, for such a position, the development of the movies turned in another direction. By the mid-twenties sound became technically possible in large movie auditoriums, and the talkie developed as one of the major American experiences of the Depression years. Progress was the watchword as movie technology began to make everything "bigger and better," eventually bringing us such innovations as Technicolor and CinemaScope.

Some of the earliest motion pictures of the Frenchman Georges Méliès achieved color by having each separate frame literally hand painted through the painstaking agency of a factory of women. Later, film was tinted various hues in the processing stage, sometimes merely for "effect," sometimes to underline a dominant emotion in a particular sequence. Similar effects were accomplished at the time of projection by interposing colored gels in front of the projector lens, a technique culled from theatrical usage. More sophisticated color experimentation paralleled the development of sound techniques. A Douglas Fairbanks swashbuckler, *The Black Pirate* (1926), was the first full-length movie to use a two-color Technicolor process. Three-color Technicolor followed in musical shorts and Walt Disney's *Three Little Pigs* (1933). Inexpensive productions in the thirties—"B" westerns, for example—used less successful color processes that made otherwise realistic scenes appear to be squirted with blue or orange watercolor.

After World War II the motion picture industry "met the challenge of television" by concentrating on those aspects of the film experience that could not be duplicated on the living room box—namely, the sheer size and sound quality made possible by wide screens and stereophonic reproduction.

Thus each innovation has marked a step forward in the inexorable march toward more accurate simulation of exterior reality, a direction epitomized at the present time by total projected environments, multiple-channeled sound, the occasional use of smells, stereoscopic viewing devices, and experimentation with laser systems. At all of this, the Golden Age movie buff wrings his hands and sheds a silent tear. For him, film that lusts after achieving an absolute verisimilitude sheds the integrity of its limitations. If film should ever finally successfully approximate reality, it would at last have abandoned the dream for waking life—abandoning any quality that distinguished it from ordinary "reality," from the very limitations that gave it artistic potential, and staging aesthetic suicide in the process. Orson Welles rests his case.

There *is* a counterposition: With every technological innovation, we have witnessed an accompanying thrust on the part of creative minds to master technology and make it serve an aesthetic rather than allow it to take over. As color came more completely under technical control (replacing those Anscochrome gouaches), filmmakers saw its potential for creating mood and underscoring narrative elements and began to make color part of their film vocabulary. Sound came not to destroy the film but to enlarge its possibilities. It has not, in fact, reduced the motion picture to a lackluster imitation of "legitimate" theater, but, rather, has created an alternative form outside the boundaries of the proscenium arch. Moreover, the soundtrack has established its independence from the visual image, with the relation of sound and picture now supportive, now dominant, now operating like two themes in musical counterpoint. CinemaScope and MagnaScope and Todd-AO have not merely broadened screen size; they have increased the cameramen's options as well. There is no reason to believe that the 3:4 aspect ratio of the older motion picture screen is the only way or even the best way. Through clever compositional schemes, wider screens can be shortened, but the smaller one could never be made larger. One can play harpsichord pieces on the piano: They won't sound the same, but they'll sound like something. Nobody plays Beethoven sonatas on the harpsichord.

We will examine some of these propositions in greater detail further on. At this point, it is sufficient to indicate the continuum of verisimilitude, running, as it were, from Charlie Chaplin to Jerry Lewis—at one extreme, a black-and-white image, sometimes jerky because of uneven hand camera-cranking, sometimes suffering today from deteriorated film stocks and long-destroyed original negatives; at the other end purrs a multicolored, broad, overpowering picture, the consonants of its sound track crisp as crunched celery, its sibilants lush and sinuous, unfuzzed and unwhistling, like John Coltrane.

The Less	The More
◄────────	────────►

Another dimension must be recognized and accounted for. We have concentrated almost exclusively on the movie image itself, as a mirror held up to nature, a representation succeeding more or less literally in reproducing what Arnheim has called the "epidermis of reality," the skin off which our sensations reflect. Such a notion seems to come to us naturally. We view film as illusion, by and large, and we enjoy the deception involved (the red dye spurting out of faces and chests in *Bonnie and Clyde* [1967]) at the same time that we distance ourselves from the actualities shown (bleeding and dying) by asking "how it's done." We conceive movies as an extension of the still camera, a collection of single, static photographs. Seen run together, they are apparently in motion, but each frame is equivalent to the still photograph—static and faithful in every detail to the scene it documents.

René Magritte's painting *Les Promenades d'Euclide* exploits spatial illusion to create its deceptive effect. *(Credit: The William Hood Dunwoody Fund, The Minneapolis Institute of Arts)*

Such a perspective conceives the movie rectangle, whatever its projected size, as a kind of window on the world. Were we to shift the vision by moving our frame ever so slightly up or down, left or right, we would do little more than affect its composition, probably (although not necessarily) for the worse. The frame serves only as a limitation on the extent of what is visible to us, just as the construction of our eyes delimits how much we can take in without moving our heads. (The same principle functions in Magritte's series of trompe l'oeil paintings that counterpose a canvas landscape in front of a window that looks out on the view from which it was painted. The painted landscape is placed within the window frame so as to correspond exactly to the part of the view hidden by the canvas and to merge perfectly with the rest. Remove the canvas and you have the identical scene. Move the canvas to a movie screen, and you have the movie.)

Similarly, if we were to move up to the screen and peer around the picture's edges, we might see just a little more, like Alice in *Through the Looking Glass,* wondering about the fire on the other side of the fireplace. (Godard used this knowledge to comic effect in *Les Carabiniers* [1963], during which a peasant soldier first experiences the movie image when he encounters a film of a woman taking a bath and wants to get into the screen.) At the same time, we realize too that this illusion would be destroyed were we to sneak a glance beyond the edges. We would very likely find not more of the same, but other, different goings-on. People dressed at odds with the screen reality would be sitting in chairs, controlling lights, and monitoring ammeters. Someone might even be pointing a fan to give the appearance of wind on the screen, or squirting a hose whose water fell on a raincoated actor. Our reality is manufactured.

Taking this a step further, we realize that there are, as it were, two kinds of manufactured reality: the one that looks like the real thing and a kind that doesn't—a product of somebody else's head, not necessarily a vision we share, at least not until we've gone all the way into it.

These are the polarities of a second continuum. On one side there is photojournalistic fidelity, as in the documentary film or the fiction film posing as photojournalism. (For the moment we beg the question of whether actualities *can* in fact be "caught" and reproduced without being distorted.) Films of this order give a kind of ultimate vicarious pleasure; in the measure that they win our confidence we participate in an

The peasant soldier in Godard's *Les Carabiniers* is frustrated by his encounter with the "real" image on the movie screen.

actuality different from our own. The acting is "real," filmed on location in settings unblemished by studio technology. We do not compare an actress with her performance in some other role ("I liked her better in *Last Tango in Paris*" [1972]). We do not recognize the rock formations of Monument Valley when the locale is supposed to be Texas. There are no mike shadows in the corner of the screen. We fail to note the jungles of *King Kong* (1933) rear-screen projected behind the picnic scenes of *Citizen Kane* (1941). At its most authentic, a film like this would probably be something on the order of Robert Flaherty's documentary *Nanook of the North* (1921)—and even here, film buffs are aware of certain "stagings." Yet any film which commands total belief on the part of any member of an audience is, in its way, real for him.

The challenge to most filmmakers, then, seems to be to have their way with the material while concealing from the audience the strategies they have used. Such techniques can assume many guises. Hollywood technicians have always been proud of their imitations of actuality: the earthquakes, turn-of-the-century Bowery streets, epic battles, aging of characters, and car chases. Studio magic is a constant battle of wits between the sharp-eyed moviegoer and the union technician. Will there be skid marks on the road before the car comes to a screeching halt? (There didn't seem

The Eskimo Nanook, from an early example of a subject treated in photojournalistic style, Robert Flaherty's *Nanook of the North*.

to be any in *The French Connection* [1971].) Will the heroine's hair turn blue as she grows older (like Elizabeth Taylor's in *Giant* [1956])?

But these illusions are a kind of lowest common denominator of the filmmaker's craft, a minimally credible scheme against which everything else must be staged. More important are those far more subtle skills by which he may advance his story, complicate a character, foreshadow a development, underline a motive, ally himself with one value in preference to another. Such devices, like fingerprints, provide the means of identifying many different directorial personalities.

The highly individualized filmmaker who has made these devices abundantly visible rather than disguising them is at the far extreme of our continuum. Here reside Jean Cocteau, Jean-Luc Godard, Federico Fellini, Alain Resnais. Each man in his own way has decided to abandon illusionism for the sake of a private vision. Each developed some form of aesthetic rationale for his approach, and some have found a political philosophy underpinning the bases of that aesthetic.

Almost without exception, the commercially financed narrative film has operated within the confines of the representational image photographed with relative clarity—that is, shot "in focus" throughout, regardless of the subject matter or behavior being depicted.* Such clarity of focus inspires our willingness to accept what we see on the screen as "real." When the story is fanciful—that is, unreal—or the terrain isn't congruent with our experience, we are increasingly required to alert ourselves to other aspects of the film, formal elements like color and the relationship between sound and picture.

Sometimes when this happens, we find ourselves locating narrative intention in what would otherwise be thought an obstacle to our experience: the fact that "nothing happens" in long stretches of an Antonioni film, that Godard appears to bombard us with incessant, strident chatter, so constantly reminding us that we are watching his film that we can never slip for long into absorbed attention. Such obvious manipulations, like the grotesqueries of Fellini players or the shifting cuts of Resnais, are for some spectators incomprehensible on first viewing. We have to reexamine the experience to find them more than a distraction and to discover that these initially irritating mannerisms really convey highly personal visions. The makers of such films are exploring unfamiliar territory. As with all explorations, the trails marked out for us may be somewhat unclear.

The second continuum, then, runs from the Eskimo Nanook to disordered, pagan Rome in *Fellini Satyricon* (1969).

---

* Privately financed ventures may, on occasion, either have so totally doctored the image before its exposure to film (parts of Cocteau's *The Blood of a Poet* [1930], for example) or depersonalized the imagery (Stan Brakhage's *Prelude* [1961]) that regular photographic orthodoxies fail to apply, but these approaches remain outside the parameters of our study. Like *The Cabinet of Dr. Caligari* (1919), they stand as solitary monuments.

Allegiance to the   Allegiance to some other

←——→

    epidermis of reality   aspect of reality

A reader with a long memory will recollect that the arrow-drawing commenced during a discussion of parallels between movie-viewing in a darkened theater and dreaming. The German film historian and theorist Siegfried Kracauer used similar analogies, concluding that movie-dreams took two directions. One was toward the screen, toward its photographic realities and the humane understandings which followed on that experience. (Kracauer's allegiances rest altogether on the left sides of our arrows, with the exception of his appreciation for musicals.) The other film-dream direction, according to Kracauer, was inward, which he regarded as unhealthy. It encouraged self-serving passivity and a withdrawal from reality. It was the daydream, the Walter Mitty delusion of glory, which might perhaps satisfy one's psychological needs, but was socially dysfunctional. It took the spectator away from his necessary active social role (*Play It Again, Sam* [1972]).

This book is not written to so doctrinaire an approach. I believe that any critical ideology that diminishes our responses to the moving image can only lessen possibilities for inquiry and hence for experience in film-going. To put it another way, what is to be gained from any film stands independent of its visible relations to the world we inhabit—so long as we connect. Herman Melville said about the novel that it was like religion: "It should present another world, but one to which we feel the tie."

We may, in fact, conclude that the extremes of the polarities I have drawn, as well as the intermediate positions, all lend themselves to equations between film and dream. Some dreams are rather vague and open; only occasional objects occupy an otherwise barren landscape. Some are vivid, demanding our attention—wide-screen and stereophonic. Sometimes, some of us dream in Technicolor. Some dreams are very much like ordinary life, with our family and acquaintances appearing as in an old photo album. Some dreams seem the purest "fantasy"—objects dissolving into other objects, landscapes shifting like rear-screen projections, or single elements of the environment appearing curiously out of place: a fur-lined teacup, a bodiless face, an apple atop a neck. This is what the psychologists call displacement, and it is a heritage of film by way of Surrealism, although the best movie displacements look least like paintings even if the effect is similar.

Certainly Kracauer touches on one truism: We go to movies for many reasons, not all of equal social utility. Just as in reading a book or attending a play, a football game, or a lecture, we operate out of mixed motives stemming from contrary needs. In all of us there is the disposition to reassure ourselves that the world is pretty much as we suspected: cruel and violent perhaps, or vibrantly attractive and puzzling; a sell-out, maybe, dominated by avarice, hypocrisy, and the hydrogen bomb; or possibly sterile and meaningless. These suspicions define our speech, our gestures, and our pleasures, including moviegoing. Films seem to provide especially convincing confirmation of our pet beliefs; they always have. So attendance at a film event, particularly what are called *genre* films—that is, types of film like horror, comedy, religious epic, westerns, thrillers—may be a way of reaffirming what we believe the world to be about.

In this respect, an unquestioning approach to film does seem at times to serve that self-inflected, daydreaming, static sort of response. Its very "realness" rationalizes passivity, and answers something in contemporary lives. For the city-dwelling, office-commuting, routinized member of the industrial age in the twentieth century, what can be fingered and smelled may be drab indeed compared to experiences and sensations in the lives of other men in other societies and other ages. However many buttons we touch, whatever the odors of the garbage, the bus, the gym locker, or air itself, we remain at one remove from many experiences that had been an integral part of earlier lives. We may buy, sell, manufacture, or transport commodities that each of us will never personally use or even see. In such a strange and unlikely world, even the shadowed illusion of more concrete realities shifting across a movie screen has special merit. It puts us in touch with different places and most especially with other people who live under different conditions, their lives dominated by different needs. We learn something about who else peoples the planet, not so much by their "story" as by their gestures, expressions, and movements. The concept "run" may be commonly applied to an Ibo competing in a track-and-field event, a ghetto Arab child racing through the streets, and a man with a briefcase rushing for his bus. Their appearance, clothes apart, is different; movements betray purpose and something of the secret self. In curious ways, film, the mechanical art of the twentieth century, has reintroduced into our modern lives some elements of nineteenth-century humanism by making available to us intimate knowledge of people who only appear to be very different from ourselves.

FILM AND SECRETS

Yet there is another aspect of the film experience, too, for the man of today. Film is what Thomas Mann, describing a dream in his novella *Death in Venice*, termed "the theater of his very soul." Whatever our suspicions, we are all equally condemned to seek our own meaning. So long as we live, experience puzzles as much as it explains itself. No matter what the lure of a particular economic yardstick on reality, or a religious or philosophic or psychological one, a man or woman who admits to no bewilderment seems somehow to have abdicated the human condition.

All art is a part of human experience. If art is not this it is nothing, and when we attend a film we always ask privately of it, consciously or no, what life is about, what we are about.

The film doesn't tell us, not very directly. It was made by men who share the ultimate ignorance. But some movies contain more of an answer than others and speak with less cant.

Movie history traces a kind of rite of passage, for gradually, haltingly, movies assumed certain responsibilities. In their capacities to touch and to excite our most primitive responses, motion pictures are disposed, not by edict but by their nature, to explain things. (The political recognition of this disposition prompted both Lenin and Mussolini to describe film as the new art, the art of the people in a new age.)

In the measure that a movie, whether Bernardo Bertolucci's or Budd Boetticher's, shares some of the qualities of the dream, it externalizes certain aspects of our private lives, casting on the screen a larger-than-life version, albeit distorted, of what for most people had been until this era largely secret, had never been inquired after before. Some of these subjects are still considered scandalous, and, even in the relatively permissive cultural atmospheres of this decade, must be disguised to become palatable to audiences. Thus sex becomes either pornography or an outgrowth of scientistic naturalism in order that love need not be confronted.

Some of the secrets are confusing, too. They sustain something of darkness and the void even in illuminated magnification. What Jungians regard as a true unity in the human disposition and Freudians think of as buried internal contradictions may be split on the screen into a duality or multiple parts, each personified by separate and distinct individuals (the good guy, the bad guy). The reconciliation of these parts, then, may be clouded in timeworn plots that are inadequate to the application. Hence some of the ambiguities and inexplicable facets to many films. Characters who ought really to be something more than representations of seventeenth-century humours may refuse to turn into full-blown personalities (the too good guy, the unbelievably bad guy). Or if they do so, they may distort the narrative by introducing complexities that work against a story's ultimate purpose.

We can conclude, then, that the film experience is more than a little complicated and involved. At the same time, the vividness, the tangibility, and the vulgarity historically associated with the movies all seem to contribute to a sort of compacted immediacy that denies this complexity. Most often, any particular movie offers a little of this and a little of that, cafeteria-style. We find the popcorn-munching kicks—laughs or gasps, a clichéd chuckle and a predictable tear. We see someone else, someone different from ourselves, and how he organizes life and confronts it. We become hero or heroine, maybe both, with all the privileges relating thereto. Even though we know better, we absorb the most absolute claptrap. Cowboy movies are most popular in Western towns.

We study the effects. We scrutinize for signs of age stars last seen when both we and they were younger. We compare this experience with others like it. We make judgments on the quality of photography, the sound, the sets, and performances. We rouse ourselves into attention now and again when we catch our minds wandering from the events taking place on screen. With luck something happens during the film to astound us or to linger in our minds to contemplate on the way home. We check out the Coming Attractions and make a mental note whether to come again next week.

FILM AND CONVENTION

The business or joy or tedium of looking at two-dimensional moving shadows undulating within the confines of a large or small rectangle is so ingrained in the habits of our lives that we give it little, if any, thought. What is involved in the perception of a movie? Since television boxes replaced radio boxes in American living rooms, many of us began watching these pictures years before they altogether made sense to us and have continued to look at them years after we made too much sense of them. By the age of twelve, the average child has spent far more time in front of a television than he has in school—more in fact than anything else but sleep.

This is the most subtle and effective form of education, for like any decent instruction, it is self-motivated and accompanied by pleasure. What else the cradle-to-grave television viewer picks up isn't always clear, even to himself; it's a question about which many minds have speculated. Marshall McLuhan concluded, in a slogan, that the medium is the message. By this he meant that in experiencing television, or any other sensory extension of ourselves—the telephone, the phonograph, the automobile— the *form* of that perception, *how* it communicates itself to us, constitutes by far a more significant element of experience than its apparent content.

Television, of course, is a cyclops that lives on cellulose acetate: reels of movie film. These days the only exceptions, "live TV," are portions of newscasts, panel shows, sporting events, and occasional public events like funerals and congressional hearings. In instances like these, the subject, the thing which happens, customarily dominates its transmission. (Exceptions include calling football timeouts to accommodate commercials.) If a television director were to indulge his artistic sense by shooting semiabstract compositions centering on the scoreboard at a time when bases were loaded, two out in the ninth inning, we would take exception. Were he to slip into fancy fast-switching from senator-interrogation to indignant witness-response during a heated exchange in a Washington caucus room, great portions of the audience would cry that they were being "manipulated," that their perceptions of the event in issue were being controlled, to unwise purpose, by intermediary, anonymous agents behind cameras, switchers, and special effects boards.

In looking at programs that are taped or on film, however, we either ignore such "manipulation," or else we openly accept it. Like willing bodies beneath a pummeling masseur, we submit to a vague understanding that, under the circumstances, this is the order of things and the experience is for our own good, that is, immediately pleasurable, or else leading soon to anticipated enjoyments—excitement, vicarious anxiety, laughter. Such strings to which our perceptions play marionette affect our understanding of "what's going on" in very literal ways. For example, they will define where a subject exists, spatially, and where the other elements locate themselves in relation to it. This kind of information is conveyed by visual variables, such as how much we see, the angle from which we view it, the composition of the shot, movement within the composition, movement on the part of a camera, movement of camera and subject relative to one another, the duration of our perception, and so forth. Whether we are watching movies made especially for TV, series, or old films, there is also a certain order, that is, temporal sequence, to our perceptions. We have been trained to expect a pattern of shots moving from long to short, from distant to near, from greater to less.

A narrative opens with an establishing, orienting scene: Marshal Dillon and Doc are talking generally about events in Dodge City in the Marshal's office; McMillan and Wife attend an art opening at the M. H. de Young Memorial Museum; Lon Chaney, Jr., and Maria Ouspenskaya are driving a gypsy caravan across the barren steppes of Transylvania. We settle into such introductions with a combination of relaxed attention and a general awareness that something is likely to happen fairly shortly, unexpectedly. (This is particularly true on TV shows, where the strategy is to capture a viewer's attention before he has time to switch to an alternative program on another channel.) We organize our comprehensions of the scene. Doc says something about delivering a baby the night before, and that he's had only two hours' sleep; Rock Hudson and Susan St. James are dressed in evening clothes, and she comments that she ought not to have eaten two chocolate mousses (she calls them mice) before coming to the opening; Lon Chaney, Jr., tells Maria Ouspenskaya that he has been feeling uneasy, that the time is near, that she must make sure his chains are tight tonight, and that he fears the setting of the sun, which we see is imminent.

With all this information, we relax. We know that each of our couples is between adventures, waiting, like us, for the next event. We know the time of day or evening or night, and its relation to the characters. We know, in literal terms, *where* they are—not only the part of the country or the world they inhabit, but its very specific geography, the location of certain rocks, or a potbellied stove, or a modishly dressed curator on the terrain. We know how much space is around each couple, and where they sit or stand in relation to one another. We may even acknowledge, on some level of our awareness, just how poised the body of each appears, ready for what may happen.

Something happens. In the Marshal's office, James Arness turns, hitches up his gunbelt, advises Doc to take the day off for sleep, and exits, screen left. In the next shot, we see him close the office door from outside, and walk across the street to a scaffold just being completed. A close shot of one of the workmen shows him eying the Marshal surreptitiously. The workman removes a revolver from his own gunbelt and hides it beneath a trap door. He looks up at the rope, seemingly measuring its distance relative to the platform. We share that view as if from the workman's eyes.

In the San Francisco museum, Police Commissioner McMillan's glance, resting affectionately on his wife's chic new outfit, strays after a statuesque blonde. Through his eyes we watch this girl from the rear as she ambles in the direction of the bar, where a bartender nervously polishes a wine glass. McMillan's eyes take in the bartender. We cut back to a medium shot of him and Sally. McMillan frowns. Sally says conversationally, "I thought she looked pretty good, myself." "Haven't seen that face in ten years," the Commissioner says. "You haven't seen the face yet," Sally replies. From behind the bartender, Mac and Sally in the background, we see the uniformed bartender draw a long stiletto from a trouser pocket.

On the Transylvanian steppes, Maria Ouspenskaya glances down at the hands of Lon Chaney, Jr., lightly holding the horses' reins. From her viewpoint, we see the beginning of a pentagram, faintly traced on his palm. Back at the original shot, we see her glance up; Chaney continues to stare at the road. Again from her view, we perceive a full moon, shining through leafless, autumnal branches that flick across the screen, for it is as if we were traveling in the covered wagon.

Now we *know* something's about to erupt. We likely know what it is, and we think we know how events are going to be resolved. The knowledge has been acquired through a kind of shorthand of visual cues whose meanings we all agree on, like the rules for basketball. We know, as one shot is succeeded by another on the screen, that time is apparently passing continuously, that in spite of the inexplicable transformation from one viewpoint to another, the screen events continue unimpeded. (Note that the fact that voices are maintained at a constant distance-volume, regardless of the relative size of the speakers on the screen, doesn't bother us.) The fact that our viewpoint relative to the speakers varies from moment to moment is a source of satisfaction, for we seem, magically, to perceive more easily what there is to take into account through the agency of these screen enlargements. When our viewpoint shifts so that it appears to enter into the perceptions of one of the participants themselves, we sit unastounded. It's not exactly that we have become McMillan, a Western renegade, or a small gypsy, yet we *have* become each in a way, exactly sharing their visions in a manner unique to this medium and altogether unlike what would ever occur in actuality. Lastly, we are unconcerned with controls exercised over the duration of our perceptions.

We do not mutter indignantly that we've not been allowed to watch anything longer, that we missed something on the screen that probably ought to have come to our attention. We saw and heard what there was.

Back at the ranch or, rather, Dodge City, a prisoner is brought out of the jailhouse by Festus and led, hands secured behind his back, to the gallows. Over the shoulder of Marshal Dillon, we see the bound man taken up to the platform. Moving closer, we hear the prisoner request a moment to kneel in prayer. From beneath the platform, we see the shifty-eyed workman raise its trap door. Gun in hand, he shoots James Arness, who falls heavily onto the dusty street. Two horses appear out of nowhere. The prisoner and his rescuer leap astride and ride out of town.

At the museum, Rock Hudson whirls, strikes his beautiful wife across the face with a blow that stretches her out cold on the floor, then twists to the side just in time to escape the swish of a long knife, which imbeds itself harmlessly in the nose of Rembrandt's *Night Watchman*. McMillan swerves forward like an enraged halfback and tackles the bartender just as the latter reaches an exit. Sergeant Enright rushes up excitedly. "Commissioner, are you all right?" "Get this guy and book him," mutters McMillan. "I've got to see about Sally."

Clearly Lon Chaney, Jr., is in a bad way. Fur has commenced to sprout from his ankles; his stubble of beard has increased alarmingly in length and coarsened in texture. Fangs are extruding from his lower jaw. He turns to Maria Ouspenskaya, snarls pathetically, and leaps from the cart, landing on all fours beside the road. "Gypsy, old gypsy," he cries despairingly, "save me with the fate of Bella. Kill me with a silver weapon. Kill me before I kill again, and give me peace."

At this point, action has defined story. We know what the ensuing thirty minutes or hour or hour and a half hold in store. What had until now amounted to inconsequential dialogue, and occasional, nonsignificant movements, has erupted into violence. These faster actions have been themselves unseen in their entireties, often truncated, their continuities unexplained or lapsed into elliptical connections. How did that outlaw get beneath the scaffold? The last we'd seen of him, he was above it. Why didn't the Marshal supervise the hanging himself, instead of leaving it in the clearly inadequate hands of Festus? What is Arness doing lying on the dirt in the middle of town at the beginning of the program? Where did those horses come from?

Why did McMillan sock his wife? Furthermore, we didn't see the bartender throw the knife. There were half a dozen other people at the bar, including the blonde, who, come to think of it, was standing directly in front of the bartender, holding out a glass to him. Why weren't they hurt, or even better, why didn't they do something about it all? How did the Commissioner get all the way across the gallery floor in time to catch the bartender at the door? He had at least twice the distance to cover, and he was twisted around facing the other direction. Where did John Schuck (Sergeant Enright) come from?

Why wasn't Lon Chaney, Jr., tied up earlier? Anyone could tell that it was getting dark. How did he grow all that fur so quickly?

In the excitement of the moment, questions are repressed, if they appear at all, by our aroused curiosities about the problems introduced. The very condensations of movement and event seem to have triggered feelings that somehow block rational exploration. Additionally, the shots have decreased in length so appreciably that we have time only to take in the minimal, necessary information before plunging on to further detail—detail that will, we know, explain some of our questions while advancing others. The design is organized to salivate our appetite for more. Crouched about the living room box, we turn to warm ourselves at its heatless glow and ask, ". . . and then? . . . and then?"

Doc and Festus rush to the prostrate form in the dirt. "Marshal, Marshal!" Festus cries. "Are you all right?" "Where did it get you, boy?" Doc questions gruffly, as he bends to examine the body. James Arness rises to his feet and dusts himself off. "Get the horses. I'm glad that guy used the gun I put blanks in, but now we've got to get moving and find where they hid that gold shipment. Tell Kitty over at the Long Branch to pack us a lunch."

Sally McMillan rises to a sitting position as her husband hurries to her side. "You were right in the line of fire, dear." The blonde hands Hudson her glass, which he prepares to throw in Sally's face, but she shakes her head and drinks it instead. "I knew you were going to take him, Mac," she says, "but gosh darn it, I wanted to see you do it." She looks over at the blonde, then smoothes the hem of her dress.

Now on all fours, now crouched on his hind legs, Lon Chaney, Jr., scurries away into a forest which has appeared in the screen background. Maria Ouspenskaya reaches into the recesses of her baggage and withdraws a cane of which the handle is made of silver. Shaped in the form of a little ax, it has a pentagram on its side. Engraved across it is *Property of Larry Talbot*. "Even a man," she mutters—

> Even a man who is pure in heart
> And who says his prayers by night
> Can become a wolf
> When the wolfbane blooms,
> And the autumn moon is bright.

2 ■ Film and Other Media

When we consider film's origins and its curious melding of two-dimensional space with the passage of time, it should not be surprising that affinities with other art forms are so myriad and apparent. Relationships exist on two planes. The motion picture may share particular formal procedures with another medium, as for example the use of the *motif*, a musical technique that also appears in literature, such as in the work of Emile Zola (who admitted he copied it from Wagner) and Marcel Proust. Film may also impose its form on another idiom by using the latter as subject matter, as when a film is made "about" a painting, for example, Alain Resnais's *Guernica* (1950). In addition, when we consider the matter of adaptation (fiction, drama or biography "into" film), it may be seen that expository techniques from the original mode may carry over into screen techniques.

FILM AND THEATER

Perhaps theater is the movies' most important sister art, and one major film theorist and historian, André Bazin, viewed movies quite literally as the modern extension of the theater.

Like film, nineteenth-century theater was a medium of the people, partly by default. Although major English-language writing talents from earlier periods such as the Elizabethan Age or the Restoration had channeled their energies in the direction of playwriting, in the nineteenth century a contrary movement was apparent; writers of note were far more likely to work in poetry, the essay, and the novel.

Nineteenth-century English and American theater were very much alike. Certain director-writers worked in both countries, and many plays produced in one were exported to the other. Because British drama was more fully developed than our own, film's initial theatrical roots are more easily traced there. In this era, theater was dominated by an approach—almost a way of life—called *melodrama,* made popular by a growing working-class audience whose expectations it seemed to satisfy. Melodrama's early development in England was affected by the consequences of the 1737 Licensing Act. This reaction to scabrous performance prohibited spoken roles except at two London theaters. All other productions had to perform without words, that is, in mime. In consequence, the nonvocal aspects of drama received special attention—a development foreshadowing the emergence of the silent film—and even after speech was restored to the English stage, the new methods of acting persisted.

Orchestras, sometimes located below the stage in the pit (as in the days of the silent film), sometimes hidden offstage (like music in the sound film), sought to give support to the actors' performances by supplying incidental music whose emotional tone might underline the feelings and drama of a given moment in the play. This is the origin of the term melodrama (*melos* being Greek for "song"), originally a form limited to nonverbal expression.

The plays themselves were sometimes original, sometimes stolen from a French playwright, Pixérécourt, and often were reworked material, constantly changed to adapt to new locales or recent events in the news. Characters were painted in broad, value-inflected strokes: heroes and villains, heroines in distress, and innocent men and women "of the people." The performances always concluded with virtue triumphant, a happy occasion resulting from a hero's courage and his skill under stress. Villains either blew up in pressured moments or simply failed because they weren't as good as the protagonist. The tests of skill thus reflected medieval contests in which strength and physical dexterity proved the ultimate integrity of a man's cause. Villains might be Byronically fascinating, but in the long run, heroes had better style.

The attributions of these good and evil qualities drew on the social problems of the day. Early in the century, villains tended to be portrayed as landed gentry, perhaps false gentry, who victimized poor-but-honest peasant folk. Later, as populations migrated to the cities—creating new problems and regrets and nostalgia for the country—the scenes of the plays shifted accordingly. Villains became factory owners or criminal cosmopolitan types who would betray the naïve and unsuspecting workers and their families, particularly the daughters.

Like political cartooning, which drew on the same imagery, melodrama confirmed the understandings of its audience. It also provided vicarious thrills for spectators whose lives were humdrum and uneventful. There were not only violent physical encounters among the principals, but spectacular and spectacularly *real* events in every performance, in the form of *sensation scenes*. If the script required a naval battle, the ambitious melodrama displayed actual ships' models in great tanks of real water, with rockets and fireworks. Live horses might be used, even replicas of locomotives in the scenes where the heroine is tied to the tracks.

The sophistications of stage sets were further developed when candlelight was replaced by gas, lime,* and calcium-based illumination, followed by lens-focused machinery and, finally, electricity. All of this led to the most striking kinds of optical effects. Fires could be simulated on painted backdrops; backlighting disclosed previously unseen effects designed on the reverse side of the canvas, and colored smoke was blown out from the wings. The use of lenses to localize lighting added a whole new dimension to the possibilities for controlling audience tension. As a matter of fact, the customs of darkening the theater and dropping the curtains became popular during this period. It was visual effects that gave special pleasure to the audiences.

Thus, the substance of the plays, the simulations of reality through stage decor and props, and such expository techniques as vision scenes (read "flashbacks") paralleling two story elements for the sake of suspense, were all available to the motion picture industry at its infancy. Theatrical influence was all the more evident in the production of early films in New York City, the center of theater in this country, where many stage actors, authors, and directors were condescendingly eager to make ends meet with occasional profitable forays into the new field.

The function of the director translated easily from one medium to another. Until the latter half of the nineteenth century, he did little more than assemble actors, run them through their lines, and see that the staging was executed and performed on cue. Then, first under the aegis of William S. Gilbert (of Gilbert and Sullivan) and later by the efforts of men like David Belasco, the director became a dominant figure, coaching his players on stage business for their roles, blocking their movements, and integrating all the elements of a performance into what it was hoped would make up a coherent and impressive total effect.

David Wark Griffith, a major figure in film's early history, epitomizes the theatrical heritage of the new medium, although it should be remembered that he was an enthusiast of poetry and prose as well, of authors like Robert Browning, Charles Dickens, and Jack London. Griffith had his early training on the stage as an actor, and he even wrote a dreadful stage melodrama, called *A Fool and a Girl*. All of his most successful film ventures adapted the melodramatic form—one-dimensional characters, adventure stories, rescue-climaxes resolved through heroism. Griffith assembled a collection of actors who functioned like a group of repertory

* Limelight was created by directing a flame onto a cylinder of lime, then concentrating the resultant illumination through a lens system.

players. He would draw on their talents for each of his short (ten-, later twenty-minute) films. Like Belasco, he taught them to minimize gesture and expression, which had earlier been exaggeratedly stylized for visibility in the theater. Such grandiosity was exposed under modern stage lighting, and it collapsed entirely in front of the close scrutiny of the camera lens. Griffith combined devices of the theater with techniques of prose continuity in organizing his one- and two-reel productions for the Biograph Company, just off Union Square on Fourteenth Street.

What parallels remain today between film and theater? They are both, in a sense, live performance media, although the actuality of an actor's stage appearance gives an impression very different from his movie image. Acting, as Norman Mailer has aptly noted, invokes a special kind of ritual on stage. Once started, a performance continues inexorably until the end and is repeated each night or matinee. Theater spectators share something of that ritual demand; theater itself grew out of religious ritual. Theater brings a sense of renewal to its audience each time it is performed. It varies in intensity (and success) from performance to performance, and sometimes moment to moment in one perforance. It is a medium highly dependent on the interactions of its principals. And however thoughtfully conceived the decor, costuming, and movements, theater is dominated by the spoken word, which hangs in the air like a presence uniting performer and audience.

Film shares some of these qualities and intensifies others. What may best be expressed onstage by the movement of an arm and a leg is often better communicated in close-up by an eyebrow. The very bits and pieces —the shots—with which any movie is constructed not only serve to fragment each performance into moments, they also wrest control out of the hands of the actor. A finished film records a single version of a performance, locked forever in photographed images, but before the final take, each moment can be played with, reworked, even improvised many times.

Equally important, words in a film are but one of many elements, more or less dominant as the occasion requires. Most often, film depends in great measure on our anchoring what we hear to what is visible on the screen. We make more sense of a soundless film than a pictureless soundtrack. The concern of its creators, from the first draft of the shooting script to the last stages of laboratory processing, is pointed toward a kind of audience perception unlike that among theater audiences.

How, then, could Bazin claim film to be the theater of a new age? For one thing, he never shared those antagonisms which enthusiasts and professionals in one medium feel toward practitioners of other forms of art. His was a centripetal curiosity dominated by an integrated vision. Unlike other French critics of the period (Truffaut, for example) he was not offended by the idea of interdependency between film and theater, film and literature. Rather, Bazin tried to abstract an artist's intentions, which he was inclined to understand as dramatic, from one medium, then to pose the possibilities of their successful execution elsewhere. He felt that theater pieces stood better chances of transformation into film than did prose. A theatrical vision could, in principle, lend itself as effectively to the movie screen as to the stage. The very capacity of film to overcome the confines of the proscenium and eliminate the constancy of distance between performer and spectator, Bazin saw as the harbinger of a new aesthetic.

FILM AND PROSE

Likenesses between books and movies, adaptations apart, can be accounted for in several ways. Most movies are first written before they are filmed, and written, moreover, by writers—that is, by people who are comfortable with and probably experienced at telling tales through words alone. More important, the narrative element of both forms has evolved from a common oral tradition. For this reason, the organizational schemes on which both verbal and visual literacy rest often derive from storytelling. Often the stories themselves are shared. The manner of organizing material into episodes, while not identical between film and prose, is very much the same. Stock characters—the Watson figure in a detective story, the brave maiden lady who defends children against villainy, the little girl who hallucinates imaginary friends—are common to both. Expository tricks, character delineation, conversations, descriptions, and sometimes an author's personal interjections appear in either form.

Ways of assembling the material in terms of space and time are also shared. The mainstream tradition of storytelling by way of the written word from the eighteenth century into the first part of the twentieth (excepting the notable *Tristram Shandy*) has been what movie animators call *straightahead*. The story will progress chronologically in time from point A to point B—perhaps (as in Charles Dickens) from Birth to Marriage or (as in Thomas Hardy) from Marriage to Death. Of course, only a few major episodes can be dwelt upon within the resources of prose, even in as bulky and epic a work as *War and Peace*. The great body of time's passage, like much of our own lives, is simply dropped out, ellipsized, by way of transitional conventions. Many of *these* are shared with film.

It is possible to arrange episodes out of chronological sequence, and these techniques too have often been conventionalized in "flashbacks," often introduced by a character's reading a letter or diary that moves into the time of an event which is then itself recounted. Some of these techniques stem from the narrative experimentations of Joseph Conrad and Ford Madox Ford, who operated on the idea that our sense of one another's lives (and our own) follows no faithful chronology as events occur to us, but rather an inner logic whose connections may eventually explain the meanings of each memory—if we are ever able to understand them at all. Film tells its stories in like fashion. The reorganization of episodes out of chronological sequence is not only technically simple (mounting strips of cellulose in any designated order onto the film reels), but also satisfactory to the viewer, in part because the connective conventions have been easily transposed from prose (and theater) to movies, in part because the circumstances of watching film, as we have considered, seem to encourage our acceptance of dreamlike transitions.

In recent years, more radical sorts of experiments with narrative time have been undertaken in both prose and film. In some cases, checkerboarding chronologies are used that lack the conventions of transition we have learned to recognize: for example, slow dissolves or camera pans up to the sky to indicate the passage of time; or

*   *   *

which tell us that something either too boring or too good has been excised.

Other experimentation with time has been somewhat more complicated and will be discussed more fully when we consider subjectivity and point of view. Let us note here, however, that events shift not only in their chronological order, but also in terms of their relative credibility. To phrase the matter in the language of language, once the element of subjectivity has been introduced into an image, we are forced to confront something akin to the conditional tense: scenes that *might* have been or that are *somewhat* verifiable by other experience.

Another point of similarity between film and prose is the general dramatic structure of the way each is organized (although here perhaps theater provides a closer parallel than either the short story or the novel). In every case, there is an effort to build the extent of audience involvement and concern as the exposition progresses, then to resolve loose ends and feeling before THE END. Or else these expectations are reorganized, subdued, or circumvented: A disposition of many current films is to finish ambiguously, as in a freeze-frame, where motion ceases, but the picture remains, held rigid in a technological semblance of permanence.

Film and narrative prose share as well that sort of omnipotence which allows an author to travel in space quite as simply as he may manipulate time. He is free to locate his action anywhere in the wide universe and to assume whatever spatial perspective strikes his fancy: looking on his creation from a distance or close up, from on high or below or straight on, moving as the subject moves, drawing away, or pulling in for closer scrutiny. (Prose can do much of this less effectively than film, but prose did much of it first.)

On consideration, it may be seen that most of the capacities shared by the two media evolve from a common linearity; that is, they proceed unidirectionally in time from a beginning (or at least a point when things start) to an end (or at least another point when things conclude). This is the reason Marshall McLuhan proposed an essential cognitive linkage between the two media. He views motion pictures as a kind of last extension (or gasp) of literacy into the twentieth century.

But for all its seeming clarity, linearity is only one of many parts of the film experience. This accounts for some of the *differences* between film and prose. Further, if we reconsider the similarities that we have itemized so far, it may be discovered that, on closer examination, some likenesses are more apparent than real.

While film and prose may draw on a common background of story material and story organization, they do not treat this storehouse in quite the same ways. An easy strategy for considering their disparate approaches is to note exactly how a single piece of material is worked: for example, a story based on a film, or more likely the movie adaptation of a literary property. Such adaptation of well-regarded novels has been carefully studied by Professor George Bluestone in a book titled *Novels into Film*. Here we shall consider a novel somewhat less prestigious than those Bluestone discusses, one that has been less obviously altered in adaptation: a detective story mentioned earlier, Dashiell Hammett's *The Maltese Falcon*.

Hammett's novel began its career serialized in *Black Mask,* a pulp magazine, and met success on book publication. *The Maltese Falcon* presents the prototype of what eventually became a dreary succession of tough, cynical, unpredictable, intuitive investigators playing a lonely game against unscrupulous criminals for the sake of clients whose ethics hardly bore close scrutiny: Sam Spade, a private eye. This book is useful to our special concerns because of its allegedly faithful rendition on film, at least in the definitive version for Warner Brothers in 1941, featuring Humphrey Bogart, Peter Lorre, Sidney Greenstreet, and Mary Astor. It was John Huston's first directing assignment.

Huston had been a writer on the Warner Brothers lot for a number of years, and *The Maltese Falcon* was supposed to have been scripted by himself and Allen Rivkin. Years later, Huston maintained that in order to have a basis for discussion of the project with the company president, Jack Warner, he had requested a secretary to type out the Hammett novel in script form, merely omitting what was not useful and numbering the shots. Warner was pleased enough with the "script" he saw to advise Huston to proceed with the project as it stood. In truth, book and picture are very similar, if on close examination not structurally identical. (Huston's Jack Warner story is, however, apocryphal, like many—not all—Hollywood anecdotes.) Hammett's novel is spare and efficient, a model of concise, economic prose, which limits itself to the world experienced by Sam Spade—his conversations and actions, the offices and hotel rooms he frequents, and the streets of San Francisco. There is no dwelling on

Spade's thoughts, except as he confides them to another person. Spade's character and his ultimate intentions are central to the story, but they are hidden from the reader's purview except as evidenced by action, speech —often misleading—and occasionally expression. ("Blood streaked Spade's eyeballs now and his long-held smile had become a frightful grimace. He cleared his throat huskily.")[3]

Huston's film, first of all, redesigns the story's elements of suspense by letting us know things the detective doesn't. For instance, we see Sam's partner murdered *then* cut to Spade receiving the information by phone. More important, the first movie scene contains a *crawl** that tells the history of the falcon, a jewel-encrusted statue dating from the Crusades. All of this substitutes "we know, he doesn't" for "he doesn't know, we don't know." Such a change to create "suspense" is hardly an intrinsic necessity to the movie form, and yet it seems inextricably linked with film as a commercial fact of life. This reminds us of a danger constantly present in film study: In reducing our subject to logical, manageable proportions, we always run the risk of defining away substance for the sake of tidy analysis. Nothing inherent in film requires its allegiance to conservative orthodoxies—for instance, conventional "suspense"—except for what was inherent in a commercial, Warner Brothers film of the forties and a director's first feature.

Similarly, sociopolitical candors in Hammett's book are blunted in the movie. Criticism of Bryan, the District Attorney, is softened. Effie, Sam's secretary, does not step on the hand of a corpse. While the homosexuality of Joel Cairo (a supportive villain played by Peter Lorre) survives (one of the earliest such portrayals on the American screen), that of Casper Gutman (Sidney Greenstreet, the chief heavy) is muted. Hammett suggests, very subtly, that both Gutman and Cairo may be using Wilmer, their young gunman, as a sexual partner. This is omitted from the film, along with Wilmer's revenge by shooting Gutman.

Feature films are less able to absorb a great detail of event and character than the novel can manage. The film condenses Hammett's events: fewer sequences, fewer trips and visits, fewer characters, fewer clues. Adaptations often desaturate their prose material by combining several sequences or characters into one.

The character of Sam Spade provides an interesting illustration both of conservative changes in the transition from book to film responses and of the differences effected by our responses to the two different forms. In the novel, Sam "cursed Dundy for five minutes without break, cursed him obscenely, blasphemously, repetitiously, in a harsh, guttural voice,"[4] after the policeman has hit him. This is absent from the film. In the book,

* Credits, acknowledgments, or background notes that move from the bottom to the top of the screen. The words first appear at the bottom of the film frame, proceed gradually upwards, and finally disappear as they go beyond the top limits of the film frame.

Brigid (Sam's client) offers herself to him quite directly ("Can I buy you with my body?") before they make love. No similar scene occurs in the film. In the book, Sam forces Brigid to strip in his apartment after Gutman has accused her of stealing a thousand-dollar bill. In the film Sam only questions her. Dashiell Hammett's Sam Spade is crueler, tougher, emotionally more explosive, more exploitative. He controls his feelings, both to survive and to increase the chances of successfully completing his assignment. He hides his feelings behind a crooked reputation. True sexual emotion cannot obtrude into his profession without diminishing his effectiveness. He stays alive.

On the other hand, there are certain ways in which the movie reveals Spade to us more completely than we can learn from the printed page. Sam is a man who never tells more than he needs to, but on the screen he communicates through body language as well as through words, providing a counterpoint between what we see and what purports to be taking place. For example, in Hammett's novel, Joel Cairo draws a gun on the detective at their first meeting and demands to search the office. Sam raises his hands and allows The Levantine to frisk him, but Cairo, clumsy at physical confrontations, is quickly and easily disarmed, a fact which underlines his very helplessness.

Then Sam smiled. His smile was gentle, even dreamy. His right shoulder raised a few inches. His bent right arm was driven up by the shoulder's lift. Fist, wrist, forearm, crooked elbow, and upper arm seemed all one rigid piece, with only the limber shoulder giving them motion. The fist struck Cairo's face.[5]

In its own way, Hammett's prose is quite visual, breaking down a simple action into the component parts, ordering them clearly and sparely into a coherent sequence of smooth movement. (One is reminded of Hemingway describing a matador's movements, and Hemingway makes reference to Hammett in *Death in the Afternoon*.)

The confrontation between Humphrey Bogart and Peter Lorre assumes a somewhat different quality. Bogart raises his hands and disarms Lorre with equal ease, but at this point, he stalks the smaller man, lapels grasped in one hand, pressing him back across the office space, skillfully directing him to the armchair into which he will fall. The gentle, dreamy smile has been replaced by a "Bogie" grimace which hints at positive pleasure. (It is later echoed when he disarms Wilmer and when he watches the thieves argue helplessly in his apartment.) He is enjoying the moment. Perhaps it is the danger. Perhaps he likes to hit people generally. Perhaps he likes to hit people with perfumed calling cards. In any case, Bogart's momentary expression supplies a dimension to his character different from the novel and important to the movie characterization.

In the same category we might locate Sidney Greenstreet's straight-armed, stiff-kneed, paunchy strut as he departs Spade's apartment, flapping like a fat, live bird, while leaving the "*rara avis*" to Miss O'Shaugh-

The cumulative impact of these separate moments from *The Maltese Falcon* builds and reveals the characters—their tempers, suspicions, seductiveness, dismay—in ways beyond the capabilities of the printed word.

nessy; or Elisha Cook, Jr.'s Wilmer darting suspicious, rodent glances throughout. When the moment of truth strikes Gutman and Cairo, as they realize their bird is valueless, each responds with a betraying gesture —Cairo by falling on an armchair to weep, Gutman with a moment of jerking, birdlike head motions, which he quickly stifles by grasping the back of his neck with one hand.

A more developed piece of business is that of Mary Astor's Brigid, who characteristically smoothes her skirts demurely over pretty knees whenever she explains that she's not always led a good life. Such an action is emphasized in Huston's staging. In one instance, Bogart brings a chair horizontally across the foreground from frame left in order to point up, then obscure, Mary Astor's gesture centrally in the composition.

Such behaviors point up other distinctions between page and screen. In prose, a character is often free to explain himself, directly or obliquely, but usually through words. Such lengthy recountings are generally rejected by film. Their dependence on speech is thought inappropriate to a form where language is considered subordinate. Whether such a premise is trustworthy is certainly open to question; in any case, it has been the stance of film writers that an audience ought to learn what it needs to know about movie characters through their actions, and conversation "works" only when it leads to further action. Generally, film tries to *show* who a character is. The visual "event" shares equal importance with set and speech.

Consequently, in crudest form and stemming from its origins in mime, movie character delineation follows a policy of requiring villains to kick dogs and heroes to rescue children. (Even this scheme can be elaborated. There is an entire system of characterization in the films of Jean Renoir, for example, structured around actors' relationships with cats.) As characterization becomes more complicated, a writer will sketch a hero who is too demanding with his horse, or a villain gallant with the ladies, so as to leave us in short-term perplexity as to the truth. Similarly, he will use betraying gestures, like Mary Astor smoothing her skirt to counteract the force of her words.

Again we return to the paradox of film analysis. Any movie is very literally expressed by its look. The "how" of acting, staging, lighting, compositions: These are even more closely entwined with what a picture *is* than may be true of prose style. Yet there always remains the open question of just who is responsible for any given effect. Returning to *The Maltese Falcon* as a case in point, we may presume, for instance, that Huston bears the responsibility not only for the behaviors of his actors and the work of his crew, but also the "look," at least insofar as the latter differs from a particular studio look—in this case, the product of Warner Brothers' shadows and lighting (often designed to hide the cheap sets) as well as film stock, decor, and contract players.

Even in his first assignment, Huston has managed certain characteristic and consistent organizations of his screen space: a tendency to compose with the lower left frame dominant, secondary interest in the right corner (Sam at a chair explaining to Brigid why he must send her over), a strong exit screen left, the character moving into close-up (Joel Cairo, "I'm in no hurry. It's getting late, and I thought . . ." Wilmer exiting with the same gesture, revolvers replacing Cairo's cane and gloves). Huston is disposed, too, toward medium shots and over-the-shoulder shots.

However, just as *The Maltese Falcon* is defined in some measure by the Warners' look, it proves to be, like any feature, whether Hollywood, Mosfilm, Pinewood, or Cinecittà, a commercial product whose substance remains somewhat independent of individual stylization or predesigned intent. A choice of camera angles may prove in the last analysis to have been more the result of a particular cameraman's working pace, or the length of time a set can be occupied, or the duration of a performer's contract than it is the consequence of either individual or corporate vision. Moving camera shots will take longer to execute. The more setups scheduled, the more time consumed. Outside, a particular kind of daylight may be available only for a few hours. And an actor may have a hangover, so that his lines must be reworked on the set for easier reading.

There is, too, the presence of moneyed minds, operating at the very inception of a motion picture's production, strategies and craft dedicated to conceiving a film so as to meet and satisfy, but never unbalance or disorder, what has been accepted as a traditional litany of audience expectations.

Such considerations should not encourage us to award ill-deserved compliments to prose writers. They, too, are not without cautious considerations of audience expectation. Many novels now held in great esteem were written, often at great haste, for mass audiences in newspapers and magazines. (A good case in point is Dostoevsky.) In recent years an eye toward the book clubs has been known to cause the incorruptible author to reconsider a favorite passage.

Furthermore, many filmmakers, through luck, perseverance, power, diplomacy, or truculence, can more completely dominate their productions. Or else they may evolve special strategies to impose personality upon their material. Some of these devices will be considered when we turn to *auteurism*.

Comparing film and prose so far, then, we may conclude that certain elements of design seem to be common: the orderings of chronology, sequence, and authorial omniscience (if this be desired). Film appears to be a medium that can tolerate a greater lack of plotted "information" while at the same time remaining very alive with the visual impact of what it does express. (Partly for this reason, film is sometimes likened more to the short story than to the novel.) Finally, since naturalistic prose and the story movie are each inflected by all of the social and sometimes political considerations that bear on highly popular forms, that fact of life becomes thoroughly tangled with other media considerations. This tension underlines all feature film production and informs any criticism that has not destroyed a movie in order to describe it.

FILM AND TELEVISION

Television is not the ideal medium for viewing films, however much film makes up its lifeblood. Film projected onto a movie screen generally gives us more visual information than film transmitted through a television receiving set and made visible on its small, phosphate glass screen. The little screen's collection of lines and dots diminishes both the gradations of color and black-and-white shadings as well as the vividness and clarity of the images themselves. This is one reason why material filmed specifically for television distribution tends toward closer shots, in which the expression of performers is not only central but exclusively important.

Film enthusiasts have often had the experience of watching on small TV screens a film they had previously seen in a movie theater. There are various social and mechanical differences in the two situations, but one of the principal differences—and shortcomings—of seeing films on television is the drastically reduced quality of background in the smaller format. Settings often seem somehow to fuzz over, as if their very focus had been diminished in the transition, which of course is not the case. To watch, for example, an old Italian neorealist film on television means almost to change the philosophy and aesthetic with which it was made. The fatalistic relation between characters and setting that comes across when the film is seen in a movie theater is not evident on a TV screen because the backgrounds are less discernible. On TV the characters, rather than blend into countryside and urban rubble as if their natures and motives had been formed by a shattered world beyond human control, seem to stand out from their surroundings, like actors in a stage play.

I have sometimes made a classroom exercise out of comparing the two media. A film prepared for television (usually an *Alfred Hitchcock Presents*) is divided in half. The first half is screened through a telecine system onto a classroom television monitor. At the point where the reel expires, the remainder of the film is run through an ordinary 16mm movie projector and projected onto a regular movie screen in front of the students. The experience is informative. The projected "movie" image seems to throw into bolder relief elements of the production less visible on television. It is rather like the effect of a harshly lit vanity table mirror used to expose a subject to merciless examination. Limitations of acting are much more apparent on the larger screen—expressions, gestures, speech intonation, and human interaction. Painted flats and artificial backdrops that escape attention on the little screen become appallingly evident when magnified. As visibility increases, more authenticity is demanded; even props face sterner eyes. The story itself seems to become exposed to more considered inspection. Encounters, tensions, and situations that will play on television seem less believable on the larger screen.

Other differences result from the dictates of commerce, where film and television industries have not pooled resources and combined functions through interlocking ownerships or broadcasting's cannibalization of old movies. Television is largely directed toward the merchandising of commodities by way of commercials. Programs, in a very real sense, amount to interludes between one "pause for these few messages" and the next. In consequence, the program supports a dual, sometimes contrary, purpose. It should guarantee a maximum listening audience while yet never distracting that audience from the commercial by altogether absorbing its attention. In contrast, film-for-theater succeeds as it holds an audience "spellbound," thoroughly engrossed. In this respect, the gaggings, faintings, and involved excitabilities which attended The Exorcist (1973) all testify to its "power," that is to say, to its commercial promise.

One solution has been to design material specifically for TV broadcast more in terms of theatrical pace (a three-act play or a five-act play) than was ever true for feature films. In this way, emotional and commercial breaks coincide. Such, of course, is not the case on noncommercial television. Here the absence of merchandising interludes not only affects narrative continuity and audience empathy, it has also opened the way for experimentation with new dramatic construction; unfortunately, that route has been little traveled.

FILM AND NONDRAMATIC ARTS

I have concentrated my attention in this book on the narrative film; the very subject implies a certain orthodoxy. Nevertheless, we may profitably spend a short time on two other elements of film that are less directly related to narrative. One of these is graphic composition, which of course is inherent in any film image but comes to the fore, as it were, in modern art. The other is the nondramatic (or minimally dramatic) performance, as occurs in some forms of modern music and poetry.

When we consider relations between the movies and painting we are thrust at once into the history of still photography and of those changes that photography and art produced on one another. The history of nineteenth-century painting is a story of less-than-friendly intercourse between the two. Almost from its inception, photography claimed a blood descendency from graphic ancestors that painters would rather have denied. Photography accomplished the representational task too easily, bypassing the arduously acquired skills and secrets of the portraitist and landscape artist in the click of a shutter. Gradually the photographer (previously the daguerreotyper) usurped the professional provinces of the easel, particularly portraits. Little studios, appearing even in prairie towns and spots distant as the Klondike, gave to the poorest citizen as well as to the rich and the famous an opportunity to have a personal likeness that made up in detailed accuracy what it lacked in flattery.*

But painters did not altogether dismiss the lessons of the new medium. Although they did not find much to inspire them in photographs of composed faces against studio cycloramas, artful "salon" arrangements of fruit in a bowl, or mountains behind birch tree foregrounds, they were intrigued by those captured moments snatched out of the rush of time when space seemed to reorder itself into new, previously unrecognized shape. These were the often accidental result of mobile, outdoor still photography by way of the Kodak camera, which followed on George Eastman's invention of roll film.

Two artists whose candid views of space were influenced by the new possibilities created by photography were Honoré Daumier and Edgar Degas. For example, Degas began to investigate the possibilities of camera-angled, pulled-out-of-time moments, and their consequences for spatial composition.

Photography seemed almost to open up the world of the painter, to reposition his subject matter so that space, outdoor space, was bounded by objects, rather than objects by space. Of equal importance was the recognition of movement as compositionally useful, important in exciting new ways. Every instant frozen in time had both direction and momentum. What the painter could now accomplish often depended on a sense of organization based on the purposeful movement that was implicit in his work. Often the painter used the borders of his easel not simply for containment but as elements that contributed to his composition, edges which "pulled" or "repelled" his objects. Later, the compositional schemes of Degas, Renoir, and Manet were reintroduced into cinematography, particularly in French films of the thirties and forties.

After the impressionists and in reaction to photography's commitment to reality's surface, painting threw off a subservience to three-dimensional "seen" actuality, which it had nurtured since Brunelleschi reinvented conventions of graphic perspective in fifteenth-century Florence.

___

* The same pattern will be remarked with increasing frequency in the mechanical and electronic age: A new medium plunders the spoils of an older form, in consequence freeing the earlier art for other purposes. Or, changes in society may reconstitute the uses of a form. The critic and novelist Brigid Brophy has written, "The nineteenth-century novel had to fill-in and anesthetize the boredom of nineteenth-century life, for which reason it was the slave of its narrative. Nowadays this function is performed by thrillers. The rest of fiction has been set free. . . . It was slavery to narrative which made novels read-once-and-throw-away consumer goods. Twentieth-century prose fiction can be, as poetry has always been, re-readable. It is free to be as serious as serious music."[6]

The effect of photography on painting composition is shown in Edgar Degas's *The Dancing Class.* *(Credit: The Metropolitan Museum of Art. The H. O. Havemeyer Collection. Bequest of Mrs. H. O. Havemeyer, 1929)*

In its place we have been rewarded with a "modern art" of intensely personal image-iconographies and experiments with color and perception; today, little photography shops document babies, weddings, and men of distinction.

With the rejection of seen actuality, however, the painter appreciably lessened his capacity to imply motion. If the object on the canvas is understood to be a woman, a dog, a horse, or a boxer, however distorted, we can ascribe action to it because we allow the figure some sort of volition, since it is "alive." When painting abandoned representational imagery, it lost one technique of energizing pictorial space through implied motion; for example, a Degas figure walking out of the frame, as in *Le Vicomte Lepic et ses deux filles,* creates the illusion of motion more vigorously than a Miró shape. We may allow a shape some certain kind of vitality arising from color relationships and intensities, composition, and even the form itself, but much modern painting, on the whole, tends toward a kind of pre-photography quiescence. (Orphism and Futurism were efforts to reintroduce dynamic force into Cubism after 1910.)

How much more attractive, then, to the modern painter are the possibilities inherent in a motion picture camera, which can always generate its own movement and does *not* need to be beholden to the seen world, with its implicit real gravities and behaviors. Such experimentation, departing as it does from the narrative mode, will not be treated in depth in the present study, but the interested reader is referred to several studies of the avant-garde (or personal or experimental or underground) film.

Many visual schemes of recent story films tend to draw on Surrealism, an early twentieth-century art movement based on fantastic, incongruous, or uncommon juxtapositions. Surrealism has been a fruitful source of movie ideas because its preoccupations with dreaming and the play of unconscious forces on human perception find a sympathetic eye in the filmmaker. Surrealism did not abdicate but rather intensified its depiction of the visible, exaggerating it with hallucinated clarity, like a too sharply focused lens. Surrealism continues as an effective instrument of artistic passion today, for it denies the conservatism of naturalism, while yet allowing the artist to use representational form to show his outrage. This is why Luis Buñuel remains a vital force in the modern film, and it explains the echoes of de Chirico in Antonioni, of Duchamp and Dali in Fellini.

An awareness of composition, color schemes, and texture in painting is immensely helpful in understanding the feature film. Equally valuable is a familiarity with the philosophic-aesthetic foundations of major movements in the arts. Later we shall consider some of the ramifications of both expressionism and impressionism as they affect the story film.

When we consider relationships between film and other temporal arts, certain characteristics of both music and poetry call for our attention. Both forms share with prose and the theater the quality of combining an event happening-in-time (the argument of a poem, the duration of a piece of music) with a particular kind of out-of-time experience (the *sound* of the music, a poetic phrase or reflexive, turning-back-on-itself combination of syllables). Film shares these same attributes (it is a *moving picture*), but unlike poetry and music, its images are much more tangible and, generally, representational. However stylized, they have a certain kind of one-to-one reference with visible reality.

In earlier times this was less true; there was something of a different quality to the image in the silent movie. Synchronous sound reinforced the "realness" of what appeared on the screen. With synchronous speech, for example, Rudolf Arnheim notes that the audience is condemned to look at mouths, at where the sound comes from. Mouths are not all that attractive in motion; they dominate their settings like spoiled, noisy children demanding attention. We do not stare at the mouths of portraits. In the theater we listen, but we never feel the necessity to concentrate our attention on the sources of speech.

Before the mouths took over, silent film seemed to occupy a more intermediate ground—between The Less and The More, to refer back to a polarity mentioned earlier. However photographically "real," the image yet lacked a kind of grounding in the concrete and the tangible which it developed later through the reinforcement of sound. Operating with images alone the filmmaker could work more freely because his formal relationships had something more of the abstract quality of musical sounds. Images could be edited into incongruent contexts without sacrificing meaning. It is probably also true that the relative ease of editing silent film made this phase of production more interesting to the movie director or writer. In consequence, editing was more integral to the manipulation of a film's design. (Later, the technologies of sound film encouraged a more autonomous editing *craft*, shielded like other professional skills from free ideological interplay.)

In any case, the idea of musical composition was once a kind of analogue for experimental movie design. Hans Richter first tried to transfer Cubism into scroll form, then seized on film as a better way to relate his images in time, like music. (He called them *orchestrations*.) Film allowed Richter and Viking Eggeling to control the duration of any image, somewhat as a musical note has its duration. The tempo at which we perceive what is presented on the screen affects how we draw relationships between the individual images.

One of the more interesting urban documentaries of the twenties was Walter Ruttmann's *Berlin: Symphony of a Great City* (1927). Its very title betrays musical preoccupations. Other directors (the Russian Dovzhenko, for instance, who built interludes like musical paeans to his Ukrainian homeland) relinquished the narrative story for less time-bound ways of expressing feeling. The term *film-poem* was once common to movie criticism. *Lyric* as an adjective of descriptive praise appears regularly in the film literature of the twenties.

It is probably significant that most such experimentation has taken place in the short, sometimes very short, film. (To describe Dovzhenko's efforts as interludes makes the same point.) In its own way, an early film by Richter or Eggeling is akin to the time in which we might examine a painting, read or hear a lyric poem, or listen to a song. What we experience is the organization of film in patterns that depart from the dramatic principles associated with forms like the epic, the novel, the play, and the symphony.

This is the pattern of a Brahms symphony, the *Iliad, The Sound and the Fury,* and *King Lear:* an introduction, development of intensities, occasionally peaked by mounting climaxes until a summit of emotionality is followed by diminution and resolution. It bears obvious resemblance to (and probably has roots in) religious ritual, the cycles of the seasons, human aging, and the act of sexual love.

However, there are other ways to organize artistic experience along the continuum of time, long or short in duration: the rondo form, for example, which is echoed in classic ragtime, or the haiku, the plays of Samuel Beckett, the music of Erik Satie or John Cage. Most such patterns still make some use of devices to be found in the conventional drama, that is, techniques of repetition, of referring back, of developing variations by playing with order and context.

Where such experiences may differ (comparing, say, a Brahms symphony with a John Cage performance) is in the expectations that an audience will bring to the event, the requirements made on the quality of time passing in the auditorium. This is one reason why narrative film sometimes shudders under the pressures of experimentation. Because the film is peopled with characters—the usual ingredient of stories—an audience usually expects that its attention to the actors be rewarded by dramatic action. Furthermore, since the experience progresses in time, it ought, in all likelihood, to organize its discrete events so that purpose—that is, meaning—is somewhere evident in their sequence. Usually the accumulation of things happening leads to an act of recognition, of understanding, perhaps even of change, however minimal, on somebody's part. •

Of course all of these rules are open to question. Each may be played upon and even denigrated by the filmmaker. And the order of their occurrence is hardly sacred; chronology especially has been subject to the most disrespectful handling in the last few years. What a large, popular audience asks for is recognition, confirmation, or some other reinforcement of meaning (as discussed above in the section on Film and Secrets).

The point of interest in many innovative films revolves about the tension between technique and tradition. The application of formal schemes once highly experimental in painting, music, and poetry but now almost conventional is difficult in the feature film when such usage traps the filmmaker between the demands of form and dramatic necessity. In this respect the motion picture continues to experience creative pressures that other art forms have shed by forsaking a mass audience in favor of smaller, more homogeneous clienteles. Increasingly, status quo theater ("Broadway") is becoming moribund in this decade; but one of the consequences is the growing popularity of playwrights like Samuel Beckett, whose work is supported by small, knowing audiences.

FILM STUDY

Movies' first appearance in the classroom was greeted with a mixture of condescension and hypocrisy; film was viewed as a kind of entertainment whose appeal lay—like other popular pleasures—below the sightlines of instruction and analysis, of educated appreciation. (We are passing over those "educational films" where omniscient narrators describe confusing, animated diagrams of digestive systems and sound as if gasoline-powered lawnmowers were lodged in their diaphragms.)

In many respects, film has been in the twentieth century what the novel was in the eighteenth and nineteenth—a vulgar form which spawned and matured largely independent of criticism and consequent "rules." Like the novel, the feature film had a direct and pragmatic relation to its audience. Success was measured in attendance. What was good was what many people experienced. What proved to be box office merited repetition, in the same way that *The Maltese Falcon's* Bogart, Lorre, and Greenstreet were rematched in *Casablanca* (1942) and *Passage to Marseilles* (1944), and a film like *Dead Reckoning* (1947) varied little from the *Falcon* plot, with Lizabeth Scott in the Mary Astor role and Bogart as a returning veteran. Gradually, the motion picture developed a coherent body of expository techniques to tell a story. Still, movies were little considered in American educational curriculums, just as the novel was not "studied" until the late Victorian or even Edwardian period.

One reason for such neglect was, and continues to be, the unavailability of films for study. Of all art forms, movies are least accessible to reconsideration, to what libraries (or "information centers") now term "retrieval." Somehow most books can be located and made available for personal use. The phonograph record and the tape recorder reproduce musical classics. The art historian has four-color plates and slide projectors.

Students of film are less fortunate. The very expense of movies—itself a consequence of popularity—has precluded general availability. Even if one lives in a large cosmopolitan center, where some theater or institution may show old films in repertory, the opportunity for personal selection is minimal. Unless a student is a college film major, he may never examine a reel of sound film (his own or anyone else's) on a viewing machine which allows him to stop, start, reverse, slow down, and take notes on the experience—as anyone is free to do with a book, a recording, or a painting in a gallery. Pictures and text in a book such as this are only a poor substitute.

Moreover, until quite recently, people have been snobbish with the scorn of the reader toward images anywhere in academia. In point of fact, all the graphic arts, and the performing arts as well, have only gradually become acceptable subjects of study in our educational system. By their very nature, they are less amenable than science and the humanities to verbal articulation. If, in fact, a picture or a piece of music could be expressed in words, it would lack that self-sufficiency which gave it an identity in the first place. Like painting, sculpture, dance, music, and theater, film can be talked about, but even the most thoughtful discussion about art will fail to approximate the actual experience of it. What can be accomplished is a broadening of our understanding about the visual event, and this in turn may define the way we deal with film.

At an elementary level, words and images share certain qualities. Both convey clusters of information. Both are somewhat open to manipulation; that is, they may be ordered and organized and subverted to special pur-

MOUNTAIN

Paul Cézanne's Mont Sainte-Victoire.   *(Credit: The Phillips Collection, Washington, D.C.)*

pose. Each has a kind of built-in unitary essence; broken down further, it becomes less than itself. Each has, too, nuances and overtones that will define secondary meanings through order and organization. In the language of the semanticists, words and images are both denotative and connotative. Both *signify*, even with regard to the same phenomenon: the word mountain, the image of a mountain, and a mountain.

But words and visual images are not alike. Whatever words may do, they can never be as specific in relating what things look like—a task performed by images with seeming ease. However elaborate, no description of a mountain will effectively convey a particular mountain's shape, its colors (and the changes in color as the light changes), the clarity of atmosphere, the design of its surroundings, the size and texture of its trees and rocks, the sense it gives to a particular valley or slope or desert, the kinds of clouds that circle above or around it. Furthermore, a mountain —in actuality or created by the painter or documented by a photograph—

has of necessity to occupy a particular space. It calls for foreground, mid-ground, background, and all the orthodoxies of perspective. It *requires* a point of view, a stance from which to be seen, as well as a frame, be it the peripheries of vision, the dimensions of a canvas, or the boundaries of screen projection.

Words do other things, many far more efficiently and effectively, than the visual image. (There are, of course, the images of choreographed and architectural space as well.) For example, words carry overtones more like music, in fashions denied the visual image by its very specificness. The bull in Picasso's *Guernica* may connote courage, pride, stability, strength, lust, maleness, the elemental, perhaps even Picasso himself; it probably suggests all of these things. Yet even in its less-than-representational style, Picasso's bull remains, defiantly and ineluctably, a bull.

Words are more imprecise. That very imprecision can be one of their strengths, because words can be the more pliably adapted to different contexts. The writer may modify his bull with adjective, metaphor and syntax. He will never approximate the exactitude of Picasso or a photograph, or a bull itself, but such a bull as he manages to create out of words *can* connote courage or pride or lust or the elemental with special vigor.

Comparison of word and image forcefully introduces another attribute of the film experience. Film is a time medium, but it is also a space medium. Painting is a space medium. Architecture is a space medium. Music is a time medium. Theater is a time and space medium. Dance is a time and space medium.

Actually every form partakes of both elements. They are—on consider-

Pablo Picasso's *Guernica*. *(Credit: The Museum of Modern Art, New York, on extended loan from the artist)*

ation—inescapably linked. When we look at a painting, our eyes move in what seems a random pattern from place to place on the canvas, and a sophisticated painter knowledgeably directs the viewer's eye movement so that it will serve his private purposes. Time is involved in any sensory response. One can only experience architecture by walking around or through it; the same holds true for sculpture. Similarly, the distance between ourselves and musicians or actors is a very real element of any performance, and players will articulate words, tones, and gestures and control their dynamics accordingly.

By the same token, a writer envisions elements of space in any narrative undertaking. Long before film, prose took particular cognizance of space, of point of view and physical movement. Nevertheless, the written word can never expect to approximate either the density of these elements as they are communicated in film, nor the speed of that transmission. Should anyone question this proposition, he can test it just by looking at a photograph or a film clip or by glancing around him, and then proceed to write down all that he has taken in. At this moment, I am sitting with my typewriter at a picnic table in the backyard of a farmhouse in an agricultural valley. It would take much time simply to itemize the number of things falling within my view—mountains, evergreens, fruit trees, vegetables, flowers (none of the last three named as distinct species), horses, dog, barn, toolshed, clothesline, and so on—let alone sense impressions like the color of the fields, the sounds of passing trucks, or the reflections on wet grass; the slant of the clothesline or the angle of a collapsing birdcage; the enclosure of a pair of beeches overhead or the movement and arcs of two lawn sprinklers. The writer selects and orders his perceptions, because to do otherwise is unendurable; a lack of order would press upon our senses and cause increasing discomforts.

We have not altogether departed the classroom for the out-of-doors, for we have been enunciating reasons why the educator tended to ignore film. It is not accessible. Film was difficult to discuss except by pretending it was literature. And films once thought worthy of consideration (like adaptations of Charles Dickens) were often, in truth, not very good.

The notion of translating a literary work into another medium ignores both the differences between each and the singular properties of prose that gave the work its special qualities in the first place. A written achievement only suffers under such juggling, and the best translation to film— Franz Kafka's *The Trial* (1963), for instance—occurs when a director like Orson Welles does not consider himself subservient to the text, but rather produces his own work "in the manner of" the author.

Otherwise the effort is self-defeating, for film can only diminish special experiences of prose fiction by reconceiving them through different eyes and foreign form. It was wisely said by André Bazin that unambitious works of fiction are far more likely to make good films than are "good books." (*The Maltese Falcon* by Dashiell Hammett is neither unambitious nor poor, but changed by John Huston so that it belongs no longer to the original author.)

With the advent of film study as a somewhat independent academic venture—a phenomenon of the sixties in most of American education, earlier among certain midwestern universities and film schools in New York, California, and Europe—there has sometimes developed a kind of reverse snobbery among film academics: that film is uniquely unique. The notion of approaching the study of film through any other discipline or aesthetic appears as objectionable as painting pictures by typewriter or analyzing poems with a T-Square.

Such posturing is understandable in any fledgling discipline. As well as being defensive, it provides the impetus to construct a vocabulary that does not draw on the ideologies of other areas. (The social sciences did the same thing, and are still mired in words they invented.) Furthermore, people who share a particular enthusiasm (or love) are likely to construct shields against a philistine world. ("Of course *everybody* thinks he knows all about *movies*.")

At the same time, film's very nature works in certain ways against the self-protective, hermetic armor of academic wall construction. Film draws on agencies beyond itself for several reasons. One is its relation to photography, which appears at times to condemn the story film to one or another aspect of what is experienced directly through our senses as "reality," however stylized that experience may become; to put it another way, movies are led inescapably into the world they depend upon.

Further, our knowledge of narrative traditions forbids any notion that the story film sprang full-blown in an extraordinary virgin birth. Movies share too much with other forms. If the present study were seriously extended to cover personal, experimental film or the documentary, it would be equally obvious that these forms have evolved in the last several decades in common directions with contemporary poetry, painting, theater, and journalism. At the moment when the arts, like science and the humanities, seriously seek shared experiences, motifs and lineage, film would be shortsighted to withdraw into a darkroom: a little citystate trying to escape nationalism when the direction is really toward One World.

Finally, there is the matter of film as "mass" medium. Stendhal described the novel as a mirror alongside the roadway, held up to passing society. As noted before, serious students of popular culture today are busy with an even broader reflection covering the whole gamut of commercial, popular ephemera from TV panels to rock lyrics. Certainly film involves, among its many attributes, a culture trying to talk to itself. (An interesting study of film comedy by the British critic Raymond Durgnat is titled *The Crazy Mirror.*) Again, we would diminish our awareness of what movies do by ignoring their social dimension, even though our attention is pointed more toward what film says than what it mirrors. (The revolutionary film raises these issues in another way, often stridently.) In any case, the relations of film to society work against anyone ever sealing it up, away from the diseases of the marketplace, which is not to say that feature film *is* the marketplace or that it is "the same as" other commodities, like television and the comic strip.

Hence the present study.

The remainder of the book will investigate why movies happen at all. First we will look at where they came from, less by way of dates and personalities than with an eye toward structural innovations and formal trends. Following this, our attention will turn toward some of the ways a motion picture is conceived, produced, and merchandised.

Next we will turn toward film theory and criticism: what kinds of attitudes have been taken toward the experience itself and how writers have tried to justify their positions. We shall think about how films may be compared, if at all. Then it is our intention to consider what may happen to the movie in the future—structurally, through different storytelling devices; and technically, through changes in production and distribution. Last of all is the matter of how the audience—that is, ourselves—relates to the evolving film experience.

RECOMMENDED READING

■ Pauline Kael's views on film in education can be found in David C. Stewart, ed., *Film Study in Higher Education* (Washington, D.C.: American Council on Education, 1966). E. M. Forster's *Aspects of the Novel* is available in paperback (New York: Harcourt Brace & World, Harvest Books, n.d.). Joseph Medill Patterson interviewed the nickelodeon operator for "The Nickelodeon," *Saturday Evening Post,* November 23, 1907. It is reprinted in Roger Butterfield, ed., *Saturday Evening Post Treasury* (New York: Simon & Schuster, 1954).

■ The address of *The Journal of Popular Film* is University Hall 101, Bowling Green, Ohio 43403. Relations between the novel and time are fully and thoughtfully explicated in A. A. Mendilow, *Time and the Novel* (New York: Humanities Press, 1972). George Bluestone's *Novels into Film* appears as a reprint (Berkeley: University of California Press, 1968), as does Dashiell Hammett, *The Maltese Falcon* (New York: Viking Press, Vintage Books, 1972). Robert Richardson compares movies and prose in *Literature and Film* (Bloomington: Indiana University Press, 1969). Rachel Maddux, Stirling Silliphant, Neil D. Isaacs, *Fiction Into Film* (Knoxville: University of Tennessee Press, 1970) traces a story, *A Walk in the Spring Rain,* from book to script to film while discussing the changes which followed. See also Fred H. Marcus, ed., *Film and Literature* (Scranton, Pa.: Chandler, 1971).

■ For a structural study of characterizations in Jean Renoir's films, see Robert M. Willig, "Boudus and Satyrs," *The Velvet Light Trap No. 9* (a film journal published at Arizona Jim Coop, Old Hope Schoolhouse, Cottage Grove, Wisconsin 53527).

■ All the Bazin observations noted herein will be located in André Bazin, *What is Cinema?* vol. 1, trans. Hugh Gray (Berkeley: University of California Press, 1967). The major study of film and theater is still A. Nicholas Vardac, *Stage to Screen* (Cambridge, Mass.: Harvard University Press, 1949). Norman Mailer's comments stem from an introduction to *Maidstone* (New York: New American Library, 1971).

■ To understand painting's relation to photography, the reader should study a good history of nineteenth-century art, together with one on photography, for example, Helmut and Allison Gernsheim, *History of Photography* (New York: McGraw-Hill, 1970) or Beaumont Newhall, *Latent Image* (Garden City, N.Y.: Doubleday, 1967).

■ Rudolf Arnheim's *Film as Art* (Berkeley: University of California Press, 1969) epitomizes the view of silent film as the Golden Age, but his remarks on painting and psychology apply to all film. See also his *Picasso's Guernica* (Berkeley: University of California Press, 1962), *Art and Visual Perception* (Berkeley: University of California Press, rev. ed., 1974), and *Visual Thinking* (Berkeley: University of California Press, 1969). Other Arnheim comments used here stem from an informal lecture at San Francisco State College, May 7, 1965.

■ For histories of the avant-garde, see David Curtis, *Experimental Cinema* (New York: Delta, 1971), Parker Tyler, *Underground Film, a Critical History* (New York: Grove Press, 1969) and Sheldon Renan, *Introduction to the American Underground Film* (New York: E. P. Dutton, 1967). Marshall McLuhan's messages are decoded in *Understanding Media* (New York: McGraw-Hill, 1964). An articulate (and sympathetic) view of television aesthetics will be found in Herbert Zettl, *Sight, Sound, Motion* (Belmont: Wadsworth, 1973).

■ John Fell, *Film and the Narrative Tradition* (Norman: University of Oklahoma Press, 1974) considers the relations between movies' expository techniques and many other media in greater detail than can be undertaken here. For thoughts on film and modern theater, see Fell, "Freeze Frame," in *Arts in Society* 10, no. 2 Fall 1973 (University of Wisconsin Extension, 610 Langdon Street, Madison, Wisconsin 53706).

■ Recent research on American television viewing habits is to be found in Robert T. Bower, *Television and the Public* (New York: Holt, Rinehart & Winston, 1973), which updates similar surveys from George Steiner, *The People Look at Television* (New York: Alfred A. Knopf, 1963).

NOTES

1. Dashiell Hammett, *The Maltese Falcon* (New York: Alfred A. Knopf, 1929, 1930, 1957; reprinted Vintage Books, 1972), p. 3.
2. Quoted in Alfred Kazin, *Bright Book of Life* (Boston: Little, Brown, 1971, 1973), p. 180.
3. Hammett, *Maltese Falcon*, p. 192.
4. *Ibid.*, p. 73.
5. *Ibid.*, p. 41.
6. Quoted in Kazin, *Bright Book of Life*, p. 179.

Part II

Film Elements

3 ▪ Space and Time

Although the present study is not a film history and does not describe the relationship of a film discovery to its cultural or sociopolitical milieu, in the work of certain filmmakers—Griffith and Eisenstein, most notably—the understanding of such a relationship is essential. In general, however, I have used a somewhat chronological approach toward components of the narrative film in order to point up how these components "worked" in the context of evolving, shifting narrative ambitions. Because movies still lack a vocabulary and critical approach that effectively separate the creative personality from that personality's contribution, this section will be found, too, to shift between discussion of general subject matter and occasional short biographical profiles.

To treat a concept like "space" separately from its obvious correlates may seem at first to do disservice to the interrelationships between all the elements that make up film experience. Nonetheless, the step was undertaken here, for to approach the elements initially in terms of their interaction would not only be overwhelming but would also tend to obscure the particular contributions each element may bring to the whole.

It may be noted, too, that what are termed "elements" can hardly be regarded as mutually consistent or like categories. (Time and point of view? Sound and genre?) Rather they are facets of film and filmmaking that the neophyte observer would do well to incorporate into his movie vocabulary. Awkward as this is at first—rather like one's first driving lessons, when simultaneously steering, shifting, signaling, and watching the road seems impossible—eventually the process of responding to and re-

57

lating these elements as one watches a film will become almost automatic.

Finally, various components—editing, for instance—are discussed from a different perspective later in the book. In this section, each is purposely limited to the development of film as a form and the broadening of its creative possibilities.

SPACE

Unlike painting, film space is defined by movement—either by the subject viewed or by the camera-spectator. Unlike that in the theater, space in film shifts from shot to shot—that is, the perspective, or the relative distance and angle of view between viewer and subject, continually changes. The history of film development moves from static to mobile, from single to multiple points of view, though hardly in ordered fashion. The term "space" itself becomes increasingly ambiguous and begins to seem more a coordinate of time.

Retrospective comprehension of the early years of film was long bound by certain pivotal titles, not a great number, available through a few key viewing and distribution sources. More recently, vast material has become available through the agency of a Southern Californian, Kemp Niver, who has rescued and catalogued quantities of early film submitted to the Library of Congress for copyright protection in the form of paper prints of each entire title. Because this relocated the images themselves on a more durable medium than the unstable cellulose nitrate stock and because Niver developed a technique to rephotograph the little pictures on modern movie film, we now have substantial amounts of early footage to study that would otherwise have escaped attention.

On examining selections from this material, one is struck first by its liveliness (as if the Edwardian world possessed, in some curious fashion, more energy than ours), and then by its variety. Contained within the format of obvious and trite story anecdote there are to be seen a body of film technical "firsts" that presage later developments. What is lacking is coherence. Shots, human actions, and camera movements, striking in their singularities, remain unintegrated into the broader contexts of the little films, which run from a few seconds to a few minutes. Later one begins to notice minimal connections—a matching piece of action that joins one scene to another, or an enlargement of part of a just-seen composition. Screen compositions, particularly those shot out of doors, are often so vivid and so admirably complex that the movie historian is encouraged to reconceive his previous impressions of narrative evolution.

Theater and prose taught film how to organize scenes into greater unities. At the same time, the older media restrained movies from exploring space. However much the written story and the stage had themselves investigated shifting views on enacted scenes, their resources encouraged different narrative strategies. In prose, for example, point of view tended to emphasize the psychological aspects of a character's perspective (Henry James, Virginia Woolf). Theater used spotlights, color, design, and the control of actors' movements the better to direct audience attention.

Neither medium was able to indulge the possibilities afforded by shifting distances and "angle" of view between the reader or spectator and the subject of his attention (the book or performance). Eventually prose came increasingly to ape film techniques, and some types of theater chose to resolve the matter by relocating the performance in such a way that distance became open to manipulation, either by placing spectators on the playing area or allowing them to move about the theater at will. Arena staging allowed actors some choice about whom they could address. Planting performers in the audience itself or rushing them into the aisles clouded the definition of spectator and player in an attempt to encourage more movie-like empathy from a sometimes nervous audience.

The lessons of the parent medium, then, encouraged film to approach space as a static perspective. Two scenes might be ordered so that a portion took over the full dimensions of the earlier screen.

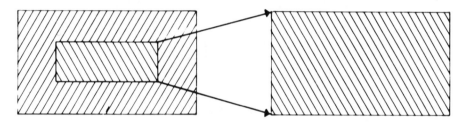

Or the reverse, in which one shot diminished into the broader context.

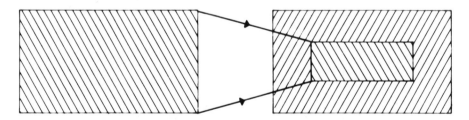

The possibilities were open to infinite variation, for any combination of separate footages will take on a time-sequence quality, defining how much an audience shall see and the order of disclosure. For example, a French director, Louis Delluc, experimented in the early twenties with what he called "Photogenic" technique. In a film titled *Fièvre* (1921), which dealt with low life in a waterfront bar, Delluc presented his audience with close shots of the saloon habitués without allowing them an "establishing shot" orientation, which we ordinarily need—in film as in prose—to understand the overall spatial geography (Lon Chaney, Jr., and Maria Ouspenskaya in the gypsy caravan on the Transylvanian steppes; McMillan and Wife standing in the museum gallery). Such an approach began to tap elemental movie uniqueness, as space became injected with ambiguity and emotion. But so far as Delluc's waterfront dive shared the single-space limitation of the naturalist theater's box-with-one-invisible-wall, its origins remained creakily evident.

The situation might be likened to an art film of the forties or fifties in which the cameraman has photographed a single graphic surface (painting or still photograph) so that its boundaries extend beyond the borders of the screen, thus creating a "world," like the Magritte painting superimposed within its own visual field. Within this special universe, the operator may move his camera at will.

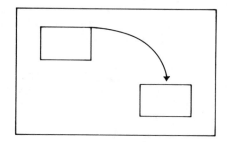

Or else he can execute a series of separate shots, each composed within the larger canvas.

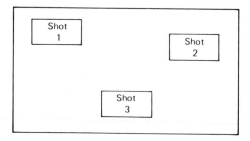

Still, the world of the broad canvas remains constant, its space impermeable to camera eye. (Painters disliked such movies because they denied the integrity of the artist's original compositions for the sake of passing effects.)

Another example of such organization would be the situation of a theater spectator equipped with opera glasses. He may supply his own close-ups at any moment during a performance. If the glasses are good enough, he may even create spherical compositions of other sizes (medium shots, medium-close shots). Nevertheless, the spectator can never vary the single perspective of his view without changing his seat. Furthermore, he has coopted a stage director's prerogatives, imposing a personal aesthetic on the performance by deciding what shall be singled out and how long each shot shall be. All such actions manipulate a single, theatrical space, which ultimately maintains its own integrities. (We document, rather than re-create, the world around us.) This approach to dramatic form should not be considered outdated or disused. It continues to dominate a great body of film work and is as well an inheritance of "live" television, particularly under circumstances where camera mobility has been inhibited by physical necessity. Football games and congressional hearings afford good examples. Television cameras are arranged for maximum coverage, usually effectively, if somewhat monotonously, because the space of performance itself is circumscribed. What occurs, then, is documented by the cameras, subject to the events and certain options on the part of the television director. He decides how long we shall look at a particular space scooped out of the larger playing area and how much of that area we shall see.

Spatial innovation in movies began with structural innovations by D. W. Griffith, which took two paths. Both originated in the same principle: that a spectator's vantage on events can transcend what is available to the experience of any of the principals. One application of this axiom confined itself to the geography of a single setting. The other switched between two or more locations.

The technique can be illustrated in the episode where Lincoln is assassinated in Griffith's *The Birth of a Nation* (1915). For our purposes the setting itself, a replica of Ford's Theatre, in Washington, D.C., is interesting because it evokes the distances between spectator and performance that we have just considered.

Phil and Elsie Stoneman are attending a performance of *Our American Cousin,* locating themselves in orchestra seats. In the opening shots we are introduced to the general overview of the theater itself, then to the couple's location and to their vantage. As from the orchestra, we see the stage and then the President's box, where we note the presence of Lincoln and his party.

Next we shift altogether, beyond the limits of our previous perspective. We note the disastrous inattention of Lincoln's bodyguard and see John Wilkes Booth outside the box, coming in to a close-up of the assassin's pistol. These events, historically earth-shaking, appear to have no special, functional, dramatic significance until we remind ourselves that they are unknown to anyone but ourselves. We, the movie audience, enjoy a dra-

And then when the terrible days were over and the healing time of peace was at hand, came the fated night of April 14, 1865.

Lincoln's assassination from D. W. Griffith's *The Birth of a Nation.*

matic omniscience denied any of the performers. Booth sees the body-guard and Lincoln, but he does not see the stage where he will trip while catching his spur in the American flag. Lincoln, for a few more moments, sees only the performance of *Our American Cousin*. Phil and Elsie Stoneman see the performance and the President's party, but the events unfolding on the far side of the box door are unknown to them.

The matter of audience foreknowledge, then, created new and fertile ground for aesthetic elaboration in defining a special audience relation to spatial shifts. In extending this largess to the audience, film divested itself of the bonds of nineteenth-century naturalism, although no one realized it for a while and matters continued to operate as if nothing had happened.

When, for example, we watch the play *Hedda Gabler,* our own experience is largely shared with the title role. Ibsen encourages us to note Hedda's changes in speech and manner as she deals separately with different members of her family and her social set. Each such encounter broadens our sense of Hedda Gabler's complexities, for we see and hear different, sometimes conflicting, moods. In a sense, we know Hedda in ways she herself cannot understand, yet all of the experience has been shared with her. Her death has special poignance for us because we have been permitted to see more of her true nature than anyone else in the play, even—or perhaps, especially—her husband.

Film interjected the possibility of audience experience independent of the performers. In consequence, our judgments are forever condemned to a certain independence, the result of the imaginative use of space. Space, as Godard said, has a moral component.

The other Griffith path, switching back and forth across distances to organize two stories into one for the sake of suspense, is something of a vulgarization of the same idiom. As in Ford's Theatre, we are given a sort of geographic omnipresence that allows us to know everything that is happening. If the hero is racing to rescue the heroine, we know he's on his way, but she does not. We know how close she is to torture-rape-vivisection, but he can only suffer his worst doubts before arriving on time. The entire design is one to encourage audience suspense— . . . *and then . . . and then . . .* —at a primitive level, and little more. Suspense is certainly not absent from Ford's Theatre, but it is accompanied by our sense of an acting-out of something we already know is going to happen.

The *switchback* ("meanwhile, back at the ranch"), which came to be known as crosscutting or parallel editing, was also used by stage melodrama, as in the tied-to-the-tracks rescue, although theatrical space worked against its effective execution, except where two staging areas might be undertaken simultaneously. Parallel editing will be found, too, in popular writers of earlier date—Frank Norris, for example. It can even be argued that the technique exists germinally in the *Iliad* and the *Odys-*

sey or in any epic, for a hero must always operate successfully against the challenge of time, and time's imminence is usually signified by crisis, shifting back and forth between events.

Further employments of space evolved from the filmmaker's sense of composing objects in such ways as to surround them with the undefined. Carl Dreyer's *The Passion of Joan of Arc* (1928), for instance, abstracts Joan's tortured interrogation out of courtroom space with an inexorable, indescribable series of close-ups. Maria Falconetti displays an anguished, psychic sickness-unto-death, almost unbearable not because she fears dying but rather because she is withheld from the sacrament and because she listens for, but does not hear, her voices. The space around Joan serves to isolate her in despair, to emphasize the emptiness that she inhabits (it is a barren space), and to remind us of the voices, which would be heard only by Joan in the very silence of the screen images.

Another famous movie moment that draws on space for effect occurs in Eisenstein's "Odessa Steps" sequence during Part Four of *The Battleship Potemkin* (1925). A crowd of citizens, sympathetically disposed toward the sailors who have mutinied on a government vessel anchored off the shore, has been brutally attacked by guards of the Czar's Winter Palace. The people flee down the palace steps (a process that seems to take almost forever), chased by the guards who descend from above and fire without cause or warning. Eisenstein has previously singled out various types from among the crowd; he now returns periodically to note the fate of each during the slaughter. One is a nurse with a baby and carriage, another apparently a student.

The nurse is fatally shot. Sinking slowly, she brushes against her carriage and sends it hurtling down the palace steps. As the carriage gathers momentum, an impression furthered by progressively closer shots, its passage is marked by one of the sequence's few camera movements. Earlier shots advised us that the bottom of the steps offers not safety but carnage by Cossack troops who have cut off the crowd's escape.

Eisenstein then returns to his "student." In the tumult, the boy's attention has been caught by the baby and carriage bouncing down the stone steps. Like the baby, he is powerless to affect events. As additional spectators, ourselves helpless, we know this to be the case not because we see the space between student and carriage, but because we do not. Each subject occupies its isolated spot. Their close-ups denote human fragmentation and connote impotence. The student's immobility contrasts with the jouncing carriage in Eisenstein's variation on parallel editing; here the victim rushes toward the crisis while the rescuer stands helpless. The sequence concludes with the student open-mouthed in powerless rage, as the carriage upturns into a mass of bodies at the base of the steps, to be followed by a Cossack swinging his saber in close-up toward the camera. Here, suddenly, space is not undefined, but danger-

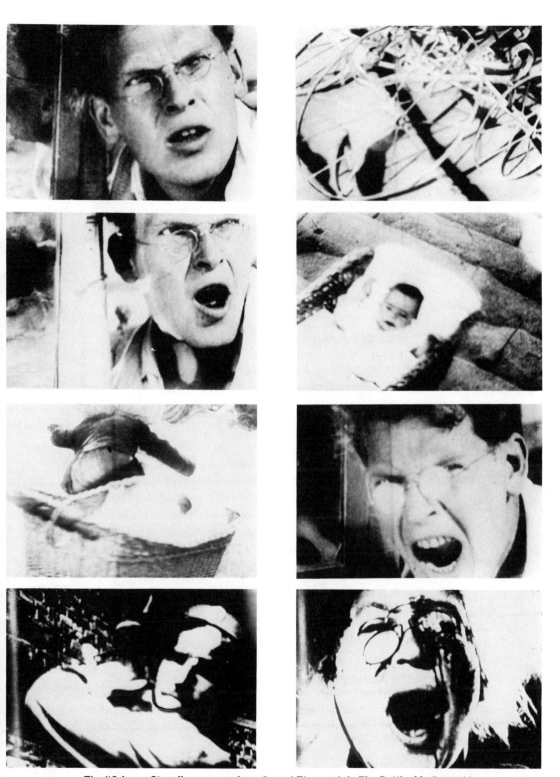

The "Odessa Steps" sequence from Sergei Eisenstein's *The Battleship Potemkin.*

ously real and occupied. Eisenstein finishes this part of the episode with one further switch. After the Cossack has swung his saber, we see his apparent victim: not the baby but another identifiable figure, a woman with a pince-nez, which is now shattered, and blood streams from her eye. In a short time—less than a minute—Eisenstein has isolated, contracted, and altogether abolished space's integrity, leading us to inject his distanced relationships with our feelings.

In contrast to the isolation of space for dramatic purpose, its coherence was emphasized as well by experiment with camera movement. In itself, the idea of mounting a camera on some conveyance, likely wheeled, began early in filmmaking and was not remarkable. Very early films located cameras on buses, cars, and railroad trains, documenting the reality that hurtled past screen edges. To maximize vistas or sometimes to follow performers, cameramen swiveled their instruments on tripods in horizontal and vertical sweeps. Allan Dwan, who himself later became a director, helped Griffith construct an elevator-truck that would descend while it approached actors walking through a gigantic simulation of a Babylonian courtyard (*Intolerance* [1916]).[1]

All these efforts sprang from the impulse to include more material without the interruption of moving to another setup and taking a subsequent shot, but they soon grew into devices with artistic potential in their own right. As camera movement became more functionally integrated into narrative, it introduced further variables for the filmmaker to consider. One of these was subjectivity: the camera operating as if through the eyes of a participant. The execution of shots from unusual angles could give the viewer a novel attitude toward the action. Another consequence of increased camera movement was the effect of such movement itself on audience perceptions.

Recalling a subject discussed in chapter 1, the left-hand, Nanook side of the verisimilitude arrow, we might extend the idea that audiences believe moving an image disturbs little more than the balance of a shot. Moving the camera underlines this confidence, reassuring the spectator that what he is watching is real. In proving the integrity of space, camera mobility undergirds our visual faith, which can be shaken by the cut. Furthermore, as long as the camera speed has remained constant, screen time coincides with clock time.

A cinematographer working with a series of static angles and varying only the relative size and perspective of his subject matter, is in a position to control composition. When he adapts to a continuous camera run and a moving base of operation, he literally faces constant, shifting fields of images, not only ones whose very transience denies him careful composition but also images different in kind, since the rules of perspective governing the static picture no longer apply. He may elect merely to start on one effective composition and to conclude his movement on another equally satisfactory. At best, the cinematographer tries to pass through interesting arrangements as well. Success rests on the speed of his camera movement and the character of what he traverses.

In its exploration of space, camera movement manages to restore some of the depth sense lost by the static shot. As a lens approaches or recedes from its subject matter, the distances between objects shift, relative to the camera. Let us begin an approach, with camera fifteen feet from an actress who is standing five feet behind two trees:

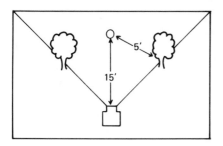 

The relation between her distance from each tree and her distance from the camera would be five feet to fifteen feet or 1:3. If the camera moves in and diminishes its separation from the woman to ten feet, the trees, remaining stationary as trees do, give the visual impression of approaching the outer screen margins, of moving toward the viewer and of increasing their separation from the actress, for their relative distance has now become five feet to ten feet or 1:2. Eventually, the trees would pass be-

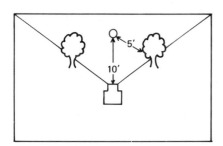 

yond and behind us, outside the lateral screen borders. This phenomenon is called *parallax*. It is accentuated by such variables as the number of objects in the composition, their relative sizes and distances, the speed of camera movement, and the possibility of the subjects themselves being in motion.

The likelihood of our falling into an illusion of movement, all the while denied by our seated muscles, is also affected by screen size, itself a consequence of the actual dimensions of the theater screen and our personal distance from it, whether we sit toward the front, where we see all the grain, or in back, where we see all the heads of the audience. As the location of the screen borders approaches the periphery of our own vision, we are increasingly inclined to equate projected image with "real" experience, for we become less conscious of edges, curtain, auditorium, and the screen itself, which is why some people like to sit in the front row. All of this contributes to the argument that wide screen ratios intensify the illusions of ordinary human perception.

There is a piece of camera equipment that gives a less adequate approximation of physical movement through space, substituting a specialized kind of compositional change. This is called the zoom and should be noted for the sake of comparison. The zoom was named after a trade product called Zoomar, once one of several such lenses on the commercial market. It varies distances between lens elements within the lens barrel, so that a manual operation by the cameraman can create a continuum of visual experience that changes focal length from moment to moment and thus magnifies or diminishes the image at will.

Because the manual operation (there are electric zooms as well) is oil-dampened for smoothness, and because the camera itself remains stable through the execution, the appearance of a zoom will be gracefully continuous. However, our sense of passage through space is much less convincing than ordinary camera movement, for the stable camera maintains a constancy of distance from the subject matter, regardless of the focal-length lens in operation at any given instant. Screen images vary in their size, but we do not experience the conditions of parallax, where spatial distances actually vary relative to one another. The zoom experience is more like that of a camera approaching or receding from a still photograph, whose constancy of nondepth is inarguable. It is useful for particular kinds of effects but not as a replacement for tracking or mobile, hand-held shots.

Studies of camera movement, perspective, and zoom remain few, although what has been called "structural film" often works from zoom principles. Alfred Hitchcock, working with his most effective cinematographer-collaborator, Robert Burks, tried once to induce audience vertigo. They contrived a camera mounted on tracks and focused on the model of a deep-welled Spanish mission staircase. As the camera approached the stairwell on tracks, its zoom was simultaneously manipulated in the opposite direction, with dizzying effect (see *Vertigo* [1958]).

There are other ways to think about camera movement. One is the beauty of the execution in itself, not the mere surmounting of technical problems but the sheer exhilaration that attends graceful movement through space, independent of what it does and what it means. Movement may be simple or complex. It is to film what the production of

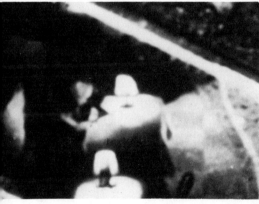

Shifting vantages provided by camera movement shape our responses to *Citizen Kane.*

sound is to music. Compare the static camera to dry sound, constant in tonality and contained, and the moving camera to a singing tone, its vibrato increasing like an opera tenor's, or to the distinctive sound of the reed or brass instrument, independent of style, execution, or intonation, although it will color all of these.

Movement in film can sometimes be enough to sustain our happy relation to the screen, independent of any other factors. It accounts for pleasures in the most idiotic western, the silliest cops-and-robbers melodrama. Its absence, too, explains some of the feelingless, intellectualized flavor of highly edited film. Even in highly skilled and imaginative animation, one is aware of the limitations imposed on movement. A film buff approaches the directors in the great tradition of movement—Murnau, Ophuls, Renoir, Welles—with special anticipation of visceral enjoyment, knowing that their skillful use of the camera will be allied to narrative function as well.

Another aspect of camera movement relates directly to a director's inclinations to strike attitudes toward his material. He may, for example, simply "uncover" subject matter for our attention as his camera comes across it in movements that have the appearance of chance, while they in fact have been subject to the most careful premeditation, the most intense supervision. In the closing moments of *Citizen Kane* (1941), for example, Orson Welles and his cameraman Gregg Toland designed a crane shot that passed over the great accumulations of Kane's collecting passion as these rested in crates or awaited disposal on the stone floors of his castle. The objects that pass beneath our view seem random. Then we realize we are reseeing items that had figured in most of the earlier story sequences, things to which the late Charles Foster Kane attached special, private emotional significance. These intense feelings are known now only to ourselves, and the emotion we carry to the objects now becomes tinged with their crated isolation: furniture from his family's boardinghouse in the West, a bird cage, the brass bed he occupied in the first newspaper office, an inscribed trophy given him by the early, affectionate journalists. Finally we settle on Kane's sled, painted with the name Rosebud.

Another instance of early Wellesian camera movement is twice executed to introduce Kane's second wife, beautifully played by Dorothy Comingore, a broken-down club singer whose last claim to notoriety is her former marriage. Godlike again, we arc across the skies, passing over the tavern roof and through a skylight to descend on the actress bent over a table with her glass. The movement intensifies our sense of spying on other people's secrets, while it emphasizes the actress's helplessness and smallness in the greater scheme of our own awareness—in further ironic contrast to her declarations that she alone was responsible for Kane's downfall.

The hunting sequence from Jean Renoir's *The Rules of the Game.*

Lastly, a moving camera shot may always be considered as an alternative to a succession of cuts in the progression from story point A to point B. It purposefully connects one thing to another.

Although we accept the conventional linkage of two discrete shots as a single continuity without necessary time break, we are just slightly more credulous of the uninterrupted connection. So long as film proceeds to run constantly through the camera, we stay the more agreeable to emotional, psychological, and narrative relations between the events pictured.

This is a pattern repeatedly used by Jean Renoir, particularly in his film *The Rules of the Game* (1939), the underlying design of which connects discrepant social elements of France in the thirties. Like Shakespeare, Renoir contrasts the behavior of his aristocracy with that of their attending servants—only, Renoir plays the servants not as buffoon-microcosms of the ruling class but as carriers of the Rules, as they have been observed, to their rational extreme.

In consequence, there is special purpose in a scene that begins in the kitchen and then proceeds, uninterrupted, into the dining areas, from one society to the other, in continuous camera execution, linked by the food itself, a nest of Rules, which has been discussed by both parties, each from his particular tastes and knowledge.

Similarly, in the hunting sequence Renoir begins with a close-up of a frightened hare who bolts as the beaters approach, to be followed by the shooting party, costumed for gunning, country-estate play. What begins as a rabbit's-eye view of human gameplaying continues through the shot to intensify contrasts between animal, servant, and aristocrat, each with his own sort of cruelties. Cruelty as a theme is then played back at the end of the sequence when the Marquis's wife looks at a tree squirrel through field glasses and then accidentally catches sight of her husband in an embrace with his mistress.

While it can hardly be isolated from every other element of moviemaking, film space carries unique, nonverbal qualities that have a special aesthetic pleasure. As with architecture, space manages somehow to escape the ravages of time, as fashions change, acting becomes dated, stories depart from original meanings, once-effective dialogue shifts into cliché, contemporary music becomes antiquarian. Space remains, defining itself by what it embraces or is contained by and through the camera movement that explores it. Of all the ingredients in film, it is the most formal and hence free of substantive issue. This is a principal reason why certain sensitively photographed older films seem never to lose their attractiveness.

TIME

Our investigation of duration in the film will be sharpened by distinguishing between *kinds* of time. Like space, time operates in separate ways under different conditions of perception.

The easiest form of time about which more than one of us can agree is clock time, the sort that can be measured through quantification, whether in terms of Greenwich time or divisions like day, month, and year. This is what A. A. Mendilow calls "conceptual time," and I shall refer to it as Time I. Often I will be using it to signify the literal duration of any film, its length converted to temporal units: ninety feet per minute if 35mm, thirty-six feet per minute if 16mm, twenty-four frames per second. Sound speed. (Every sound projector shows its pictures at that standard rate.)

Next there is the apparent time of the film experience, termed by Mendilow "fiction time." This is Time II, the time or times that filmmaker and audience agree are being shown: Napoleonic France; 2001; World War II *then* the Korean War, *then* Vietnam, *then* Indonesia; and so forth.

Finally, we have the time that seems to pass in the viewer's mind as he watches the movie, a sensation that varies among individuals and one that may shift during the course of a single film. This "experiential level of time," our Time III, is greatly affected by editing decisions relative to shot lengths (Time I) and their organization.

Clearly, each Time is unlikely to coincide with another, although this is possible. Generally, it is out of the discrepancies among the times that expository film conventions have arisen, as in other temporal arts like the novel and drama.

Most often, Time II is "shorter" than Time I. That is, we see episodic versions of "real life" events. Were the two to coincide, the duration of any film would amount to an unaffected representation of some other, previous or invented, conceptual time. Occasionally this has been undertaken. Agnès Varda's *Cleo from Five to Seven* (1961), for example, traces part of an afternoon during the life of a young Parisienne while she awaits the reports from a medical laboratory that will confirm or deny a diagnosis of cancer. Varda actually flashes a subtitle of the movie's clock time onto the screen every few minutes. Although the film does not consume all of two hours, its Time II remains very close to what would have been the actualities of conceptual time if, in fact, Cleo really existed. A strong ingredient of Varda's film is the sympathetic equation that the audience draws between its own perception of the passage of time (Time III) and Cleo's sense of her personal experience, while at the same time she is unmasked from a mannequin, a groomed and coiffeured figure, and revealed as a woman of warmth and great personal charm.

An early deviation from straightforward storytelling in Time II was enlisted to explicate motive, as when a character's next considered action

A Time II conversation from Agnès Varda's _Cleo from Five to Seven_. *(Credit: Zenith International)*

could be intensified for spectators by allowing them to share what he remembered in a *flashback*. A *dissolve* (the simultaneous onscreen replacement of one image by another) cued audiences they had better prepare to time-travel. We never doubted the accuracy of an actor's memory, even if, on reflection, his reminiscence didn't credibly fit the experience in terms of what he could or could not have known.

The memory enacted, we would return to the face of its originator and proceed with the story, wiser about the character and impressed with the thoughts and emotions that would affect future action. Flashbacks had the effect of interrupting a story, and a filmmaker had to organize his exposition carefully enough that the memories would further, not frustrate, audience interest, as when warring Greeks sat at evening campfires and told sad tales about the death of kings. This effect was usually accomplished by working special drama into the remembered incidents. In fact, flashbacks often made up the more interesting parts of a story.

The whole technique of the flashback has been reconceived in recent years, partly because of its creakiness as a device, partly because of the interjection of subjectivity in the players' relationship to past events. Flashbacks are manipulated and enjoyed to savage satiric purpose in a Polish film called *The Saragossa Manuscript* (1964), directed by Wojciech Has. Its story is an incredible succession of substories recounted on the least pretext. Indeed, the storytellers will sometimes bully an audience into listening. Each actor's tale proceeds until a point in *his* story when *another* person requires an audience to tell *his* story, and the overall narrative turns into a convoluted design of story-within-a-story-within-a-story, like a Chinese puzzle. Finally, each tale has to work itself out and return to *its* listeners to free *them* to conclude *their* tale for the next listeners.

There does appear to be a kind of compulsive fascination we give to the dramatizing of our stories and dreams, a tendency that Luis Buñuel also satirized in *The Discreet Charm of the Bourgeoisie* (1972), where a recounting of dreams has the magnetism of scandal among middle-class French couples. *They Shoot Horses, Don't They?* (1969) was perhaps the first commercial film to use the *flash forward* (the recounting of a future event) to give added meaning to its characters' actions and motives, with arguable success. (The device was not used in Horace McCoy's novel.)

It is often the case that Time II is a selected series of occasions, isolated out of continuous clock time. Perhaps we might experience certain key events in the life of a lovable old schoolteacher—the moment he decides to teach, his graduation, a proposal, marriage, the death of his wife, and the occasion of his retirement. Or the same moments might mark episodes in the history of a tyrannical and despised professor. In this respect, the organization of material will be formally independent of story.

Each sequence can have Times I and II coincide or not. The filmmaker might regard an actor's walk across a campus as significant to the exposition of the story, in which case that action could be followed in its entirety. On the other hand, the filmmaker may be interested in the man's destination and what follows—beating a poor schoolboy or patting him on the head. Consequently, the screen images might show no more than the professor's closing his office door, then opening another into his classroom. *The Blue Angel* (1930), for example, made much of Professor Unrath's departure from Lola-Lola and then his tardy entrance to class, but it did not document the intervening journey.

Alternatively, a filmmaker may choose to lengthen Time II in contradiction of actual time, although this is hard to maintain for long. He could show the great difficulties in a mortal's passage to the underworld by filming part of the journey in slow motion, as Cocteau did in *Orpheus* (1949). He may even drag out a suspenseful moment by so manipulating a photographed clock that it no longer documents Time I (as in *High Noon* [1952]). He may so intercut isolated objects or events that the moment is prolonged. In any case, it is likely that the Time I passages between each episode (or sequence) will be dropped out and the connections between sequences somehow formalized so that the audience will be able to organize its understanding of what has happened either at that moment or in retrospect.

Just what sequences are selected will define the kind of narrative recounted. This may seem to be less a province of time—that is, a structural problem—than one of substance—"content"—until we consider the fact that choices of sequence define plot. Plot is very functionally related to time.

For example, a characteristic approach to one kind of gangster film, *Rififi* (1954), or *The Asphalt Jungle* (1950), emphasizes first the preparation, then the execution of a well-planned heist. Selection of sequences are engineered so as to dwell on "slow" matters, building up the intensity of Time III until it is resolved in part by the burglary itself and finally completely resolved when a character's fate is determined by his behavior under the pressure of escape, a behavior that we come to understand by way of the earlier, slower sequences.

At the other extreme, a filmmaker may choose to point up only those moments of high intensity that are customarily "developed" by buildup. Good instances of this can be found in Richard Lester's Beatles films: Consider "the escape" sequence in *A Hard Day's Night* (1964) and Ringo's escapades in *Help!* (1965). They are also apparent in *The Knack . . . and how to get it* (1964) and *How I Won the War* (1967).

Such an approach often lends itself to vaudeville bits and variety-show turns, as on *Laugh-In*. It is often found, both live and animated, among directors who spent the formative years of their careers in television where there is less Time I to accomplish what one must do, particularly during commercials.

Another approach to sequence is epitomized by the Antonioni of the black-and-white Italian period, when he was often disposed to dwell on the facial expression of an actor after the dramatic moment has apparently concluded. By this decision, Antonioni diminishes the overt happenings visible to us by way of character interaction and thrusts the real event into the minds of his actors. What would dilute the Time III impact designed by John Huston or Richard Lester becomes central to Antonioni's purpose. Tension may be created in part from audience discomfort in experiencing Time I and Time II overlaps, as in Antonioni's *L'Avventura* island sequence. Antonioni is trying to intensify our sense of each character's psychic isolation by stranding us in time, as it were, by literally dispensing with a character we had thought central and by minimizing human movements within shots, while playing them against the rhythmic cycle of beach waves.

Time attitudes may also mark cultural variation among the films of different countries. A psychological study of entertainment films of the forties proposed that the British characteristically miss trains and appointments, leading to unhappy consequences. French films were inclined to condemn their actors to victim roles, powerless under time's whim and chance. Then as now, American melodrama assumes heroic proportions, the protagonist arriving "in the nick of time" to defuse the bomb (*Experiment in Terror* [1962]) or to interrupt the wedding (*The Graduate* [1967]).

The Italian movement known as neorealism encouraged a blending of Times I and II. One of its major spokesmen, screenwriter Cesare Zavattini, called for a direct approach to the "reality around us," not filtered or purified like American films. He wanted "unstoried" films that would in theory eliminate the screenwriter himself and concentrate on the banal "dailiness" of everyday events, like a woman undertaking to buy a pair of shoes, which would assume significance under such close scrutiny.[2] Such an attitude toward narrative is really part of the literary tradition of naturalism. Zola said the novel was "simply a monograph, a page of existence, the recital of one single fact." Nonetheless, the effects of neorealism's energized approach to the storied nonstory continues to be felt in later filmmakers like Truffaut and Satyajit Ray, and among the sequence choices of many younger directors (George Lucas in *American Graffiti* [1973], for instance), who eschew the dramatic moment for the seemingly insignificant one. In some respects, this is part of the less-is-more aesthetic.

Another approach to Time II is cross-sectional. Drawing again on experimentation among novelists—Virginia Woolf in *Mrs. Dalloway,* John Dos Passos in *U.S.A.,* James Joyce in *Ulysses*—some filmmakers have approached the matter of time horizontally rather than longitudinally, cutting across a given moment to show how it is lived by different characters.

The problems of simultaneity have preoccupied our culture since Romantics such as Wordsworth intensified our awareness of the past as a constant element occupying the present. In some respects narrative solutions to simultaneity are as inimical to the single-image film as to the page, because we must continue to concentrate on one event at a time, and each event consumes its own moment. Earlier we encountered one solution in Griffith's parallel editing, the last-minute rescue, but even here time eventually has to pass, and the two elements of the story merge into one.

What is customary in the cross-sectional narrative is either some variation of the flashback or a kind of temporal zigzag back and forth along the time continuum, establishing a convention agreeable to the audience, which pretends that time is standing still. *Rashomon* (1950), the brilliant movie by Akira Kurosawa that introduced Japanese films to the world market, used the recounted flashback technique. Four versions of a single incident, the rape of a young woman and her husband's death in the forest, are told by several parties: a bandit, the wife, the dead husband (through a psychic medium), and a woodcutter who happened to observe the episode. Although the events are repeated in their entirety four times, as experienced by each principal character, the situation is here complicated by the vested interests maintained by each speaker, so that the actions in each episode are not in fact identical. Even the woodcutter has some obvious motive of self-protection for telling his version quite as he does.

An experimental French short of the twenties, *Rien que les Heures* (1926), by the Brazilian director Alberto Cavalcanti, tried in its own way to confront the passage of time by showing the clock time of different parts of the world, each echoing a moment in Paris, then introducing rapid camera movement plotted against the contrary movement of the subject matter, as if to overpower time with spatial frenzy.

The so-called City Documentary often approached cross-sectioning by moving from subject to subject in the urban setting, but these films are usually Time II–bounded by the span of a day. *People of the City* (Arne Sucksdorff [1947]) caught separately located citizens of Stockholm setting their timepieces against a ritual noon cannon-firing. A British documentary, *Waverly Steps* (John Eldridge [1948]), approached the problem in documenting life in Edinburgh. The enacted lives of different people, mostly unknown to one another although a few meet accidentally, are connected from moment to moment by clever, nontemporal, associational transitions. For example, an amphitheater lecture on heart disease is followed by a trial scene in which a nervous, little man is confronted with the clear evidence of bigamy—another affair of the heart. *Diary for Timothy* (1944–45), the narration of which was written by E. M. Forster, made similar connections through free association of word and image. Such designs seem to lend themselves especially to an older form of documentary, which was structured in terms of ideas rather than events.

Jean Cocteau tried to isolate the experiences of his protagonists both in *The Blood of a Poet* and *Orpheus* so that they might be understood to exist altogether outside Time I. The artist-poet of the first film explores the passageways and rooms of a hotel, emblematic of an interior investigation of the creative imagination. Orpheus dares to penetrate the underworld in order to meet his death, represented by a beautiful woman, and to rescue Eurydice, his wife. Both Poet and Orpheus pass through mirrors to reach the other realms. The journey of the Poet is marked, at the film's inception, by a shot of a collapsing tower. At the end of the movie, the tower completes its fall. In Orpheus's adventure, a postman drops a letter into his mailbox. On the return through the mirror, the letter resumes its passage, and the mailman's ringing the bell announces the completion of his action. Ambrose Bierce's story *An Occurrence at Owl Creek Bridge,* filmed under that title and also as *The Spy* (1932), uses a similar framing narrative.

There is a further dimension to Time III, which might be called the "tense" of a movie. Knowing that what we view is time past, we nonetheless experience it as a continuous *now.* In this respect, all moviegoing dwells in the present, unlike prose conventions, which may use past tense or even invent a historical past. Some filmmakers have experimented with sight or sound cues to advise us of different time, while we yet experience film as continuous and current. Perhaps the most effective is Alain Resnais's *Night and Fog* (1955). A concentration camp is revisited and filmed in color, which accentuates the overgrowth of weeds and the deterioration of the buildings and grounds. Then, before our eyes, the movement of the camera along a rusted railroad track is matched to a like movement caught in black-and-white documentary footage of the camp in World War II. Our self-protective awareness lowered by the earlier footage, we are thrust into the monochromatic horrors of another time, which yet remains time present. It is difficult to deny the presentness of time in a film, just as it is hard to disavow its "reality."

Finally, some mention needs to be made of an author's "visible" relation to his material, which defines his relation to time. In turn, this hinges on an additional element, a variant on Times I and II. A contrast always exists between the putative time at which the events of the film take place—its fictional time—and its production date. As the production date recedes into the past, we become increasingly and unavoidably aware that any film is an historical artifact. Time's passage seems to strip away certain planes of narrative texture once available to the film's contemporaries and to bare the stylizations imposed by the past itself. Film is not exactly a beetle trapped in amber.

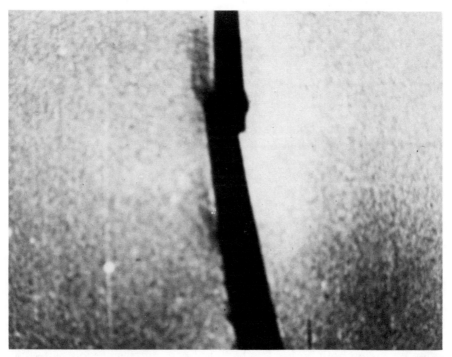

A falling tower brackets the beginning and end of *The Blood of a Poet*, emphasizing Cocteau's rejection of Time I.

For example, there are blatant differences between the *Napoleon* of Abel Gance (1927, or, its sound version, 1932) and that enacted by Marlon Brando in *Désirée* (1954). Some of these distinctions may be located among the director's conceptions and some among the acting skills, and certainly it is difficult to compare an ordinary sound film with one whose speeches were originally shot without sound and then, five years later, dubbed in, where possible by the same actors. Nevertheless, other, very clear dissimilarities remain as a kind of desideratum. Some of these may be traced to a traditional kind of French histrionics, others to the mumble Brando brought West from the Actor's Studio and which sounds somewhat odd to our ears today. The intentions of graphic design rested very differently on each art director's vision. The romanticisms of the earlier version sit curiously now.

As soon, therefore, as a film is no longer "current," we become distant from a certain part of it, and some movies seem to fall into rigor mortis before our eyes. Every filmmaker, regardless of his talents and their deployment, is the inescapable victim of time's passage. Some bear up better than others, this occasionally by purest chance and fancy. For example, the highly verbal, surreal, and fast-paced comedy of Preston Sturges, a Hollywood director of the early forties contracted at Paramount, receives a sympathetic reception today, while his treatment of women and his stereotyped black clowns become increasingly offensive to the same audience.

The omniscience of a filmmaker—his knowledge of the events in the film and control of them—defines his relation to time. If he elects freedoms of time and space travel, he sacrifices a certain kind of naturalistic verisimilitude for the sake of sequence juxtaposition. On the other hand, he may decide to limit himself to the experience of a single character, as Dashiell Hammett did with Sam Spade in his novel and Agnès Varda in *Cleo from Five to Seven*. Such self-limitation, while removing the author from his godlike perch, allows a viewer to experience but a single time continuum: one time at a time. This more restricted view, though it may still permit the filmmaker a certain authorial point of view toward the narrative, prevents him from asserting himself as a separate and distinct element of the exposition.

On the stage and in fiction to a greater extent than in films, a writer may intrude upon his creations. The eighteenth-century novel was rife with such editorial interventions, often because of its didactic intentions (which Henry Fielding ridiculed by the facile moralizing he interjected into novels like *Tom Jones*). Such ethical impulse, serious or comic or often balancing both on ironic edge, has been effectively represented on stage by Bertolt Brecht and in the films of Jean-Luc Godard. In either case, the artist chose to interrupt and literally to destroy at some point in the story the audience's sympathetic identifications, which had been based on conventions that allowed them to pretend that the unreal was actually taking place. The interruptions permitted the author to speak directly to his listeners, to inject himself into the performance like an additional character. These intrusions have usually been undertaken either to discuss the events "pretended" (as when actors speak to the audience in *The Threepenny Opera*) or else to attack the conventions themselves because of their effect on the spectators and because of their sociopolitical ramifications. In *Wind from the East* (1970), Godard tries to ravage the full arsenal of illusionary conventions as bourgeois agencies of conservatism and self-delusion. In *Weekend* (1967) he injects characters out of the past, like Emily Brontë, and then destroys them before our eyes (he burns one pair).

Yet all such intrusions enable the filmmaker to do no more than create new conventions, since his innovations, if successful, are critically celebrated and in consequence repeated by others. When, in a Marx Brothers movie, Groucho turns to the camera with a hand-to-mouth aside, "Pardon me while I have a strange interlude," he is in fact having fun with Eugene O'Neill, who drew on popular expressionist stage convention in the twenties to have his characters speak alternately to one another behind masks and then directly to the audience. From our perspective today, Groucho just seems to be doing another aside, throwing himself in and out of character like any television comic.

4 ■ The Impact of Editing and Sound

EDITING

More than any other aspect of film production, editing, the act of joining two pieces of film so as to form a continuous passage of footage through a projector, carries connotations of design and organization. By facilitating changes of perspective, editing first made it possible for the movies to reorganize space. In permitting the filmmaker to join together different moments, editing then gave him a tool to manipulate time.

The possibility of editing introduced a new form of selective control into filmmaking; for example, different versions of the same moment might be filmed and only the most successful chosen. (Griffith did this.) In essence, editing allowed movies altogether to escape still photography, for until the editor's intrusion, film was quite what its name suggested: moving pictures.

The first impetus to order a series of scenes so that it told a structured story originated elsewhere. It had been undertaken with picture post-. card series and by the stereoscopic photographs that were enjoyed sequentially in Victorian parlors. Stories were told with series of pictures in communal peepshows at fairs. They were projected on theater screens to illustrate popular songs of the nineties. Alexander Black even photographed actors posed as in a stage performance, then projected them as slides in commercial "photoplays."

82

Gradually it was realized not only that different camera angles might be used while preserving fictive continuity on the movie screen but also that the photographer could go as far as to change the setting itself from one location to the next, even from exteriors to interiors. (This seems to date from as early as Méliès's *Bluebeard* in 1901.)

The next step was one of combining two story elements, distant in space, simultaneous in time, into continuous narrative. (Again, representations of simultaneity were common before the moviehouses.) This method of organization, appearing primitively in Edwin S. Porter's *The Great Train Robbery* (1903)—its melodrama burlesqued a decade later in *Barney Oldfield's Race for Life* (1913)—was developed to create suspense in countless titles by Griffith. Griffith furthered the editor's control over audience anxiety by manipulating the duration of each perceived event. Alternating shots of Story One (the heroine tied to the railroad track, the train in the distance) and Story Two (the hero en route) were shortened and often brought increasingly into close-up until a climax marked the joining of both elements into one scene.

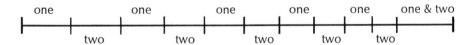

It may be noted that we have gradually slipped from the notion of *editing,* one of several movie production processes, to the idea of the *editor* as independent agent. As with directing, camera operation, and film processing, these functions became individualized during the century's first decade, at the time when more ambitious production and more demanding schedules separated out the various activities. Later I shall discuss these operations in greater detail.

As audience understanding and anticipation figured more prominently in the editor's mind, he realized that stage conventions of completing one action before beginning another were unnecessary, too, unless specifically desired. Once accustomed to the movie image, a spectator might, it could be shown, "read" necessary information from any particular shot in the space of a second or less. In recent years it has become evident that we can consciously "take in" minimal stimuli on screen from two or three frames, and sometimes even from one frame —that is, from less than one-twenty-fourth of a second of sound film (not exactly one-twenty-fourth because the shutter time takes the extra fraction away from the picture). The practice of breaking off any enacted film moment therefore became the editor's, not the actor's choice. After the interruption, the moment could then be continued with a separately angled shot, or else ignored, its remainder either nonessential or the interruption itself useful in stimulating audience interest. Once this step had been taken, the editor found his understandings of screen time and of audience perception neatly intermingled. In the first place, screen time had come, literally, to exist. An event projected before an audience now assumed its own duration, independent of how it might ever, if at all, be marked in actuality by clock time.

Generally what took place on film amounted to condensed, truncated, or elliptical happenings, created by joinings of separate shots that discarded irrelevant clock time. But this was not necessarily the case, and an editor could as easily elongate the suspenseful moment by stretching out its execution through repeated changes of angle. (A common and usually effective student filmmaking exercise is that of dragging an ordinary normal movement, something as simple as sitting down or swinging a tennis racket, beyond the endurance of an audience to tolerate its incompletion.

The editor found that he enjoyed a curious power, unwittingly imparted by his audience, through his handling of the interrupted event. He might, for example, leave a heroine struggling to reach a knife, which the villain had dropped just beyond reach on the gravel beside the railroad track, and switch to the hero on horseback racing a locomotive to the scene. The editor could then return to the exact moment he had departed the girl, as if the time consumed by the rider had no actual relation to his fiancée's plight. Or else he might presume that the horseback shot was real time; on coming back to the heroine, she became the more endangered (especially if he kept the locomotive in the background of her shots so that we could gauge danger by the engine's constantly increasing size).

Customarily, the editor would opt for the second alternative, for its emphasis on the diminishing time against which the hero had to contend. Eventually, the editor learned to squeeze an extra squeal from his audience by showing the knife fall even farther away from the heroine's bound hand as she strained to touch its handle. Whether the geographic space was single (Ford's Theatre) or multiple (the rescue), he called this intermingling "intercutting."

The Russians, following their 1917 Revolution, studied the accomplishments of American silent film, particularly the work of D. W. Griffith. Their own observations and experiments (the most interesting compounded in Lev Kuleshov's studio workshop) led to an isolation of the movies' formal designs from the substance of the stories. They concluded that joining separate strips of film could produce narrative denotations, independent of any evidence implicit in the individual shots so grouped. For example, each of two figures, photographed at far-distant locales, might seem to be approaching each other by a combination of screen directions (one proceeding left to right, the other right to left) and by the expectations that an audience predictably imposes on the material by reason of its juxtapositions. (If they weren't headed toward a meeting, what in the world was the purpose of the events witnessed?) The pair might then in fact meet, but at a spot altogether foreign to the city they had earlier occupied. They might stop before the steps of one building, to be followed by the shot of another piece of architecture. Without visual contradictions, an audience would believe as much or as little as its eyes advised. Similarly, a human body itself was constructed out of close-ups assembling the different anatomical parts of several women. And the face of a famous actor of the day, Mozhukin, was juxtaposed as if in reaction to different scenes: a child playing, a plate of soup, a dead woman. Although the actor's face in fact maintained a constant expression throughout, in context his "reactions" gave audiences the impression of distinctive if subtle responses.

By such experimentation, the Russian filmmakers raised the "art of editing" to a kind of aesthetic apotheosis. In joining shots together, the filmmaker was thought to have imposed his own formal impulses onto the raw materials of life, to have created something where before there had been nothing. By this measure, editing enabled moviemaking to consume its own materials—that is, so to alter the elements with which it worked, the exposed and processed snippets of film, that these lost their original, photographed "meanings" and assumed intentions that had previously existed only in the mind of the editor.

One great Russian director, Vsevolod Pudovkin, underlined this point in his theoretical writing. In an early thoughtful study of motion pictures, *Film Technique* (1929), Pudovkin discussed creative editing by likening it to the work of a painter with his canvas, palette, and brushes. Just as the raw materials there were transformed by an artist's skill and inner vision, Pudovkin said, the film editor could create a new reality. As an example, he explained how, on finding that photographing an actual explosion failed to provide the impact he wanted, Pudovkin "invented" an explosion that had never actually occurred, piecing together minute lengths of film whose images, ambiguous in isolation, produced in combination the requisite effect. (In fact, almost all Pudovkin's impressive record of feature films affects the viewer not in such terms, but instead as fluid, well-acted narrative not a little in the manner of the capitalist Griffith. For Griffith's "literary" adaptations and melodrama, Pudovkin substituted stories indigenous to his own culture, alternately intimate understandings of working-class life and manners and hortatory propaganda. Essentially, Pudovkin draws on the "raw materials" of the photographed image without consuming their original meanings, but rather refining these into a lean, linear narrative.)

Sergei Mikhailovich Eisenstein carried the Kuleshov workshop premises to further extreme, evidencing their utility both pragmatically and in essays that sought to provide an intellectual foundation for his accomplishments with the Hegelian ideology of the dialectic. Like Griffith, Eisenstein's previous background had been in the theater, but unlike the American and in stated disagreement with his friend Pudovkin, Eisenstein opposed the now orthodox narrative scheme of stringing together significant details pulled out of the "master shot" for any given sequence. Eisenstein's alternative constituted a direct challenge to the illusory storytelling of film. Eventually it was rejected by the Soviet authorities as "formalistic" and too "intellectual," but before this happened, the director had several opportunities to put his schemes into practice.

While working on the stage, Eisenstein had evolved a theory he called "montage of attractions," based on then contemporary psychology and current attitudes toward revolutionary art and toward the devices by which an actor might elicit the requisite responses from his audience. Unlike the smooth, "invisible" film editing that had preceded him (even Pudovkin's "explosion" pretended to be a real one, as the Kuleshov experiments were illusory "tricks"), Eisenstein proposed that the film joinings should not appear unobtrusive to the audience. Rather, he said (and showed), the editing ought to constitute a series of explosive shocks. This was to be accomplished by placing the expository flow of separate shots into various kinds of opposition to one another, like the Marxist thesis-antithesis-synthesis dynamic.

Eisenstein's impulse was thus to "break the flow" of narrative. Even, for example, in the "Odessa Steps" sequence from *The Battleship Potemkin* we can see that the succession of images omits certain "vital" parts of a straightforward story continuity, while yet following the usual one-after-the-other temporal order. The soldier, the baby carriage, the Cossack, and the wounded lady—each is isolated and thrust into edited relationships that confound story continuity as much as they explicate it. The cause-and-effect relationships of narrative are manipulated and hinted at, rather than spelled out. We do not see the lady struck across the face. Indeed our first impression of whom the Cossack attacks has been, we soon realize, misinformed.

At Eisenstein's command, stone literally rises up.

If the "Odessa Steps" sequence has been successful in Eisenstein's eyes, our audience reaction is one of shock leading to outrage. The sequence itself concludes, after the last shot noted, with a title advising us that the *Potemkin*'s guns are being trained in retaliation on the Czar's buildings. After part of the architecture has been blown up, Eisenstein mounts a three-shot series of pictures showing carved stone lions, progressing from prone to upright position. It is his intention thus to suggest that the "very stone" has risen up in indignation and outrage at the depredations of the Czarist forces.

However, such an audience recognition is not at all likely, which serves to point up the extent of the problem Eisenstein posed for himself. More often than not, spectators seem either bemused at the trickery, confused that the lion follows the *Potemkin*'s gunnery, or nonplused that lions were interjected at all into an experience sufficiently busy with Cossacks, catastrophe, guards, palace, and a wayward battleship. Eisenstein's films were avowedly not pursued for experimental self-discovery, but rather for propaganda; hence they are altogether dependent on his audience. In its way, his efforts to control audience perception, comprehension, and behavior were even more demandingly authoritarian than Griffith's chase sequences because they were more premeditated.

Other evidences of Eisenstein's tactics show an even sharper departure from the usual narrative scheme. Eisenstein's interest in opposing two apparently disparate images (the thesis-antithesis) for the sake of a comprehending reconciliation of the two (the Hegelian synthesis) found a parallel technique in the rhetorical strategies of language, particularly the simile. Simile in speech or poetry, if sometimes rejected by schools that find its overambitious imagery distracting, serves often to sharpen our perceptions by calling attention through likenesses to special features of the subject described. In film, the problem of its employment is magnified in the degree of our commitment to illusionistic narrative. In his film *Ten Days That Shook the World* (1928), for example, Eisenstein satirizes Russia's provisional leader, Alexander Kerensky, by pointing up (or inventing) his vanity and mounting ambition.

Kerensky's rise to power is summarized in his ascension of the stairs leading to the Czar's former quarters. Dressed in military finery, Kerensky's climb is noted in a series of shots intercut with busts of ancient rulers set along the stairway landings. Such drawing of similarities, however heavy-handed, has the merit of locating all its images in the seeming realities of a re-enacted scene and Czarist decor. In the upper hall, however, Eisenstein shoots Kerensky executing an 180-degree turn toward his bedroom door, the camera showing only a close-up of his polished boots during the turn. This turn is intercut with shots of a preening peacock, the movements of bird skillfully matched to those of man. Our response to this image may be alternately one of amusement, of pleasure

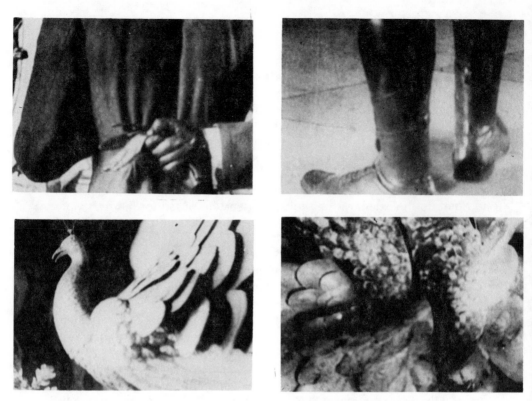

Eisenstein's symbolic intercutting of Kerensky and a preening peacock provides a heavy-handed clue to the director's assessment of Kerensky's character.

at the facile connections between the matching actions, or of profound disturbance at the imposed likenesses. If stone lions were hard to assimilate, what is a peacock doing in the Czar's palace? In the measure that he demands illusion, it's enough to make any well-behaved spectator irascible.

By such example, we may place Eisenstein's silent films (his sound ventures tended toward another kind of stylization—namely, opera) somewhere toward the right side of our verisimilitude continuum. Other aspects of Eisenstein's imagery drew on his sophisticated eye for painting (the compositional imagination) and his skill as a caricaturist (the emphasis on exaggerated postures and features; the use of physical types to trigger audience sympathies). He profited, too, from the development of the poster as a medium of agitprop in the early days of the U.S.S.R.; advertisements for Eisenstein's films often seem to encapsulate his approach with special energy and aptness.

One linguistic consequence should be noted. Because of the success of his films and the ardor of his writings, Eisenstein became one of the earliest Soviet artists to espouse the new revolutionary aesthetic abroad, both by way of personal travel and in his published writings. Eisenstein's essays were much translated, and collections of his work appeared early. Thus his theories were widely discussed by the English-speaking world in the thirties.

The British equivalent to editing drew on the French word *montager,* meaning "to mount or join." In consequence, the term *montage,* as in Eisenstein's earlier "montage of attractions," became synonymous in critical circles with creative approaches to editing. Initially, montage connoted the "Russian School," where editing enjoyed special prestige. With the advent of sound, montage seemed to broaden in scope to describe any imaginative editing technique.

Later in Hollywood, a Yugoslav editor, director, and teacher named Slavko Vorkapich became associated with another, very particular, kind of editing technique, one in which a succession of images is vigorously compacted and imaginatively organized, often with impressive optical effects and supportive music, to convey some concept while shortcutting story exposition. The technique could be spotted in feature narratives. It can be seen at its most clichéd, for example, in a gangster film when, accompanied by effects like sirens, newsboys, jail doors, and the pounding of a judge's gavel, some actor, innocent of the crime of which he has been accused, is sentenced to die in the electric chair. We see him stopped by a plainclothesman in the street, booked, and taken to a cell, where he sinks his head in his hands. A newspaper with eight-column headline comes whirling from nowhere to the front of the screen. Rotary presses are shown running at full speed. Newsboys run shouting "Extra, extra!" down the street, soon surrounded by eager customers, mostly men in raincoats shot from above. A prosecuting attorney with a small moustache mouthes imprecations in close-up, shaking his finger at the audience-witness-lens. Shot from a low angle, the judge pounds his gavel and pronounces sentence. The prisoner is led away to Sing-Sing. He's had it.

A more sophisticated example of this editing scheme makes up the concert-tour sequence in *Intermezzo* described earlier. The technique came to be known as a Vorkapich, Vorkapich montage, or simply montage. Thus when we encounter the French term, the speaker might refer to Eisenstein's principle of "dynamic editing" or to Professor Vorkapich's technique; or perhaps it is being used to distinguish between "movies" (mundane film) and "film" (Film Art) as the critic John Simon employs these two words in his book title *Movies into Film*. Or it may just be a synonym for "editing" or the even more workaday "cutting" to carry overtones of personal sensitivity and appreciation. ("Ah! The cinematography! The montage!")

Initially sound had deleterious effects on editing. It curtailed the freedoms of the poetic film by concretizing its images, and it at first seemed to curtail the advances made by Eisenstein and others to broaden sequences of shots into wider frames of meaning. The situation might be likened to a comparison between juxtaposing words on a page and doing the same with recorded speech. In the former case, all dialogue, whatever its source, carries at least a commonality of atmosphere about it by way of its typography. In contrast, when we edit recorded speech, we face the variables of sound quality, including the ambiance that surrounds the speakers, dynamics, tempo, accent, dialect, and intonation. Recorded speech can be edited, but it operates by way of different organizational principles. Unless a sound editor sets up a particular aural sensation to be interpreted a certain way, we are inclined to accept it simply as "meaning what it is"; that is, signifying the identity we customarily ascribe to it, and nothing more. A wolf cry is a wolf crying; it does not connote anguish or pleasure unless we have been prepared to interpret it as such.

Similarly, early sound film was limited to the long but immobile take and to some extent has remained so. But as technical developments facilitated camera mobility, sound film progressed along with it—for example when it supported the visual aesthetic of the continuous-run silent camera in the last films of Murnau. Imaginative approaches to editing were reintroduced when relationships between sound and picture had advanced both technically and aesthetically to the point where each had gained some independence from the other.

For instance, sound might be maintained as a constant with different images juxtaposed for effect. Rouben Mamoulian did this to comic purpose in a musical sequence of *Love Me Tonight* (1932), where two lyric lovers, separated by miles, gaily bellow a common song. Alternatively, the integrity of the image might be held constant while the sound varied. This is common to the situation in which a character's mental process is "visualized" by playing variant, sometimes antagonistic, elements of his thoughts and memories on the soundtrack as the audience watches his expression. Mamoulian elaborated this technique in *Dr. Jekyll and Mr. Hyde* (1931) during the transformation scenes. The two sides of Jekyll warred by way of imaginative sound mixes while his face grew fangs and prognathous jaw. Or else the two elements could be played in more fully developed counterpoint. Pudovkin provided an extraordinary instance of this in a tour-de-force introduction to *Deserter* (1933). The film is a story of workers in the Hamburg shipyards, and Pudovkin develops awesome interaction between dock sounds, music, and scenes of the early day, each element reinforcing the underlying narrative mood in a kind of sound-picture ballet.

In recent years, editing has operated usefully as a way to emphasize or to foreshadow elements of plot and character by the juxtaposition of images. Their visual relationships advise us of more than the characters know. For example, in one of his early and best films, which is variously known as *The Naked Night* and *Sawdust and Tinsel* (1953), Ingmar Bergman has the proprietor of a traveling circus (Ake Groenberg) sitting in his wagon playing solitaire while waiting for the return of Harriet Andersson, his mistress, who is a bareback rider in the troupe. We know that she has just left an assignation with a local actor, impressed by his sophistication and vaguely motivated to escape the tedium of her life. Groenberg is unaware of this and is preoccupied with unsuccessful efforts to extricate himself from his mistress and effect reconciliation with his wife, who lives in the town and whom he abandoned by running off with the circus.

A close-up of a playing-card king is dissolved into a close-up of Groenberg's face, the images so composed that the king's crown seems to blend into the live actor and to sprout horns from his head. By this means, Bergman very subtly and efficiently tells us that cuckoldry will play a part in the story, while the actor's expression advises us that his first suspicion has just now reached consciousness.

Similarly, there is a moment in George Stevens's *A Place in the Sun* (1951), which is based on Dreiser's *An American Tragedy,* when Shelley Winters has just left a telephone booth. She was phoning Montgomery Clift, by whom she is pregnant, to tell him they must meet the next weekend. Clift has been occupied with the attentions of Elizabeth Taylor, the daughter of a wealthy factory owner. Shelley Winters is a poor, ill-educated working girl in the plant. Clift, ambitious and deeply attracted to Elizabeth Taylor, is becoming desperate at the impossibility of his situation. A murder plan has begun to form in his mind. Shelley Winters advances to the center of the screen in a shot that composes her image small enough that her vulnerability is emphasized. In a dissolve, Stevens overlaps the lake where she and Montgomery Clift have agreed to go boating on a picnic. The combined image shows the girl alone in the middle of water in which she soon will drown.

SOUND

Film sound was intended to accompany screen pictures from their inception; we remember Edison's impulse to wed his private viewing machine to the cylinder phonograph. But when movies became a public, auditorium-bound medium, film sound had to await two technical developments before it could operate with full success. First, a means of ensuring constant and accurate synchronization had to be devised. Although this was approximated with accompanying records and transcription—for example, Warner Brothers' sound on disc system—the sound-picture relationship could not be predictably maintained, particularly when the film was broken and then spliced, in which case the film's duration was shortened while that of the phonograph disc remained the same. Finally, during the twenties, systems were evolved that literally printed the sound onto the edge of the picture film, providing a tightly synchronized composite as sturdy as the cellulose nitrate on which it was printed.

While these events were taking place in the United States, filmmakers in Germany were experimenting with a sound-on-film process they termed Tri-Ergon, a system that in fact supplied the basic design for Warner Brothers' Vitaphone. Such sound was experimentally used here in newsreels and short subjects and appeared in feature films as musical accompaniment in John Barrymore's *Don Juan* (1926) and then the talking-singing sequences of *The Jazz Singer* (1927) with Al Jolson. Germany's early accomplishments help to account for the imaginative character and superior sound quality of *The Blue Angel* (1930), which clearly "sounds ahead of its time."

Although movie speech had developed hand in hand with electrical recording in the phonograph industry and with radio, early technical demands, particularly in the initial recording process, placed serious obstacles to sound film's picture quality and editing freedom. Cameras were immobilized in soundproofed areas outside microphone range. Actors had to operate within firmly fixed staging areas so that their voices might be successfully captured at constant volume.

During the thirties, further technological advances in camera design, lighting (the old carbon arcs emitted a recordable hiss), rerecording, studio simulation of exterior locations, and microphone apparatus somewhat freed the movies from a reversion to domination by theatrical dialogue, but more important to our present concerns was a developing sense of the sound aesthetic itself: independent sound, and sound as adjunct to an accompanying picture.

We perceive any sound source somewhat differently than we do a visual subject. The binaural accommodations of our ears enable us to locate one or more sounds in space (for instance, loudspeakers) relative to ourselves, but our ears do not characteristically separate several simultaneous events by distance between one another as sharply as the binocular capacities of our two eyes can manage. We often define the conditions of a sound source by way of hints, like volume, echo, and sound quality, somewhat as the flat movie screen simulates depth. We cannot consciously focus our ears as we do our eyes, yet we are constantly screening out "noise" and "focusing" on the meaningful sounds in our environment, since we cannot close our ears as we can our eyes. Sound is thus much more defined by way of its ambiance, the environment in which it operates. When recording sound material for a film, the technician, wherever he is located, will tape amounts of "silence" in the field to intermix later, as necessary for dead spaces, for all silences are not alike, and no silence is total.

Archibald MacLeish's phrase "the ear is poet" reminds us that sound may carry connotative overtones. Because sound isolated from its visual source, as in a recording, maintains something of a quality of nonspecificity, and because hearing is a less consciously controlled sense, it is more open to a listener's personal meanings than visual presentations. This is why ambiguous sound effects are often useful to the filmmaker in securing emotional responses. Val Lewton, a talented producer of low-budget horror pictures, called one such effect "busing," based on a particular moment in his first film, *The Cat People* (1942). A young woman is hurrying home, late at night on the outskirts of a city park. We fear that she is being followed by a large leopard. Although we never see the cat, we sense its presence by way of shadows and the rustle of leaves. The pursuit is built up in intensity with accelerated parallel editing, alternating between the girl's heels tapping on the sidewalk and a silence marking her possible pursuer's noiseless paws. As she steps out of the pool of light from a street lamp into the darkness, a loud soundtrack screech is accompanied by a huge form that intrudes from behind, blocking out her image. After a panicked moment, we realize it is a bus.

What is interesting about the effects (for there are two) is the sound's capacity momentarily to confuse us by drawing on a different reference in our mind, facilitated by a sudden, ambiguous image. This is possible only as long as the sound source remains clouded or unidentified. When sound and picture are visibly linked, the filmmaker speaks of "sync sound," as with the jabbering lip-synced mouths noted earlier. There are other alternatives. Sound source may be seemingly visible but not actually so, an effect René Clair played with by leading us to believe a singer and her song were identical until they became increasingly mismatched and we realized the music came from a phonograph.

We may also define sound by way of its narrative relation to the picture. The two may be supportive or complimentary to one another in either a simple or complex design, or they may be at odds. In Alain Resnais's *Last Year at Marienbad* (1961), a narrator, who is perhaps one of the characters shown, often describes scenes that do not altogether substantiate his own assertions against the visual evidence. In *Diary of a Country Priest* (1950) Robert Bresson's narrator reads passages from his journal while visuals repeat the events. Such a technique may strike the audience as an irritating redundancy until it is realized that one source subtly contradicts the other at various times, as when the priest describes what he believes himself to have experienced. When this occurs in either film, we are pressed to reconcile the differences, either by denying one for the other, or by accounting for some condition that will allow disparity. Bresson is especially sensitive to the evocative power of sound. In *A Man Escaped* (1956), a long last sequence concludes with the screen almost entirely black. Our aural sensitivity is made more open, and the soundtrack guides many listeners into an intensity of feeling and understanding about escape, whatever form of imprisonment the escaper may flee. (Others are frustrated by the ending, and "want to see more.")

To the extent that sound echoes and reinforces the reality of the screen, it supports the movie's illusionistic functions. Partially or entirely independent soundtracks are more characteristic of highly personal stylizations, but even the use of natural sounds may be put to special purpose. Some directors, for instance, bury human conversation in the noise of locale (waves, machinery, city sound pollution). Such an effort may point up the impotence of human beings in an environment beyond their control. It also underlines a director's assignment of equal importance to living and nonliving parts of his "world," just as the visually inclined Josef von Sternberg gave like treatment to his actors and to pictures on the walls behind them.

Because of its special characteristics, the soundtrack has enjoyed less exploration and "building" than the picture, this despite the high skills of studio technicians, who will mix impressive numbers of different sound sources to produce a single composite where each element is properly balanced and timed. Sound tolerates less density than picture; it is harder for us to separate its various parts when they occur together, for all are equally in focus.

Sound is also cheaper than picture. Even a high-salaried dialogue writer will cost a production far less than those moments terrifying to a producer during shooting when actors and director stop and try to fix speeches that are not working, while the crew sits, thinking of overtime. It is usually better to pay one man than many. U.P.A., a unit of imaginative animators who broke away from Disney, realized the value of sound by dressing their inexpensively produced cartoons with extremely clever, minutely planned voice and effects tracks.

The circumstances of production will also define a movie by way of its sound. Studios draw from different libraries of stock sound, not only "canned" music, if that should be used, but effects. Different studio libraries approach sound quality variously, so that a western from Twentieth Century-Fox may compare favorably or not to one from Paramount in terms of the sharpness and echo of its rifle pings and the virulence of its dynamite.

Many European productions are disposed to postrecord the dialogue of a film, or *postsync*. The procedure is less expensive, because sync sound does not then figure as a major factor in the shooting circumstances, and execution can be speeded up when the director and actor have to contend with fewer variables. On the other hand, postsyncing has its drawbacks. The ambiance of shooting stage or location cannot be simulated effectively, and studio recordings always sound somehow out of touch with the visuals. Since most such recordings are done with actors seated in front of the microphones, distinctions in volume that would better match the locations of the visual images relative to the audience are sacrificed. Everybody has the same "presence." It is hard, too, to reconceive the emotionality of an earlier moment, especially the effect of posture and movement on one's speech.

Postsyncing may be used by a director the better to control or to maintain the design of his film, for he has escaped the dangers of misinterpretations and misuses of his dialogue on set. He is granted a last opportunity to unify an entire production and even to correct earlier mistakes or his own lack of clarity. Federico Fellini is notorious for this approach. He will go so far as to tell the actors to recite numbers, the alphabet, or meaningless gobbledegook on camera, perhaps not himself having altogether refined to his satisfaction what they will eventually be saying. Orson Welles has done most of his later productions in Europe and is said to be quite proud of what he can achieve by way of postsyncing. (Welles was an active part of thirties and forties American radio.) Nonetheless, critics periodically comment on the technical inferiority of his soundtracks, which they contrast unfavorably to the quality of his images.

The matter of postsyncing brings up the question of printed titles versus translated voice tracks for foreign language films. It is not an issue that is easily resolved. Those in favor of titles will contend that any violation of a director's soundtrack clearly deteriorates the film itself, for the two are not, properly, separable. Translated dialogue is usually done by anonymous actors of greater or less talent, but they are hardly capable of duplicating either the skill or the appropriateness of an original performance. Sync can never be ideally matched. Witness any spaghetti western on the Late Show. And the words themselves, however ably a translator has done his job, cannot duplicate the nuances of the original tongue. It is far better to tolerate titled intrusions and benefit from an original soundtrack, which has its own rewards even for one who does not understand the language.

On the other hand, certain films could never even get to this country in the first place without dubbing. They are otherwise too expensive to import, since the market is too limited for titled prints (neighborhood audiences don't like to read subtitles). Millions of people saw films like $8^{1}/_{2}$ (1963) and *Two Women* (1960) because of the dubbing. Further, as we have noted, the original sound itself is likely to have been done in a studio, often with other actors than those on the screen. The titles themselves are a visual abomination, and half the time invisible. Not only do they intrude on a picture so that the camera's intentions are destroyed, but also the spectator's total time and attention are occupied just keeping up with what's being said, forcing him to ignore the major part of the experience. And titles on television are impossible.

Until all of us speak all languages, the problem is insoluble, but, in order to understand exactly what is lost in translation, everyone should sometime attend a foreign moviehouse and hear some familiar star like Paul Newman or Marilyn Monroe burst out in Italian.

All good film dialogue is written to be heard. We often fail to realize that the most natural-sounding language in film has been itself carefully rewritten and polished for effect. Just as ordinary speech in prose rarely sounds as it reads, the screenwriter's conversations must be refashioned, usually in the direction of economy. Consider a Faulkner sentence on film. Dudley Nichols, who wrote many of the early sound films by John Ford, said that the screenwriter must learn to practice "dialogue in a synoptic fashion, which may show itself to the eye when printed on a page, but should never reveal itself to the ear when spoken from the screen."[3] On stage, the actor projects, which necessarily colors both the character and intonation of his speech. On screen, even more so than in actual life, his entire presence, the shifts of his body, his expression, and the distance maintained from his listener are all literal aspects of the conversation. The closer one is to another person, the fewer words one is likely to use. The more one shows, the less one need say.

The ear-attuned filmmaker may use both words and sounds in certain kinds of musical pattern, for in this respect, the soundtrack is not necessarily held to its own logic of dramatic form. Sounds may be developed as motifs, their recurrence and variations making the narrative more concrete. Important elements in *Last Year at Marienbad,* for example, are footsteps and pistol shots, both ingredients of a story that is obsessively told and reworked by the narrator. A girl listens for footsteps on the gravel but does not hear them. A man approaches her on carpeted stairs, and we hear the sound of his steps as if on gravel. We see footsteps on gravel but hear nothing. Guns are fired at different times. In the pistol range, their report is sharp and ominous. When a girl is shot in her bedroom, the sound is different, muffled, like a muted kettledrum, and it seems to deny the reality of the event.

Music has a particular tie to period. We may date a film almost as easily by its music track as its images. For this reason, the filmmaker may thoughtfully select his music sources to locate a story in time, as Eddie Cantor's closing radio theme song was used in *Bonnie and Clyde.* In the late forties and early fifties, the French accepted Sidney Bechet, a great American jazz soprano saxophonist, with high enthusiasm after he emigrated. In *Murmur of the Heart* (1971), Louis Malle has his adolescent hero steal a Bechet record on the Vogue label from a record store. The music effectively defines the period of the film for the French and other Bechet lovers.

Stanley Kubrick is inclined to use the dated edge of popular song. When giant planes meet and mate for refueling in *Dr. Strangelove or: How I Learned to Stop Worrying and Love the Bomb* (1963), to the tune of "Try a Little Tenderness," humor rests not only in the image evoked but also on the contrast between the two mechanical beasts and the tearful wartime ballad. Similarly the very incongruity of a Strauss waltz and space flight gave particular exuberant charm to *2001: A Space Odyssey* (1968). The attractions of Beethoven to a futurist thug are central in *A Clockwork Orange* (1971), which also uses "Singin' in the Rain" in ways Gene Kelly never dreamed.

Just as Asiatic audiences grew up with the *benski,* a live narrator who provided linkage between themselves and the screen images, we have been provided with movie music since film's earliest days. Much movie music continues to serve this early purpose, itself an outgrowth of incidental music in the theater, especially at melodrama, then of silent-film pianos, and, in the larger theaters, orchestras.

The uses of music in film, however, extend far beyond a disposition toward overblown extensions of audience feeling in baths of emotionality. Much of the best film music is marked by its economy, as with language. Music is especially powerful when employed sparingly on the screen; a little goes a long way.

Music appears at times almost to escape the ideologies and theoretical rubric that may color all other aspects of a film. In many cases, a fine director simply has a bad ear for music, a truism underscored with the unfortunately sentimental harmonies in Roberto Rossellini's early neorealist ventures, like *Open City* (1945) and *Paisan* (1946); the bathos of the music belies the integrity of other aspects of these productions. Even among the socialist realists, where the use of words or a high stylization of images to convey inner states is anathema, music is condoned. Pudovkin demanded the employment of music relative to picture in the manner of counterpoint, to call up the interior meanings of screen action rather than supporting or duplicating them.

Music can interject meanings in a screen experience that are unavailable to speech or picture. A music passage may work, for example, where a spoken interior monologue cannot. Because music occupies a different meaning dimension, it has a special independence as well, if so deployed. Or music can lend particular unity to a film. The clean blend of classic line and Kurt Weill–like orchestrations in Hans Eisler's music track for *Night and Fog* makes the film in one sense endurable, despite the music's anguish.

The film composer has an entire tradition of music history on which to draw, and although we still have Quincy Jones bass figures in accompaniment to our thrillers, there is growing experimentation with orchestrations of varying size, electronic music, and even improvisation. The Modern Jazz Quartet was used to good effect in Louis Malle's *Frantic* (*Ascenseur pour l'Échaufaud* [1957]), and Stan Getz improvised against picture in Arthur Penn's *Mickey One* (1965), evoking a fleeting memory of the nickelodeon piano player who would shift his melodies to conform with the changing scenes that flashed above him.

The Impact of Editing and Sound ▪ 97

5 ▪ Color

Even black-and-white film is affected by color, in the sense that any film emulsion requires chromatic response to every hue it photographs. The early emulsions (termed orthochromatic) recognized blue, green, and ultraviolet, condemning the red end of the spectrum to darkness. Further, ortho film stock was grainy (grain is the visibility of microscopic particles in the emulsion), which combined with a "slowness" (emulsion requiring maximum exposure) that needed high illumination and made contrasty images that clung to the extremities of the black–white continuum. In consequence, theater-like makeup was applied to give expression visibility, despite its masklike appearance under the camera eye. Our impression of early films today is further affected along these same lines because the prints we see have often been copied not from long-gone original negatives but from later-generation projection prints, which were purposely made more contrasty than the original source for projection purposes.

Panchromatic stocks, sensitive to red light as well as blue, green (somewhat), and violet, had been developed in the early 1900s but they were not seriously used in the industry until the twenties. Filming a South Seas documentary, *Moana,* in 1923 and 1924, Robert Flaherty took both a color camera and some new panchromatic film stock he had secured from Eastman. The color camera did not stand up, but Flaherty, who processed his own film and even got sick from the cave water he used, responded with such enthusiasm to the rich skin-tone variations of the islanders as captured on the panchromatic stock that he completed his picture with it. Orthochromatic stock, in contrast, suited the world of Nanook the Eskimo.

As faster emulsions were developed, so that panchromatic film finally surpassed ortho in this respect too, it cut back on necessary light and altered the character of artificial illumination. Incandescent light, which gave off more reds, became practical, replacing arcs. Makeup could now be put to more natural effect.

Hand-colored film has been mentioned before. (The flag of brotherhood raised by mutineers on the battleship *Potemkin* was stenciled in red on some prints.) Laboratory techniques involving dyes at the fixing stage simulated color. In the century's first decade, the Lumière brothers invented a colored "monochrome," which they used to make some lovely still photos. But conceiving a film that would respond accurately to the light spectrum of the world was complicated further by problems of reproducing the original prints in quantity. The technique that finally became prevalent involved a camera that split the field into three images: cyan (blue-green), magenta, and yellow. Each impressed itself either on separate negatives or on different layers of one emulsion. This three-color process is what we call Technicolor. In the early fifties, Eastman Color improved color qualities in the release prints (the version exhibited in theaters), and this encouraged increased use of color. Some wide-screen processes lessened color quality by the degree of their magnification. Today network television has largely condemned all productions to color, appropriately or not, for every feature now hopes to spend its declining years intercut with deodorant commercials.

There are differences between the color we watch in a movie theater and color in real life. For one thing, both camera lens and film emulsion may not record quite what the eye views. Our brains ask us to see color presences that do not exist in fact. For example, a shirt, white in sunlight, literally turns yellowish under incandescent illumination that has more reds and fewer blues than daylight. Film emulsions are composed, too, for particular color balances in light (what is called "color temperature"), and when these formulas are out of phase with actual illumination, the exposures register this disparity one way or another. So color rendition bears no easy one-to-one relation with any outside "control." The filmmaker, then, manipulates effects through filters, lighting, choice of film stock, costuming, even by applying cosmetic correction to the surfaces photographed.

Begging the crucial commercial determinations of the choice between black-and-white or color, the thoughtful filmmaker needs to confront the question of why he ought to choose one process or another in the first place. Rudolf Arnheim wisely construed hue's relation to narrative by proposing that black-and-white places all of reality on one continuum. Because these shadowed conventions are acceptable to an audience, the filmmaker is free to pitch his narrative to a single, controllable value scale, just as Herman Melville, say, developed the underlying metaphysic of *Moby Dick* by pitting Ahab's black heart against the whiteness of the whale, or placed Negro slave against white slaver in *Benito Cereno*. When color is introduced, said Arnheim, it adds so many variables of hue, brightness, and saturation that the greater part of every vivid moment has escaped the aesthetic control of the film artist.

Our relations to color are blunted, too, by eighteenth-century carry-overs, attitudes represented by Sir Joshua Reynolds, first President of the British Royal Academy. Reynolds viewed color as an afterthought in painting, a patina to content rather than intrinsic to form. Color was used to emotionalize a portrait or landscape, and to render it attractive, but nothing more. Certainly color can carry high emotional overtones, so great, in fact, that their effects on us are like the atavisms of primitive imagery. Modern painting, departing from representational form, has returned color's precedence, but the narrative film, which continues to operate with photographic fidelity, stays somewhere within the biases of Sir Joshua.

In most cases, movie directors are content to settle for fixed emotional tones in color renditions, as when John Huston tried to evoke the qualities of Toulouse-Lautrec's posters in *Moulin Rouge* (1953). Producers of well-financed M-G-M musicals often experimented with color in special production numbers where fantasy was permissible and techniques of high-fashion photography and advertising might be used. See *That's Entertainment* (1974).

There is some tradition for singling out one color or a simple color combination in order that a film audience may be cued to story and theme. In *Becky Sharp* (a 1935 *Vanity Fair* and the first color feature to use the three-strip Technicolor camera), Mamoulian used this approach. Soldiers are called to battle during a dance. The director had costumed only these men in blazing reds, so that as the hall emptied of their presence, the audience felt the departure. Hitchcock cues color to our, and his characters', emotions: red as a trigger to Marnie's deep-seated childhood trauma, for example. Eisenstein once wrote an essay that traced the connotations of yellow through history, and while there appeared enough variation in its "meanings" to keep connections between certain colors and emotions from being readily apparent, the area remains open to investigation. In the days before Soviet color film, Eisenstein intercut black-and-white photography with translucent splashes of red during a bull-mating sequence in *The Old and the New* (1929).

We bring more circumscribed associations with color as well through shared iconographies: patriotic combinations, for example, or the qualities of printers' ink known through the comic strip. Stanley Kubrick used these familiarities just as he employed popular song, if somewhat more subtly, in *A Clockwork Orange*. The white-pants "uniform" of Alex and his droogs is enough like professional medical garb to link an ironic sanitariness to their cool cruelties. White underlined the youths' repressed emotions and worked into the narrative by way of the drug-and-milk bar, where we are introduced to Alex and his gang. As Alex's plight worsens, the growing filth of his uniform corroborates a mounting anxiety as "feelings" come closer to eruption.

In *The Beggar's Opera* (1953), Peter Brook helped to dominate his screen with the avarice that riddles John Gay's play by suffusions of bright green, like the color of pool-table felt, and of golds. In *Shadows of Forgotten Ancestors* (1965), the Russian director Sergei Paradjanov used red skillfully during an ax murder. What appears to be blood falls across the lens, changing then to a kind of leaping flame that has the semblance of fiery horses passing overhead like fleeing, manic spirits.

In all such cases, it is a single color that falls within technical control. Arnheim's dictum is evidenced by Ingmar Bergman and his cameraman Sven Nykvist in *Cries and Whispers* (1972). Here the Swedish director in effect substitutes red for black at the distant end of the value scale, to which the other colors play nonfunctional support. The entire film is organized along red and white variations, sunlight serving as correlate to occasional moments of bliss and childhood innocence. Scarlet dominates the home where Harriet Andersson is dying. In fact, Bergman has even replaced black with red in his fadeouts, so that each sequence concludes on a note of implicit emotional fervor. The two sequences with a softer color scheme occur as memories of the dying woman. As a child, she watches her mother in a garden, unseen and worshipful. On a later summer day, she plays on a swing with her sisters and their maid, happy in a naïve world of kindness and love. Here the dominant hues are soft whites, as in the women's summer gowns, the whole done like the pastel palette of an impressionist painter working in bright sunlight.

Francis Ford Coppola puts color to interesting use in *The Godfather* (1972). It is employed as a plot cue in the meeting-of-the-families truce, where oranges are located around the conference table to spot the enemies of Don Corleone. On a grander scale, there is the "framing" black-and-white that introduces and concludes what is otherwise a color film. As indicated by Judith Vogelsang in a study of image and sound motifs,[4] this relationship of color to black-and-white might be seen as a forewarning of the story itself, in which Michael, the son, learns to reconceive his own value system. What had first been a black-and-white view of Mafia enterprise and the American "way" adapts altogether to new perceptions colored and broadened by understandings of the family business and its behavior. We might also substitute our own ignorances for Michael's so that the film opens a personal awareness of Corleone ways. We could also propose that the film is paying passing tribute to its genre heritage: the black-and-white gangster world nurtured in Depression movie palaces, a notion that more easily accounts for the black-and-white conclusion.

Years back, when a Dutch documentary cameraman/director named Joris Ivens was filming the poor Belgian mining country Van Gogh had known (*Borinage* [1933]), he discovered dangers in beauty. Ivens said a large amount of his footage had to be discarded because its visual attractions counteracted his intentions. One imaginative solution to color's attractiveness was attempted by John Huston when filming the black-and-white world of *Moby Dick* (1955). Huston employed a laboratory process that subdued the colors to extremely low saturation. Then the color original was printed in combination with a monochrome image to make the final product "more" black-and-white. The result is a somber sea world that almost succeeds in reconciling one to the presence of Gregory Peck as Captain Ahab.

As color emulsions have become faster, the possibilities of further controls fall within the domain of cameraman and laboratory, for film which can be exposed under wider variations of light and at different times of the day or night is more subject to color alterations. Some recent films have used these new options to achieve kinds of "washed-out" effects, although a running concern rests with the editor, who must find reasonable color matches between shots that were executed at different times. Color may vary considerably during any particular feature, but its changes have to be accomplished gradually, unless abrupt contrast is intended. In any case, the color qualities of *The Godfather* evoke some sense of the world of the forties, and a film like Robert Altman's *McCabe and Mrs. Miller* (1971) worked especially well in its snow scenes, where a white landscape was balanced by somewhat whited-out browns and reds of tree trunks and the ill-fated, leather-coated McCabe. In *Catch-22* (1970) Mike Nichols used a different picture quality in Yossarian's nightmare trauma with the dying gunner. The washed-out plane and uniform surfaces helped to point up both Alan Arkin's hallucinating memory and the gunner's spilling innards in this uneven version of Joseph Heller's fine novel.

6 ■ Point of View

Like time, point of view is open to several interpretations and raises even more convoluted structural problems. First, we recognize attitude-taking on the part of the filmmaker himself toward his material as a whole, analogous to what an author of plays or novels can choose to assume. Some of these attitudes have been noted in passing. In a sense, they are implicit in even the most "removed" relationship between filmmaker and his material, say certain *cinéma vérité* productions. The cameraman must select what will fall in or out of his lens field. A documentarian camera angle itself is a point of view, and it may be argued how far the very presence of movie machinery and crew will affect the behavior it seeks to "observe." For example, two Frenchmen, Jean Rouch and Edgar Morin, approached this problem by adding their own visible presence to the production (*Chronicle of a Summer* [1961]) and then incorporating what happened into the story. One way or another, we are exposed to a designing presence in every film, which we shall term "director's point of view," presuming in this instance that the camera is the director's eye.

Next, three possible points of view stem from the movie's exposition. These alternatives may be likened to our first, second, and third person verb forms. The recounted story will give the impression of being told: (1) by a person who experienced it, directly or indirectly, and who talks to us as if we were strangers; (2) as if the film, in the form of soundtrack and/or visuals, were addressing itself immediately at the audience, like Mr. Peacham in Brecht's *The Threepenny Opera;* or (3) as an "impersonal" representation that cannot be identified with any known character.

Under possibility 1 we number all those motion pictures that use a first-person narrator—*Great Expectations* (1946), for example—who tells us his experiences as we watch them unfold on the screen. This practice amounts to first-person narration, third-person picture. In theory, we might have both first-person sound and first-person picture, although such attempts have been rare, for either the camera must then maintain a continuous posture of being the speaking character (posing problems we will soon investigate), or the speaker's absence in the picture must otherwise be accounted for. (How can he describe it as participant without being there?)

Second-person camera-to-audience is unlikely, too, because we know that what has been recorded is time past, and film cannot in this respect simulate the immediacy of theater any more effectively than can prose. Perhaps Godard has come closest to this stance in his film *Wind from the East* (1970), which contains one sequence in which a character, standing in front of a rural stream, is said by the commentary to invite a pretty girl in the audience to join him. Godard enjoys the complexities of performers falling in and out of roles, and here the event is marked by a simultaneous awareness that what is being asked of us is known to be impossible to all concerned (actors, film crew, and audience) and that it has a parallel reality in the actor's relation to the crew members present at the time of his purported speech.

Insofar as the director assumes an attitude about the material of his film, this will be accomplished either by spreading his postures toward the production "overall," or else by injecting himself literally as a visible presence. Fellini makes somewhat comic use of himself as a performer in *The Clowns* (1970), which is in this respect a sort of recap of *8½* (1963), playing "Fellini" for laughs. The matter of a filmmaker's relation to his film is the substructure of illusion, as Pirandello showed in the theater. Its problems were displayed in *Man with a Movie Camera*, made by Dziga Vertov in 1929. Burlesquing something of the documentary style, Vertov runs variations on the filmmaker's presence by introducing the camera itself as a visible character. In one effective sequence, he shows us a scene, then shows us an editor filing away the film of that scene, and then shows us the footage of the same scene edited into a new context. The visible presence of a filmmaker in his film momentarily provides us a glimpse of the production process itself, then buries it again as we realize there yet remains an unseen director directing the visible one.

The credibility of the camera as first person depends on its plot integration and on the point of view itself. Panoramic views would not "work" for very long, although the moving camera, as noted, may so involve us that its use in the lens-eye equation can be very effective on a short-term basis. In his introductory sequence to *Dr. Jekyll and Mr. Hyde*,

Mamoulian has the audience travel from home to medical school as if it were Dr. Jekyll, journeying to a lecture on human atavisms the doctor then delivers. The sequence is full of shots angled through coach windows, along the London streets, tracking through door frames and down corridors to intensify the parallax phenomenon while associates turn to address us as if we were the good doctor.

Second-person camera angles as they might relate screen to audience have been described. A common convention that does not work as well on wider screens is the close-up/reverse-angle/close-up of a two-party conversation. We see Character One speaking directly to the camera lens, which gives us the impression that we physically occupy the ground where Character Two stands while being addressed. The angle then shifts more or less 180 degrees, so that we seem to have taken the perspective of Character One watching Character Two. This cut-and-dried formula will be varied at times so that the audience watches one party's face listening rather than speaking (which may be the point of dramatic interest anyway), and the camera angle may withdraw to a medium shot that neutrally includes both characters. At no time do we identify with either actor, any more than we mistake the direct address of a writer as pointed uniquely to ourselves instead of to the anonymous "reader."

The third-person camera vantage carries its own ambiguities, for an audience finds itself party to an experience where its presence is not acknowledged (the camera as peephole) and safe from the events and responsibility for them (the camera as security). Such a situation lends itself especially to the proclivities of a director like Alfred Hitchcock, who encourages us to identify with his murderers, even those as deranged as the criminals of *Psycho* (1960) and *Frenzy* (1972), so that we are both relieved when these men have escaped apprehension and guilty for the sympathy we have extended.

Objectivity and subjectivity in the film experience operate in both broad and narrow confines. In one sense, every film is an objectified, or removed, event by reason of the circumstances of its production and our perceptions of what is projected on the screen. At the same time, all such moments are subjective in that we empathize with the events despite all we know about their artifice. In narrower terms, a director's point of view, the "tense" of the exposition, and the choice of camera angles all contribute to some specific degree of audience commitment on the objective-subjective scale. Either we take no sides with relation to the characters and their author, or our sympathies have been elicited —literally, as when we become a character, or figuratively, if we are "for" one screen image in preference to another.

Narrative film at its most conventional asks that we be "for" a protagonist but elicits our sympathy almost exclusively by way of the story's events. Many directors who grew up within the confines of the large studio systems have maintained that stance in terms of camera-angle–editing designs, while yet seeking to affect us covertly by defining what we will see in any particular scene. Howard Hawks and John Ford, for example, draw support toward the heroes of their masculine adventure films and comedies by thoughtful plot twists, character delineation through revealing little acting "bits," and a skilled sense of pace that is especially evident in mimed action sequences. Their camera angles tend to the human, straight-on, eye level that does not take evident sides, close-ups only for special tension and intimacy, distance at time of epic behavior (stagecoaches and Indians, plane dogfights).

In extremity, the subjective camera becomes a character and, if successful, engages our attention (first-person narration, first-person camera angle). Seeing as he or she does, moving with him or her, addressed as if we were one, we feel, ideally, part of the plot. The experience itself is curiously bisexual. Movies do not require us to identify with our own sex, age, and race. In this way, our fantasies can escape many social and psychic rubrics that operate elsewhere. Just as human sexuality is itself mixed, we may locate identification binds with hero *and* heroine. Our empathy can lodge itself on pursuer *and* pursued. Young people may take to today's wrinkled John Wayne not for the quality of his private opinions but because he seems rough-edged and authentic, free of evasion and the usual adult subterfuge.

The problem with subjectivity as an expository technique of any duration is the difficulty of keeping it going. A camera can track and swerve and jounce only so many times before the mannerisms become distancing—that is, they remove us from identifying with the process, remind us we are sitting in an auditorium. A first-person commentary (the camera eye speaks as I) can continue only so long before we begin to question motivations and behaviors that are patently not our own. The notorious

Filming a love scene for the first-person The Lady in the Lake.

instance of this was a version of Raymond Chandler's *The Lady in the Lake* (1946), in which Robert Montgomery, camera, and audience jointly shared the role of Philip Marlowe, private eye, throughout the adventure. All of us were slugged, smoked cigarettes, drank booze, questioned suspects, shaved, and were even kissed by Audrey Totter. The experience, while interesting, failed to hold spectator empathy with any consistency.

Strong feelings of audience identification are often elicited by camera shots that eschew the first-person posture while maintaining the excitement of immediacy. For example, the footage of wartime combat cameramen working with hand-held equipment first acclimated large audiences to a sense of "nowness" that grew out of jerking, bouncing, sharp-angled shifts in the visual field as photographers experienced the very battles they documented.

Objectivity and subjectivity need not be extreme alternatives. A filmmaker will often elect some camera angle that "favors" one character— that is, falls into the general province of his personal sight lines. Over-the-shoulder shots permit an audience to watch an actor's speech and reactions while they remind us that a second party is a constant, tangible presence to the exchange. As Character One faces the lens, we take a position behind Character Two, so that his back (head, neck, shoulder) obtrudes in the cornered foreground.

If there is a visually evident relation between two parties on screen, the camera may assume any posture of relative sympathy. If we draw a

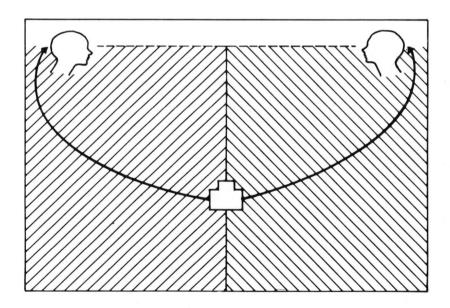

line between two characters that acknowledges their interplay (perhaps a sight line, perhaps a knife on the ground for which they are vying), the camera can then undertake any choice of angles (high, low, left, right, near, distant) or movement as long as it observes a relation to the "action line" that avoids reversing the position of each character onscreen relative to the other (unless that's what is wanted).

Sometimes it is possible to shift from one point of view to another in the same shot, without relying on a cut. This experience may have singular effect, advancing our experience not only by story and visual information but also from meaning implicit in the shift itself. Murnau's *The Last Laugh* (1924) does this in a night sequence in which an old man is walking through the corridors of a hotel, lighting his way by flashlight. The camera tracks next to him, so that at times we follow torchlight down the halls, watching its moving beam as if we were the performer, then withdrawing just enough that his stooped back is visible on the right side of the screen. In this way our sympathies alternate between the character's own anxiety (alone and trespassing) and a reminder of his age and shuffling gait.

In like vein, the filmmaker may himself play in-and-out with his audience, now pointing up with more or less subtlety, an item, a gesture, a sympathy he wants us specially to note. In *Mother* (1926), Pudovkin estimates the power relation between proletariat and imperialist forces now and again throughout by use of camera angles. In most of the film his angles point down (high-angled) with respect to the people, up (low-angled) toward authority, so that judges, officers, and soldiers dominate the screen frame and their victims are literally downtrodden. As the people organize, revolt, and mass themselves into larger and larger units, the relation of class to camera is reversed. Authority drops down in the camera's sight, epitomized by the statues of equestrian leaders, and the people visibly rise up.

The great director Leni Riefenstahl manipulated symbols toward similar purpose in the staged "documentation" she made of the first Nuremburg Convention that served to consolidate Nazi power in Germany (*Triumph of the Will* [1934]). Early on, the film places the eagles of the Weimar Republic high up with relation to the swastikas of National Socialism—on flags, on banners, and set against the great cloth backdrops of the massed forums. As speeches and pageantry continue, the eagles slip down visually. Finally they are out of sight altogether, leaving the swastikas high and triumphant.

The device of acquainting the viewer with information either known only by himself (for instance, the last shots of *Citizen Kane,* earlier discussed) or shared with a single character is a common and effective technique of suspense, for it enlists the threat of disclosure. Hitchcock once said that he would like to film the sinking of the *Titanic.* "But everyone knows what will happen. Where is the suspense?" he was asked. "Ah," said Hitchcock. "Everyone knows the *Titanic* will sink, but no one knows when."

In *Rope* (1948), which draws on the circumstances of the Leopold-and-Loeb kidnaping, James Stewart plays a professor whose Nietzschian espousals have inspired two students to kill a child. The body is hidden in a living-room chest visible to Stewart, who is visiting the students. Much of the story is developed on this knowledge, shared with the audience but unknown to Stewart. In *North by Northwest* (1959), James Mason plans to kill his mistress, Eva Marie Saint, as they escape in a plane and then dispose of her body in midair. Cary Grant discovers the plot and tries to warn her by way of a note written inside a matchbook on which his initials, R.O.T., are printed. (Discussion of the matchbook was planted earlier.) He knows; she doesn't. Then she knows, Mason doesn't. In *Psycho*, after Tony Perkins, as Norman Bates, has cleaned up his mother's mess in the bathroom and sunk Janet Leigh's car in the mud, we and he know, but the police don't. We know the money was in the trunk, but he doesn't. But he and Hitchcock know about Mrs. Bates, and we don't. And so on and so forth.

Point of view may also be considered in terms of two aesthetic positions that derive from elsewhere in the arts: impressionism and expressionism. Each describes an approach to creating perceptions and feelings in an audience that I have examined until now in terms of camera angles and plot disclosures. Since much of their stylizing effect is graphic, impressionism and expressionism are most apparent in matters of staging and composition. Because these elements do not always rest easily with other aspects of the movie experience, we are reminded of the complications sometimes posed by film's catch-all relationship with so many of the arts.

Impressionism grew out of certain tendencies among realist French painters. Emphasizing a far more direct relation to nature, it brought artists out of their studios and into the field, like early movie documentarians. This world was viewed with a kind of artistic innocence that intensified the paintings in a hedonism of the retina. Impressionism concentrated upon our fleeting perceptions of the moment; the special interest of these painters was in the passing effects of light on objects. Subject matter retreated back to a kind of motif, servant to its surfaces.

Neo-impressionism, a subsequent movement, countered the earlier indistinct, large-brush-stroked forms with more intricately executed, ordered canvases based on what were thought to be laws of visual perception. The neo-impressionists emphasized an internal harmony of elements (composition, form, color, shape) and defended their actions with the science of the day.

What has all this to do with movies? First there is the direct influence of impressionists and neo-impressionists on cinematography and on film aesthetics—the sometimes debatable ideas that in canvas and screen composition, horizontals are calming, verticals strong, and diagonals active; the efforts to relate color, line, and tone to particular and definable emotions. The neo-impressionists' belief in grounding their aesthetic philosophy in science (Seurat, for example) is echoed in the very character of photography as an art technology where visual experience depends altogether on laboratory formulas and the physics of lenses.

More important is the personality of the impressionist artist as a presence obtruding between us and his work, similar to our earlier discussion of director's point of view. His pictures were not "finished" like those of his realist predecessors, which, however identifiable by style, were all equally "representative" of the outside world. Each painting by each artist of the new school constituted a singular, private vision. It was the artist's impression that was shared, growing out of one special moment. The energies of impressionism inflect narrative film in the measure that an audience views any scene as singularly and visibly perceived by some eye, either the artist-camera's or, in terms of dramatic point of view, that of a character, but never by a machine and never "unreal."

Unlike impressionism, expressionism does not indicate by emphasis how things truly are seen but rather gives structure, hence visibility, to the unseen-yet-experienced. Expressionists stressed the externalization of experience itself; feelings experienced by the characters were manifested in staging, costumes, and decor, rather than simply through the actors' portrayal of them. Edvard Munch said, "For realism, it was the façade that counted, for impressionism the character. Now it is shadows and movements." Shadows and movements took graphic forms of simplicity, big dimensions, undulating curves, and jagged-angled design.

Expressionism found voice, too, in prose, poetry, and theater and passed into motion pictures largely by way of German films of the twenties. In its early stages, expressionist film bore a strong visual resemblance to painting: shadows, exaggerations, highly stylized set pieces, the most "unreal" studio flats, like the sharp-angled roofs and doors in Robert Wiene's *The Cabinet of Dr. Caligari* (1919), which were in fact executed by expressionist painters. Expressionism sought to make manifest a performer's feelings or sometimes the general atmosphere of a production, and it lent itself, particularly in the German film, to bizarre, fanciful tales of horror and menace.

At the same time, difficulties arose in adapting so highly stylized a design technique to a medium that is bound by lenses to apparent visual realism. Thus, as Arnheim has said, however jagged the parallelogram Caligarian walls and however out of the ordinary its chairs, these must still be occupied by flesh-and-blood humans. How to seat a real man at an expressionist table and give the appearance of stylistic consistency?[5]

Fritz Lang utilized painted scenery to heighten the expressionist approach of *Metropolis*.

Theater did not place the same demands on the relation of performer to set, but film could no longer merely document "screenplays," and the exaggerated behaviors of expressionist actors, however deeply felt, carried something of Victorian melodrama about them.

Expressionism reappeared in the American horror genre, often because Hollywood technicians had been imported from Germany. It underlies some of Hitchcock's graphics, like grotesque faces in close-up, comic-book gesture, and unreal backgrounds. Hitchcock himself worked at the German UFA studios for a short period.

The style also insinuates itself into later film by way of writers' and directors' theater experience. Expressionism colored Depression-era American theater, where, for example, Orson Welles assembled his Mercury Players (the unnatural angles of *Citizen Kane* and *The Magnificent Ambersons* [1942], particularly up-angled shots of actors against enclosing ceilings; the manipulations of light to shift playing areas; Ray Collins's theatrical train departure and goodbye to Tim Holt). On occasion, expressionism has been adapted with a play itself, like Arthur Miller's

Death of a Salesman (1951), in which Frederic March abandoned some of his usual restraints in film, perhaps because of the direction by Laslo Benedek, who had been an editor in Germany.

Today expressionism is evident most often in staging and use of color that depart from accustomed vision, not because these elements are "really there" on examination (impressionism) but for the sake of emotional effects or else as evidence of a character's inner state. In *Red Desert* (1964), Antonioni painted props and sets to indicate Monica Vitti's depression. Thus she lived in a world of somber browns and grays, although Arnheim's "Caligari problem" re-emerged in the actress's complexion. Rosy-cheeked, Vitti stood at visual odds with her environment, and visual style and point of view were at irreconcilable odds. Expressionism is also manifested in the brightly painted green of David Hemmings's park grass in *Blow-Up* (1966) and the fades-to-red in Bergman's *Cries and Whispers*.

Such techniques are inclined to intrude in the staged, rather than scenarioed, moments of production. In illustration, let us examine two scripted episodes from Hitchcock's *Marnie* (1964, shooting script by Jay Presson Allen).

(FADE IN)

1. EXT. UPPER PLATFORM RAILROAD STATION—DUSK—CLOSE-UP
   The screen is filled with a bulky yellow handbag held under a woman's arm. The CAMERA MOVES along with her for about ten or fifteen seconds. Then the woman begins to gain on the moving CAMERA until she is waist high and we see that she is hatless with black hair hanging almost to her shoulders. Slowly the CAMERA comes to a stop. The young woman who continues walking is consequently completely revealed to us. She is carrying, in addition to the yellow handbag, a rather heavy suitcase. The CAMERA remains stationary as the young woman continues to walk. She walks to the far end of the platform until she is a tiny figure in the distance. Through the whole of the walk, the yellow handbag stands out—the only spot of color in the general grayness of the scene. Finally the girl comes to a stop and looks expectantly in the direction of an oncoming train, which we HEAR approaching. Through all this we have never seen her face. We see the train approaching in the distance.

In viewing, the film's opening shot closely duplicates the script, except that the yellow handbag's unnatural brilliance assumes special significance. We begin to register conflicting Eisensteinian sensations about cowardice and money toward the young woman whom we have not yet identified. Further, the exaggeratedly contained perspectives of the station platform give one an impression that she is entering an enclosed, confining space. The train arrival carries overtones not of escape but some more restricting future.

Later, Marnie is described riding her favorite horse.

441 MED. SHOT

MARNIE AND HER HORSE. The CAMERA is now traveling with her as she gallops. It PULLS AWAY until it reaches a VERY HIGH SHOT showing MARNIE, a tiny figure on the horse, galloping over the terrain. Some distance back we see LIL after her.

442 CLOSE-UP

MARNIE—now head bent, her expression beginning to become a little wild. She loses her hat. Her hair blows in the wind.

443 CLOSE-UP

THE FEET OF FORIO galloping over the ground.

444 CLOSE-UP

FORIO'S HEAD stretched forward, mane streaming back.

445 CLOSE SHOT

MARNIE stretched forward toward FORIO'S neck. In the distance, a long way behind, we see LIL coming after her.

446 CLOSE-UP MARNIE—SIDE VIEW

The THUD of FORIO'S hoofs beats with tremendous speed.

447 LONG SHOT

A FORWARD VIEW shows the HEAD OF FORIO in the foreground and beyond the countryside. We are approaching a low mound and a brook. The CAMERA leaps over it.

448 CLOSE-UP

SHOOTING ONTO MARNIE as FORIO makes the leap.

What cannot be recounted in the script is all the impact of Hitchcock's effects. The long countryside (shot 441) impresses with its overview of riders on undulating, grassy terrain, but the following close-ups become the more artificial, rear-projected in a studio with Tippi Hedren bouncing on pretend horseback. The ensuing unreality of the experience, rather than distancing us from story by a break in illusion, points up Marnie's mounting terror ("her expression beginning to become a little wild") with its dreamlike exaggerations. She isn't even getting anywhere, and fear mounts as she fails to remove herself from the traumatic splash of red, which had triggered her childhood phobia and flight.

Impressionism is identified less often through filmmaker intrusions than by way of first person subjectivities: the camera eye as participant and witness, as when the woodcutter wanders through the intermittently sun-splashed forest in *Rashomon*.

As impressionism and expressionism intermingle and as they assume character point of view, we are more likely to face contradictions between different images. Some say one thing happened; some say another. In one sense, all images are equally true; each carries a like accuracy through focus and the integrities of lens systems. And even though we have been taught that pictures often lie, we remain inclined to accept the experience of our eyes at face value until further experience forces us to reconsider the credibility of what we see.

In consequence, then, when a character or camera-eye report may be understood to have actually happened "differently," the wedding of present and conditional tenses poses interesting artistic possibilities. For example, *Rashomon* reported several differing versions of the same event, like Browning's *The Ring and the Book* or a Henry James novel. Some accounts could be awarded greater credence than others by internal evidence or through the weight of conflicting testimony, like evidence in a court of law. Even so, one is left with a perplexing residue of lying images, images which, however tightly focused, fail to make sense in the broader narrative strain, either through visions so colored by emotional involvement as to render them suspect, or because of private motive. In *Rashomon,* the bandit insists the wife flirted first, he bested her husband in fair swordplay, and she gave herself to him. The wife insists she was raped. The husband claims the duel was unfair. All this is film's effort at approximating the novelist's ability to make his narrator the true focus of reader interest although the narrator himself thinks the events he reports are most important.

As narrative departed its nineteenth-century naturalist conventions, the bases of credibility became increasingly unstable. Recall the observations of Brigid Brophy in chapter 2 as to how the novel had been "freed." We are less likely to come across last-minute plot resolutions to explain ap-

Ingmar Bergman's *The Seventh Seal.* *(Credit: Courtesy Janus Films)*

parent contradictions. Rather, the explanations of inconsistent images remain buried if they exist at all. In *Cries and Whispers*, Harriet Andersson's corpse comes alive, cries for warmth and comfort from her terrified sisters, and finally settles in the arms of her nurse, who suckles her like a baby. To account for this sequence in a film that has ostensibly been naturalistically credible requires a spectator to strike much deeper attitudes toward the picture. Perhaps it is a ghost story, in which case it doesn't have to be "real." Perhaps the whole film is a broad, expressionist "statement" on isolation and the terrors of death, another piece of Bergmania whose garish conclusion witnesses the director's inconsistencies and not our faulty perceptions. Perhaps this particular sequence is wish-fantasy from the maid who, we know, has lost her own child and at the end of the film settles down, alone and content in the house with Harriet Andersson's diary in front of her. She "has her all to herself."

In similar vein, Marcello Mastroianni as the frustrated director of *8½* seems finally to shoot himself beneath a table. Or does he? He reappears, megaphone in hand, to assemble his players in a joyful explosion of life. Or is it an echo of the dance of the characters into death, the great image of *The Seventh Seal* (1956)? The inconsistencies are most easily reconciled by viewing it all as Fellinian whim. Mastroianni is but another of his, the ultimate director's, players, goaded into a last performance.

It may be seen that impressionism and expressionism serve both as devices to "subjectivize" point of view and as techniques in the service of a director's purposeful ambiguities. In either case, they are two graphic ways to broaden a film narrative so as to include implicit (rather than plot-explicated) values and narrative subtleties. However disguised, they underline much of the modernity of contemporary film.

Federico Fellini's 8½. *(Credit: Embassy Pictures)*

7 ▪ Genre

Earlier we spoke of genre as the sort of film that lends itself to categories. As a descriptive term it loses utility as it is expanded toward overbroad usage, as in the "American genre." Nevertheless, genre is a helpful concept in viewing American movies, especially because of the light it throws both on commercial strategies and their target—large-audience sensibilities.

Since the beginnings of narrative, stories have fallen into types (adventure, romance, histories), their relative importances often skewed by cultural factors. Our particular sense of genre as popular art grows out of the commercial development of popular theater and print that accompanied the rise of the middle class, industrial technology, and the development of the modern city in the nineteenth century. In that time acted melodrama refined such specialized entertainments as religious stories, love stories, crime stories, naval adventures, and tales of exploration. Within each area there developed specialized bodies of convention—for example, the animal tales where trained horses and dogs would raise a flag, warn the regiment, save a child, or untie the hero's bindings in time to romp with him to a rescue.

Similar material was to be found in throwaway prose—the tradition that runs from penny dreadfuls, dime novels, and the pulps to present-day drugstore paperbacks, "men's magazines," and "confession magazines." Spawned in popular culture, genre thus preserves early narrative forms, which can be traced back to folk tale and myth.

The conjunction of the terms "popular culture" and "myth" poses a central issue of genre study and restates a disagreement we have skirted by other language: successful and good, daydream and dream, and movie-as-mirror/movie-as-expression. In the context of primitive societies and early civilizations, myth had clear social function. On a basic level, it entertained, preserved a cultural heritage, and socialized the young through its common experience. The stories carried warnings and examples that maintained the ethical precepts by which the society cohered.

Finally, myth, allied with the ritual out of which it grew, added a metaphysical plane to human awareness. Stories often appeared in cycles, leading their audience through a variety of experience that corresponded to the culture's particular rite of passage. By way of these, young people were brought to fresh understandings and elders reminded "how it is." Myth congeals and renders tangible all a people's fears, suspicions, anxieties, and communal joys. It explains what cannot be explained, whether through tales about mischievous gods or the stories of tribal heroes long gone.

By the time such elements have found a place in movie plots, their early character has likely diminished to cliché, for commercial writers (distinct from taletellers) have served as agents of transition from the preliterate past while at the same time squeezing story into formula. Formula is based not on form but on corrupted form. The enmity of good and bad brother (*Horizons West*, 1952) calls up myth so universal and basic that cultural anthropologists have a name for it: the Mar Plot. Pure hero versus pure villain (say, *The Adventures of Sherlock Holmes* [1939]) re-enacts the battle of good and evil when Professor Moriarty is bested by the denizen of Baker Street and thrown off the Tower of London.

But such relationships are drawn by writers and professors, not movie audiences. The question must be asked: Do we, watching such films, see anything beyond a thrashing mud puddle of stereotypes, outmoded by time and dependent on audience apathy? Does our industrial age *require* these pacifying circuses of escape?

To make a case that these films are more than soporifics, one has either to find continuing social utility in such experience or else locate some bases of interest and pleasure within the formula plots, characters, and settings. In fact, this is what genre partisans maintain. With a kind of reverse snobbery, they reject the director-stylists whose personality is quite visible (later Bergman, Pier Paolo Pasolini, and Jerzy Skolimowski, to pick randomly different directors) in favor of the tried and true. The genrist accepts untrammeled conventions. He opts for the directing personality who ideally shows himself subtly and covertly within the structural forms. This is a position we shall examine in greater detail when we consider *auteurism*. But the genrist maintains enthusiasm toward the forms themselves. He finds them still viable, still, as it were, mythic rather than clichéd at this point in the twentieth century.

It is often the case that the genrist view depends upon a particular cultural persuasion and social philosophy. For example, like the Soviets, we may know national ills to result from erratic, individualized behaviors or from sloth and self-serving motive. Stories accordingly can be designed so that the issues are joined to highlight these premises, for good and bad are genre's exoskeleton. An American audience may contend that world problems, perhaps even inflation and hurricanes, can be worked out in one-to-one confrontations, if only a responsible party can be located and held to account, perhaps in a shoot-out on the Queensborough Bridge or a dusty main street in old Laramie. On the other hand, a young audience will confirm its suspicions in a movie world where the old are the enemy, inclined to blast motorcyclists through truck windows (*Easy Rider* [1969]), shoot their own kids in the back (*Joe* [1970]), or destroy them by chance on the highway trails of the urban jungle (*Medium Cool* [1969]).

The films of oppressed minorities cast antagonism in similar confrontational genre melodrama, whether slickly, in the commercially minded Shaft series, aimed at frustrated blacks who returned to movie theaters seeking what they could not find on television, or else in more political terms among filmmakers like Glauber Rocha, whose *Antonio das Mortes* (1969) welds folklore, politics, and genre into a Brazilian form that throws classes into bristling antagonisms, casts the downtrodden as hero. By this token, Marxism itself is inherently melodramatic.

In each case, audience response locates some satisfaction—either triumph or I Told You So—in the resolutions of films that follow genre rules. The underlying aesthetic is Aristotelian—that is, drama as catharsis—except for those elements of education that, as in early myth, are passed along so as to affect future behavior: Don't sleep out of doors in the Deep South; don't let your dad catch you in a New York State commune; stay off the Chicago highways.

There have developed whole complexes of conventions—patterns, iconography, speech, and behavior—for every particular kind of film. Gangster films, for example, require a certain twenties costume for each criminal, its style and quality based on his position in the gang hierarchy. Together, the gang members form certain geometric patterns on the screen. Their conversations reveal the relative power of each man. A storefront must be bombed, a rival shot on the street. Period cars figure heavily in the plot. Someone's sister is likely to be misused and must be avenged. The central character is personable enough to command our interest and even our sympathy, although he must die in the end. One policeman is corrupt, another a servant of justice even though he knew the gangster as a friend when they were young. And so on.

The rules are not confined to gangster films; they permeate all moviedom. During the thirties, for instance, the "college musical" gained favor, itself growing out of theatrical musical comedy. This subform surfaced more recently in stories centering on bands of rock musicians. A variation is the sensitive young artist who "hears a sound" or "wants to hit that note." Such a form permits one part of the audience, young people, both to enjoy one of their own entertainments and to satisfy their desire to criticize the older generation. Like most movie formulas, it has been taken up by television, in such a series as "The Partridge Family."

Genres also intermarry and produce offspring. Gene Autry made a career out of the wedding of western and musical. Horror and comedy, never far apart, often join (*Abbott and Costello Meet the Mummy* [1955]). Jerry Lewis is an interesting example of a comic who allies himself with various genre forms, from detective to the supernatural, in order to establish his "character" in the context of conventions against which he may play antic variations.

The conventions of genre sometimes tap interesting social sensitivities and may pass across formula boundaries. The blonde-as-a-girl-to-have-fun-with-but-not-take-seriously is developed in the earliest musicals, institutionalized as moll in Depression gangster movies, and given wisecrack repartee in situation comedies. She will play a villain in light cowboy films where a heavy need not be overweighted with menace. In the detective traditions, she is often disclosed to be a murderess of special cunning, motivated by hatred and self-interest and disguised by her golden tresses until unmasked by the hero.

Commercially, the genre film has always been a mainstay of production companies because it is one of the few ways by which attendance can, at least sometimes, be predicted. For example, RKO found itself in financial straits during the early forties. Although its detectives were doing all right, Astaire and Rogers had broken up, terminating a series of successful musicals. Ambitious projects like Welles's *Citizen Kane* and *The Magnificent Ambersons* had fallen flat at the box office. The success of rival companies was considered, and someone was reminded of how well Universal had done with its horror series, inexpensively produced, and extremely popular: *Frankenstein* (1931), *Dracula* (1931), and *The Mummy* (1933). A young writer-executive, Val Lewton, was contracted at small salary and charged with the job of producing a horror series, each budgeted on the minuscule level of $150,000. Titles were market-tested and assigned to him—*The Cat People* (1942), *The Leopard Man*, *I Walked with a Zombie* (both 1943). Within these strictures Lewton was free to make whatever horror films he wished. The movies were marketed as "programmers," the second, or bottom, half of double-feature bills, running no more than seventy-five to ninety minutes.

The programmer nurtured American genre films. Their very budgets, requiring short production schedules, inexpensive actors and technicians, and the use of available stock resources—like sets and costuming—encouraged simple, time-tested devices for audience entertainment. Speed and stereotyped approach encouraged predictability, hence formula, hence genre. Fortunately for film history, Val Lewton was an uncommon figure, exceptional as a producer, and in his role as creative center of his RKO series, eschewed formula and the pat response for the sake of other effects.

One reason for the popularity of genre study has been that it facilitates film categorization. (Another reason is that many titles can be seen on TV, or cost less for teachers to rent.) A particular director may have been identified with a particular type of film, like John Ford and the western, but one may also organize movie titles by chronology, era, studio, or even invention (the lyric western, the historical western, the epic western, the Indian-sympathetic western, the Reconstruction western, the western and justice, the western and women, the farmer and the rancher, stereotypes in the western, the western and territorial expansion). Any out-of-the-ordinary juxtaposition should lead the student to new relationships, and his problem then becomes one of defining the significance, if any, of what he has pinpointed.

Genre study is appealing, too, because it encourages film students to examine each movie within a wide range of contexts. Historical aspects, for example, permit one to consider how a particular characterization has been shaped in part by currents of opinion operative when it was composed: the movies as *zeitgeist*. When *High Noon* came out in 1952, some critics viewed it as a disguised statement of America's traditional isolationism (Grace Kelly urging Gary Cooper to withdraw from an impossible and unappreciated law-enforcement role) in a postwar world where such return was inappropriate (Gary Cooper "doing what must be done" even when deserted by the people he had been enlisted to protect). Now we can see the film not only within the context of the McCarthy era, but in light of Vietnam.

Similarly, a student may become aware of certain kinds of evolution within any particular genre form, as when the detective moves from an eccentric private citizen with a private income (Sherlock Holmes, Father Brown, Nick Charles) to an ill-paid professional, doing his job on the commission of a client (Sam Spade, the Continental Op) to a hard-boiled, cynical, wisecracking romanticist more punished than punishing (Philip Marlowe) to the glib, well-groomed, handsome figure who moves gracefully after his adversary in a world of Playboy girls (Peter Gunn). The stylizations of a particular genre era have life cycles of their own, and a filmmaker is even more vulnerable to this mortality than the writer of prose because it is the more inescapably visible. If the stylization cannot be adapted to changed conditions (like turning Marlowe into Peter Gunn), the form itself will disappear.

When genre crisis occurs and if a genre fails to marry (the detective musical?), it may spin off into subspecies. Detectives had sometimes busied themselves with state secrets, while maintaining their independent or professionally commissioned role. The decline of the detective film in the fifties and sixties was accompanied by a corresponding rise of international secret agents. In his new role, the agent or detective was freed from the messy moral issues attendant on his shooting antagonists or passersby. He was enveloped in a broader value system, for he was now a representative of some particular country. Thus his efforts in the arena of melodrama had a significance exceeding personal motive, and his skill under fire became again courageous rather than a mere matter of artisan know-how.

The international agent better enjoyed Playboy dalliance than Peter Gunn because his globe-hopping way of life might explain it. The government gave James Bond a lot of money to kill people, but where did Gunn get the price of all those drinks at Mother's, where his girlfriend sang? Further, everything and everyone fell under reasonable suspicion from James Bond. He operated in a vast, complicated scheme of great powers in unannounced war with one another (just like the real world). If the enemy was periodically personalized as a single grotesque like Goldfinger, it might as easily be a network of disguised agents; it might be anyone. Even Goldfinger and Dr. No controlled worldwide systems. So it was all right for Bond to sleep wherever he lit, since *she* might murder him likely as not, or he might need her later (both interesting statements about relationships between men and women).

Later, as Bond became clichéd, the detective re-emerged but maintained the secret agent's "cover" by locating himself within the Police Department. Frank Sinatra moved from the independence of *Tony Rome* (1967) to Joe Leland, a municipal investigator in *The Detective* (1968). Again, the detective appears enveloped in a broader social-value system. He is operating as an arm of the law, hence an appendage to society. However, these were the years of military-like police emergency squads, and his own relationship to the rules and behaviors of the parent society became increasingly the very matter at issue.

Unlike Bond, the new detective finds reason to question the integrity of the people he takes orders from, like the young person who comes finally to hold his own parents up against the light of personal values and sees them at fault. The detective then finds himself at sea, caught between two agencies at war with one another, neither of which he can reconcile himself fully to accept. When the detective throws his badge into San Francisco Bay in Don Siegel's *Dirty Harry* (1971), he is admitting, like other investigators, this quandary, which must be resolved in later films if the genre is not to fall again into stagnation. In *Magnum Force* (1973), Harry returned to defend individual freedoms against a vigilante group developing within the police department itself.

RECOMMENDED READING

Some useful film histories include:

■ Joseph Anderson and Donald Richie, *Japanese Film* (New York: Evergreen, 1960)

■ Roy Armes, *French Cinema Since 1946*, 2 vols. (New York: A. S. Barnes, 1966)

■ Eric Barnouw and S. Krishnaswamy, *Indian Film* (New York: Columbia University Press, 1963)

■ C. W. Ceram (Kurt W. Marek), *Archaeology of the Cinema* (New York: Harcourt, Brace, 1965)

■ Peter Cowie, *Sweden,* 2 vols. (New York: A. S. Barnes, 1970)

■ Lotte Eisner, *The Haunted Screen* (Berkeley: University of California Press, 1969)

■ Dennis Gifford, *British Cinema* (New York: A. S. Barnes, 1968)

■ Penelope Houston, *The Contemporary Cinema* (Baltimore: Pelican, 1964)

■ David Stewart Hull, *Film in the Third Reich* (Berkeley: University of California Press, 1969)

■ Lewis Jacobs, *Rise of the American Film* (New York: Harcourt, Brace, 1939)

■ Vernon Jarratt, *Italian Film* (New York: Macmillan, 1951)

■ Arthur Knight, *The Liveliest Art* (New York: New American Library, 1959)

■ Siegfried Kracauer, *From Caligari to Hitler* (Princeton: Princeton University Press, 1947)

■ Pierre Leprohon, *The Italian Cinema* (New York: Praeger, 1972)

■ Jay Leyda, *Kino: A History of the Russian and Soviet Film* (New York: Macmillan, 1960)

■ Rachel Low, *History of the British Film,* 4 vols. (London: Allen & Unwin, 1948–71)

■ Gerald Mast, *A Short History of the Movies* (New York: Pegasus, 1971)

■ Georges Sadoul, *French Film* (New York: Arno, 1972)

■ Kemp Niver, *Motion Pictures from the Library of Congress Print Collection 1894–1912* (Berkeley: University of California Press, 1967) catalogues and cross indexes all designated Library of Congress holdings by title, subject and director. For Eisenstein's explorations of Dickens and other arts, see Eisenstein, *Film Form* (Cleveland: World Publishing, 1949). The essay "Color and Meaning" is in *The Film Sense* (Cleveland: World Publishing, 1949).

■ For Sir Joshua Reynolds on color, see Note 54 in his *Notes on the Art of Painting* (London: 1783).

■ Orson Welles material includes Pauline Kael, *The Citizen Kane Book* (Boston: Little, Brown, 1971); Joseph McBride, *Orson Welles* (New York: Viking Press, 1972); and Charles Higham, *The Films of Orson Welles* (Berkeley: University of California Press, 1970).

■ An excellent study of Jean Renoir is Leo Braudy, *Jean Renoir: The World of His Films* (Garden City, N.Y.: Doubleday, 1972). See also André Bazin, *Jean Renoir* (New York: Simon & Schuster, 1973). Good works on Hitchcock include Robin Wood, *Hitchcock's Films* (New York: A. S. Barnes, 1965) and François Truffaut, *Hitchcock* (New York: Simon & Schuster, 1967).

■ Discussion of more editing relations to narrative will be found in Karel Reisz and Gavin Miller, *The Technique of Film Editing*, 2d rev. ed. (New York: Amphoto, 1968).

■ Vsevolod Pudovkin's *Film Technique* is bound with *Film Acting* (New York: Evergreen, 1960).

■ Transcriptions, sometimes a mite muddled, of a Slavko Vorkapich lecture series appear in *Film Culture* 38 (Fall 1965). (*Film Culture's* address is GPO 1499 New York City 10001.)

■ Again, A. A. Mendilow, *Time and the Novel* (New York: Humanities Press, 1972) provides a useful catalogue of many, not all, film-time phenomena. An interesting link is drawn between Resnais and Bergsonian time concepts in John Ward, *Alain Resnais, or the Theme of Time* (London: Secker & Warburg, 1968).

■ A forties psychological study of forties films is Martha Wolfenstein and Nathan Leites, *Movies: A Psychological Study* (New York: Atheneum, 1970).

■ Joel E. Siegal recounts the story of Val Lewton in *Val Lewton: The Reality of Terror* (New York: Viking, 1973).

■ For a study of Kubrick, see Alexander Walker, *Stanley Kubrick Directs* (New York: Harcourt Brace Jovanovich, 1971), which has some interesting material on his earliest directing ventures, some of whose themes reappear later.

■ Robert Flaherty's adventures are recounted in Arthur Calder-Marshall, *The Innocent Eye* (London: W. H. Allen, 1963).

■ Joris Ivens titled his autobiography *The Camera and I* (New York: International Publishing, 1970).

■ A genre study of the gangster movie is conducted by Colin McArthur, *Underworld U.S.A.* (New York: Viking Press, 1970). For the western, see Jim Kitses, *Horizons West: Studies in Authorship in the Western Film* (Bloomington: Indiana University Press, 1972).

NOTES

1. For information on the origins of Griffith's Babylonian courtyard shot, see Peter Bogdanovich, *Allan Dwan: The Last Pioneer* (New York: Praeger, 1971), pp. 35–36.
2. Cesare Zavattini, "Some Ideas on the Cinema," *Sight and Sound* 23, no. 2 (October 1953). Reprinted in Richard Dyer MacCann, *Film: A Montage of Theories* (New York: E. P. Dutton, 1966), pp. 216–28.
3. Quoted in Roger Manvell, ed., *The International Encyclopedia of Film* (New York: Crown, 1972), p. 450.
4. Judith Vogelsang, "Motifs of Image and Sound in *The Godfather*," *The Journal of Popular Film* 2, no. 2 (Spring 1973), pp. 115–35.
5. Rudolf Arnheim, informal lecture, San Francisco State College, May 7, 1965.

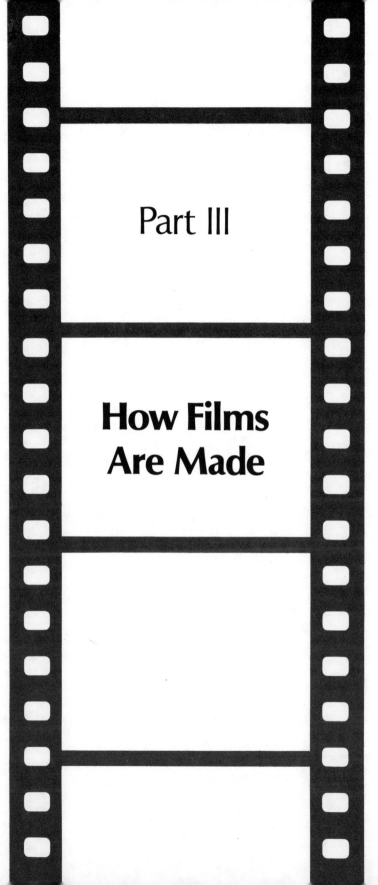

Part III

How Films Are Made

8 ▪ Conceptualization

Because film is a technological art, its production confronts both mechanical and aesthetic problems. Since many movies are put together under chaotic conditions, these confrontations are not always resolved in the best way. I could attempt to describe the making of a film by listing first the various roles performed, perhaps using the craft unions as a guide: the Writers Guild of America, the American Cinema Editors, the Directors Guild of America, the Screen Actors Guild, and the International Association of Theatrical and Stage Employees. All these unions are represented in every highly financed, overpopulated production. But categorization like this fuzzes our sense of the dynamics of filmmaking as well as obscuring overlaps among participants. There may even be moments when the question of who's in charge of what is genuinely at issue.

Because film is such a communal medium, the substance of any particular production is very likely to change appreciably between its early idea stages and the final release print. These changes may be dominated by some individual's vision, ordered by his own evolving understanding of what the movie *is,* but such a happy circumstance is never altogether the case, nor is it necessarily true at all, even if most of the time someone pretends to be in charge.

If a movie were to have a single author, the ideal production crew would be a unit of one, performers included, and that man never at war with himself. This is not impossible, for one person of much patience and high talent might draw, write, shoot, edit, score, record, and conceivably even process an animated film. The San Francisco experimentalist Jordan Belson, a man of great talent and patience, makes films almost entirely in his home, and John Whitney and his sons, for example, do computer films in Southern California. Such artists, however, remain beyond the confines of this study, for they chose other routes than ordinary narrative film. If a story is to be peopled, it must of necessity have some kind of a crew. A filmmaker who photographs himself still cannot be in two places at once, unless he shoots nothing but mirrors.

The independent American director Shirley Clarke has said that if she is ever able to realize as much as fifty per cent of her original vision of a production, she considers herself fortunate indeed. Ms. Clarke is a person of awesome will and tenacity, who usually operates on shoestring budgets, which, whatever their drawbacks, afford her maximum controls. Her remark becomes the more pointed if we compare her filmmaking circumstance with a studio production, where the different stages are far more regimented and defined. Films differ altogether in how they are conceived and mounted, but they are alike in never fully becoming quite what they were first intended to be.

If some single vision is to be maintained, production has to operate coherently enough that the responsibility for its execution may be designated. Such patterns of authority delegation may range from the most autocratic domination (like stories of Erich von Stroheim wandering about the set, peering through the rectangular frame made by holding his hands in front of his face, thumbs touching, and finally stamping once to indicate a camera location) to the most communal sharings of ideas and talents. Any figure who assumes the responsibility for a production in part or whole will have his own personal strategy for success.

The man who paid the piper called the tune in the old studio systems. The studio not only usurped directors' prerogatives through contract stipulations but also willfully colored each production to give it a certain institutional identification: by lighting, choice of story, sometimes costuming and characteristic editing formulas. On the other hand, long-term collaborations may inure a filmmaker to outside influences. A director who, like Bergman, works with a kind of repertory film-and-theater group will reach special depths of understanding and communication with his talented actors and production crew. In the several years Luis Buñuel worked in Mexico, he used a particular cameraman, Gabriel Figueroa, himself a director, to good collaborative effect, just as Alfred Hitchcock worked with Robert Burks, whose contributions to Hitchcock's fifties films have become the more apparent since his death in an automobile accident. The tightness of such relationships will help to give any production sharper identity.

Without strong domination by someone, a production may pursue the course of least resistance with vitiated results. Often an analysis of the viewer's sense of irresolution in a movie experience can be pursued to the unavoidable conclusion that coherence simply failed in production, either because problems inherent in the first conception were not recognized and resolved or because of later tinkering on someone's part. If one were to witness the confusion that attends much feature filmmaking, he would be naïve indeed to think that there was orderly pattern "beneath it all," invisible to the eye. It's a wonder that many movies ever get finished, and some do not.

The entire matter of a film's authorship is further confused by today's director cults, which are inclined to obscure our recognition of decisions by editors, cameramen, and other functionaries. A director is not necessarily the final vision and energy behind every film. Of course it is understandable that every other movie craftsman wants to be considered important—"creative"—if only because he has always been unremarked except among his peers. But each production agent *does* color every production as it passes through his hands. We shall proceed now to examine just how this is effected in practice.

A film script is neither more nor less than the way things begin. Whether that script is quite finished when production starts may prove foolhardy (*Cleopatra* [1963]) or it may be of no consequence (*I. F. Stone's Newsletter* [1974]). The character and importance of a script is affected by the kind of production in question and the relation of cameraman and director to what they are asked to shoot. Some directors, Howard Hawks, for example, are said to rewrite each day's dialogue that morning. Others, like William Wyler, may painstakingly run over and over the given material until the footage has quite captured what was proposed on paper. In the long run, all that anyone is doing—writer, cameraman, editor, sound man, director—is trying to effectuate an idea. For this reason, we elected "conceptualization" as a more useful heading for this section than "scriptwriting."

If a scriptwriter is in fact party to the production, his objective is a shooting script—that is, a very specific outline of the movie's eventual form and substance. From this outline, a myriad of decisions are forthcoming—locations scouted, costumes ordered, sets constructed, actors hired, cameras and lenses designated, dialogue memorized, and so forth. It is difficult to talk about film writing without giving the impression that the process is largely a matter of typing orders in capitals and margins as if assembling a bomb or some mighty engine.

73. EXT. UGANDA VELDT. TWILIGHT. HELICOPTER SHOT. CAMERA MOVES IN ON ELEPHANT who is protecting a small NATIVE BOY from RAIN with his giant hoof.

The very act of spelling out such material conjures up the power to send great production crews vast distances and direct men and animals through their paces. ELEPHANT will never lower his foot an inch unless the typewriter so commands him.

Writing is one of the few film professions that is more or less solitary.

The culmination of thousands of production decisions: "CLEOPATRA enters ROME."
(Credit: Copyright © 1963 Twentieth Century-Fox Film Company Ltd. All Rights Reserved.)

Editing is another. The degree of a writer's latitude depends upon whom he is writing for and whether he is beholden to the requirements of some particular star or play or novel. Most often, writers are presented with something: a book to adapt, a situation to develop, a personality to enclose in story wraps. ("Do a piece for Goldie Hawn. Put in one bathing suit scene and two bedroom scenes. Sex, but not explicit. Make Goldie's dialogue dumb-smart, more like Judy Holliday's in *Born Yesterday* [1950] than the lines she got in *Cactus Flower* [1969].")

The ways a scriptwriter can create are as varied as writing itself. He may work from pictures (Val Lewton conceived scenes in *The Isle of the Dead* [1945] from Goya sketches), an impression (Bergman said, "A film for me begins with something very vague—a chance remark, . . . a hazy but agreeable event unrelated to my particular situation, . . . a few bars of music, a shaft of light across the street"),[1] a situation, an idea of character, or the taste of the morning coffee.

In any case, the writer, probably more than any other functionary in the film's production, bears special responsibility for its underlying design. Other elements can be altered and rethought at later stages—dialogue, names, locations, movements—but it is the elusive "situation," which forms a kind of narrative backbone to the finished production, that lodges first in the screenwriter's head alone. A situation establishes what matters are at issue and who represents them and what will cause these matters to resolve: just when character finally changes or what ultimately causes someone to act or whether an early motive is really strong enough to have made the hero take the steps he did.

Beyond these elements, the extent to which a writer may impose discernible style on a finished movie will be subject to many variables. The question underlying the effect of all these variables is, To what extent will the writer's style be carried through, taking into account even those resources within the writer's control? The staging of a sequence, for example, may be independent of the shooting script (recall the Hitchcock illustrations). The most important variable is the director's final relation to his script.

Writers are very proud of their contributions to film and sensitive to the diminution of their role as the director's stock rises. (A Hollywood story has writer Robert Riskin handing director Frank Capra a folio of blank paper and saying, "Here, let's see you put the famous Capra touch on that.") One of the subjects at issue in a recent Writers Guild strike was the matter of screen credits in terms of their size, location, and relation to the credits of director and producer. Credit is not only an economic weapon in film's highly competitive world; it also determines in part a writer's sense of his own worth.

Many early directors wrote their own material (Griffith, Dreyer, Chaplin, von Stroheim), but sound introduced an increasingly writer-dominated scripting phase, as authors of repute were brought West, usually to invent winning dialogue. As directors began to dominate production, some writers elected to depart the lower order for the higher. They became directors. John Huston was an early figure to move from one rank to the other, followed by such American men as Elia Kazan, Richard Brooks, and Stanley Kubrick, and the Europeans Michelangelo Antonioni, Federico Fellini, and Ingmar Bergman.

Another basis for repeatedly successful film ventures has been writer-director teams, like Billy Wilder and Charles Brackett or later Wilder and I. A. L. Diamond. Collaborations are useful not only to maintain the importance of script and the writer's role but also to help those directing personalities who need to talk out their problems from inception. Differences at this stage are sometimes irreconcilable. The detective writer Raymond Chandler collaborated with Hitchcock in one film, *Strangers on a Train* (1951), and later expressed his sense of dismay about the encounter because, he said, Hitchcock thought altogether in terms of cardboard figures, denuded comic-strip characters he had in mind to dress at later stages by actor's expression and Hitchcockian effects: the evil young man, the rich and foolish woman.

What a successful screenwriter must always realize is that his shooting script bears a relation to the final production altogether different from that of the manuscript that will become a book. His script will be read by various people for many different purposes but will never itself be anybody's final aesthetic experience. Instead, it is at best a jumping-off place, as often as not a sort of punching bag against which other people must energize their own ideas.

Godard, for example, is notorious for seeming to improvise on the set, either ignoring or radically changing earlier material with which he until then had been thought to be working. *Masculine-Feminine* (1965) is ostensibly based on two short stories by Guy de Maupassant, "La Femme de Paul" and "Le Signe," but few resemblances are visible. There are no like characters, no similar plot situations; the setting is a different place and another time. Whether the central meaning of one of the stories—a man's despairing comprehension of a woman he had until then only mistakenly understood—is translated to the film will depend on our response to Godard's movie.

In the same fashion, Antonioni, a former writer who, like most, works very closely with his scenarists, altogether reorganized the Julio Cortázar story on which *Blow-Up* is based. The movie photographer of the story becomes a fashion still photographer in the movie. The setting is moved from Paris to swinging London. The self-reflecting, philosophically inclined protagonist is turned into a young man whose thoughts and feelings are almost unknown to us except as externalized erratic spurts of impulse and blurted, oblique conversation. But the core is identical: A man with a camera thinks that he has documented one thing, then finds on examination something quite different, which leads him to rethink earlier understandings about his relation both to his profession and to the outside world.

In sum, the scriptwriter prepares a body of material that will be more or less reworked and more or less useful to the film production. If great amounts of money are involved, a shooting script is likely to remain intact, for the words will prove bases for production schedules, costuming, acting contracts, locations, transportation, promotional campaigns, and everything that has then predictably to ensue. This is partly why actors in films where money has been lavished so visibly on "production values" have the quality of stone figures trying desperately to come alive.

The man at the typewriter may appear romantic (William Holden holed up with Gloria Swanson in *Sunset Boulevard* [1950]), but he shoulders responsibility for the fortunes and careers of people he may never even meet. Added to his burden is the sense of partialness and incompletion that inevitably accompanies his task. No one but an animator can ever accurately foresee the finished version of what he conceived in isolation. The screenwriter can never preplan exactly how the contours of a location or of some supporting actress finally will impress their own unique character on his words. At best he executes a plan for camera eye, microphone, and editor to work from, something that need not *read* but must *play*. His speeches must *sound* all right; the transitions must work as pictures. One of the special difficulties he faces is organizing a sense of pace (our Time III) from shot units through sequences and onto the film overall. This is not altogether possible where camera angle and location may determine the visible speed of movements, but in any case his capacity to "see" such behaviors cannot be equated with the prose writer's ability to create a sense of pace, which depends on sound and sentence and word choice. In a sense, the screenwriter is not really a writer at all.

9 ▪ Direction

Briefly stated, the director's job is the choosing of a film script or other conceptualization and solving the problems it poses during the realities of production. His relation to the project before and after shooting varies from nothing at all to the closest supervision. His relation to the production's finances will vary just as widely. His sense of a direct and personal connection with the story may be nonexistent (it's a "job," he's a "professional") or total, like that of the dedicated garret artist.

Before the actual shooting has been started, agents of the producer will have undertaken the most careful and practical examination of what the picture's shooting script requires. If a scene calls for LONG SHOT. CROWD, that language must be translated into a given number of bodies to be dressed in a designated fashion and located in a particular spot at a specific hour on a stipulated day. The number of people who constitute a crowd is no longer a philosophical issue but one of camera angle and focal length of lens. How many will be seen?

Actors must be hired, and the length of their contracts meshed into a production schedule. Locations will be scouted in order that their peculiarities of geography, climate, and perhaps inhabitants not pose insurmountable problems when visited by the full production. The order of scenes must be so organized that it is open to revision as necessary. If a script calls for sun but the outdoor location is deluged with rain for five days, the production must either be able to absorb this delay or move into interiors and reschedule its first location.

Whatever assistance the director might have, he ultimately bears the

By conscious design the ambiance of its resort locale contributed to the haunted, ambiguous quality of Alain Resnais's *Last Year at Marienbad*.

brunt of such problems. Since his responsibilities include environment as well as performance for every camera exposure, he will also enter into the closest planning with set designers, costuming, and properties. Each decision will have its ramifications for other crew members. If a set's lighting calls for a particular floor space, that plan must adapt itself to a certain range of lens focal lengths and perhaps of camera movement. If a scene calls for the actors' breath to show on screen, someone has to create the proper conditions for that breath to be made visible, even on a hot, humid shooting stage. Part of *The Magnificent Ambersons* was shot in an icehouse; *The Exorcist* (1973) used a refrigeration unit.

The film director heads a production unit the size of which depends on the ambitiousness of his project. An assistant director will be responsible for production logistics, expenses, and scheduling, and may also serve as liaison, perhaps buffer, between director and producer. When he is absent, his functions may be assumed by a unit manager, who is in a sense the business boss of a production on any given location.

A script girl (who may be a middle-aged man) will take notes on each run of the camera, with comments dictated by the director, describing such visual detail as the length of an actor's cigarette when the shot was cut, so that continuity may be maintained and the butt will not be longer in the next shot. The camera crew is responsible to the director, but through the cinematographer. If a prop had to be moved one or two inches on the set, the regulations of the industry's heavily unionized world would likely require a director to advise his cameraman, who would advise a subordinate to tell a grip, possibly through his gaffer (or chief electrician), to move it. The gaffer may have a small crew of his own, and there may be additional grips to lay camera tracks, make minor repairs, and such. The camera crew may include, besides the operator and cameraman, a camera assistant and someone to perform the duty of securing the day's raw stock, loading and unloading the cameras, and getting the exposed raw stock to the laboratory.

Depending on the requirements of synchronous sound, there will be a man to secure, wire, and set up microphones, perhaps moving them on boom extensions as necessary, a man to work the tape machines, and a mixer to compose multiple sound sources into a single, balanced signal. The crew may have a still cameraman as well, to maintain a continuous photographic record of the production, sometimes for publicity but more often as a basis for necessary reconsiderations of costume, set design, and the physical location of actors and props in the event that scenes have to be reshot. Of course, union requirements of crew size excepted, smaller production units will double up functions and responsibilities.

We tend to think of a director's main job as evoking successful performances from his actors. In fact, this is but one of many responsibilities and may receive more or less attention. Actors themselves may require much or little guidance for any given scene. The days when Charlie Chaplin mimed each actor's role for him on the set are gone, like the twenties director with his puttees and megaphone (for proof, see *A Countess from Hong Kong,* 1966). An actor's needs will be defined by his approach to performance. He may want no more information than how strongly he should come on at a given moment and what, if any, business with hands or body he ought to undertake. Some actors are one-take performers, whose work will predictably deteriorate under repetition. Others painstakingly repeat and repeat the smallest action until it works. Some actors simply take longer to succeed, as when Marilyn Monroe flubbed a set of lines through forty-six takes on *Some Like It Hot* (1959) while Jack Lemmon and Tony Curtis stood about in drag waiting for her to bring it off.

Actors may have so immersed themselves, Stanislavski-like, into a role that they require the greatest explanation of motive and past history for the smallest recorded action. It is not to a director's advantage to meet such needs if his film style is other than naturalistic.

Some directors will ruthlessly exploit their performers, pressing them to stages of exhaustion or frustration until they are closer to experiencing feelings correlative with the scene's demands. Carl Dreyer, the Danish director, was notorious for this strategy, most famously with his direction of Falconetti in *The Passion of Joan of Arc* and of the old woman burned at the stake as a witch in *Day of Wrath* (1943). He is said to have left that poor lady bound and suspended, exposed to the hot sun until she had reached the quality of rage and despair he was after.

Actors will be sensitive to a director's working techniques and his openness to their needs, less out of fear of physical danger than because they are most satisfied when their performances benefit from the special work involved. Hitchcock's comment that actors are like cattle is not so much inhumane (he apparently said they were *like* cattle, not cattle) as it is an indication of a particular working method in which a film is so carefully scripted that the remainder of its production falls into place with utmost fidelity to the original intentions.

Other directors may be far more receptive to suggestions, and this attitude continues the creative (or havoc-wreaking) process of working out the story far into production. Huston and Truman Capote were said to have improvised *Beat the Devil* (1953) as they went along. George Roy Hill was very open to the suggestions of Paul Newman and Robert Redford in *Butch Cassidy and the Sundance Kid*. Robert Altman proceeded similarly in such films as *M*A*S*H* (1970) and *McCabe and Mrs. Miller,* working constantly with actors and crew to shape a film so that it reflects a common effort rather than some single intelligence. Warren Beatty likes such an approach and says he wrote most of the lines for his part as McCabe. In *Bonnie and Clyde,* in which he also had a leading role, actor participation was equally intense, but it took place at the scripting stage. Beatty argued strongly for a particular characterization for Clyde Barrow,

Maria Falconetti in
The Passion of Joan of Arc.

sometimes against emotional opposition from scriptwriters David Newman and Robert Benton.

Such factors do not necessarily diminish the accomplishments of a director, but they do ask us to readjust our understanding of his talents. Just as one teacher may instruct most effectively by lecture, another through guided discussion, and either may be good or bad, screen directors have not necessarily abdicated their responsibility by sharing it; disaster is possible either way. What a director cannot shirk is the requirement that his production finally evidence some common vision and coherent structure rather than defeat itself in welters of inconsistency, that he maintain an attitude toward the material throughout, even if it is a strictly observed neutrality.

After the last scene is filmed, if a director leaves his production, its future is out of his reach. One factor affecting its later shaping will be the amount of footage provided for the editor. Hitchcock boasts that his films have been so shot that an editor cannot do other than assemble them according to Hitchcock's original design. Like Hitchcock, other directors may abjure quantities of pickups, close-ups, and alternative angles on a given action, first because such work is time-consuming, second because the editor, faced with fewer alternatives, has less opportunity to impose himself on the material. Even here, the director is never altogether safe, because he is unlikely to have any say in how his own material shall be treated. Unless he is one of its owners, the director's footage may be added to, reshot, overloaded with bathetic music, or even scrapped if financiers decide it lacks commercial appeal.

Since a director's prestige is judged by his last picture, he embodies certain circumstances of the medium itself. If he is dedicated to doing an effective job for his employers, he may be the more likely to subordinate all else to commercial values in the material. To the critical eye, such values need not be altogether at odds with other accomplishments. This depends on the production, and it would be shortsighted to criticize a film not for what it is but for what it is not, except if it is apparent that what was attempted has not been realized. In this sense, a director is faced with two alternatives respecting his career. If he submerges his personality and becomes a respected artisan in the "trade," he may gain a reputation for dependability allied with skill that will secure him a long, lucrative, unspectacular tenure in the Directors Guild. As Allan Dwan has said, "It's the fellows who stick their necks above the crowd who get their heads chopped off."[2]

Since most films are controlled by the money sources that finance them, the director whose attitude toward that money finally proves destructive to its interests is a man in trouble. When Erich von Stroheim's name was spelled on a Broadway marquee with a dollar sign in place of the "S," Hollywood was attempting not to laud his extravagant behavior

Alfred Hitchcock directing Rod Taylor in a scene from *The Birds*.

on the shooting stages but to maximize its return on the money he had cost them. Von Stroheim's directing career was short.

On the other hand, the very presence of a name in lights that is neither a film title nor a movie star suggests another merchandising ploy. If the director himself figures in a movie's promotion, as a book is "a new John Barth," or a play "the latest Edward Albee," then his presence may figure in a production's early guarantee on investment return. Hiring a name director is like promoting book sales before the film version is made, or requiring an actress to participate in postproduction plugging (appearance on panel shows, television interviews) as part of her contract. Under these conditions, the director is well advised to become a star himself. Film money men are willing to commit millions if it multiplies profits. Spend a lot, make a lot. Therefore the name director may be guaranteed both money and latitude in its dispensation . . . provided his last picture made a good profit.

It is likely, too, that such a director will, in time, develop some kind of protective persona, a public version of himself. The very magnitude of a film imparts equal portions of power and anxiety. In this respect, a movie like 8½ is one accurate indication of any director's discrepant senses about himself and his coworkers. Unlike the editor, cinematographer, or writer, he lacks the security of anonymity before a vast audience. His work will be commented on by others besides his peers, whose opinions he at least understands and perhaps respects. Unlike the movie star, he cannot see his own tangible image from rushes to rushes, to evaluate and refine it personally. The director exposes himself to an unknown public. Orson Welles has made this distinction between film and theater: when one directs a play, he knows generally who will attend it, not by name, but well enough in terms of their sophistications, biases, income, even residential area, so that responses may more easily be premeditated and affected. Movie audiences, by contrast, are vaster, more anonymous, and far more heterogeneous. Of course, a director may opt for the X-rated clientele or the family audience. Both are efforts to predefine responses by categorizing the sensibilities of the spectator. Other audiences are less easily defined; they differ from place to place. When the British films of the thirties and forties were imported, for example, they were merchandised only in major American cities, because more rural audiences did not respond favorably at all. As a little group of businessmen said in a New Yorker cartoon after looking at a new picture, "It's too obscene for Georgia and not obscene enough for New York." But perhaps it would play in Pennsylvania or Michigan.

The final nature of a film will always stand as evidence of a director's relation to its various stages of production, or else of the decisions enforced by other artisans. While in the most successful films the director has maintained this kind of overseeing throughout, other films clearly show an emphasis on script, shooting, or editing. In some measure the strengths of one area may compensate for weaknesses elsewhere. However, unsuccessful films are often evidence of problems in a script that were not recognized or successfully overcome in shooting or the failure of photographed material to disguise a poor performance or prosaic photography unsuccessfully jazzed up by self-conscious editing. The editor, in a sense, is the man left holding the bag, told to "cut around" some insufficiency when he knows full well that there is not enough footage to compensate. But the final responsibility is the director's.

We might try to reflect something of the director's situation by counterposing three statements, the first by the late French director Jean-Pierre Melville, the second by his countryman Jean Renoir, and the last by their younger colleague François Truffaut.

The most important quality needed by a film director—or as I prefer to say, a film creator—is the ability not to work through his intellect, otherwise he ceases to create a spectacle. He must also have a feeling for observation, memory, psychology, and a fantastically acute sense of sight and sound. He must have the instinct of a showman. A film is a spectacle, just like the circus or the music-hall; when it's well done, it becomes a work of art.[3]

•

We are obliged to please too many people because it's the condition of the job. If you start out with the idea of pleasing everyone, however, of course you end up satisfying no one. One has to start with the idea of achieving a certain objective, uncovering a certain truth, and if the mass public accepts it, so much the better.[4]

•

What is direction? The sum total of the decisions taken in the course of the preparation, the filming, and the putting together of a film; it seems to me that all the choices that confront a director—of scenario, of ellipses, of locations, collaborators, actors, angles of view, lenses, of takes to be printed, of soundtrack and music—enforce on him a number of concrete *decisions,* and what is called direction is obviously the common tendency of the thousands of decisions made in the course of six, nine, twelve or sixteen months of work. That's why "partial" directors—those who only deal with one stage of all that—however talented they are, interest me less than Bergman, Buñuel, Hitchcock and Welles, who *are* completely their films.[5]

10 ▪ Visualization

Like writers, cinematographers generally consider themselves unappreciated and misunderstood. Their own sense of personal and craft contribution to "the industry" is ambitious, their memories colored with directors, famous and obscure, who "only knew how to deal with the actors," "were writers or theater people," or "didn't know anything about camera." Exceptions include Orson Welles, Rouben Mamoulian, Charles Laughton (who directed one picture), and sometimes Josef von Sternberg.

Undoubtedly the contributions of creative cameramen are as myriad as their credits and their working relations with various directors. They seem to take to directors who "let me alone." William Daniels said he thought the movie cameraman should be an "inventor of detail adding to the imagination of a director with his own scientific skills," and, too, "we try to tell the story with light as the director tries to tell it with his action."[6]

The earliest moviemaker was not just writer-producer-director, he was cameraman and lab technician too. These men profited immensely from their work in the darkroom. For the imaginative, each day was an experiment that would press the resources of primitive equipment to extreme limits. The laboratory provided a cameraman with immediate, pragmatic evidence of his success with light and exposure, educating him to the practical ranges within which different film emulsions would provide acceptable picture quality.

Changes in emulsions and the design of camera lenses, as well as conveyance inventions like cranes, booms, and crab dollies, resulted from the efforts of film photographers to meet the special needs of directors and scripts. Sometimes the innovations, as with different sorts of lighting equipment, served to cut down time-consuming workaday problems as well. When Hal Mohr laconically mentions seeing his old crane resting in a back lot at the Universal studios, he cannot avoid sounding the least bit like a man who has recognized a dear friend on the Bowery. It was Mohr who pressed Eastman to improve the gray renditions and speed of its early panchromatic stock, so that picture quality might not suffer under adverse light conditions.

As the technical complexities of film production mounted in the twenties, the cinematographer became an increasingly specialized member of the production unit. Even his fancy new name betrayed the status that evolved from growing differentiation of function. Where a "second cameraman" was first employed to set up his machinery next to the "first cameraman" to expose a duplicate negative for the foreign market, he now became the first of several supportive assistants to one figure who managed a developing variety of jobs.

In essence the final responsibility of a cinematographer is so to manipulate set illumination (inside or out) and his camera that a final projected picture will prove agreeable to the director. Basic to the cameraman's decision-making is the matter of what his lens will see. The camera lens is not a human eye. The glass is more accurate and less selective.

How much a given lens will view is affected by the size of the picture it shows on the unexposed film, which is to say by the size of the film frame. Each film gauge (16mm, 35mm, 70mm) measures the magnification of its pictures relative to a standard lens of normal perspective (or "normal lens"); that is, images viewed by the camera through such a lens will appear the same size and relative distances from one another as if viewed by the naked eye from the same location. For the 35mm film camera, this is a 50mm lens; for 16mm film it is 25mm. Lenses of shorter focal length will take in broader expanses of view and are referred to, at the extreme, as wide-angle. They keep a larger area in front and in back of their subject within relative focus, and so are said to have a longer depth of field. Object size diminishes relative to vision in that broader field.

Orson Welles used deep focus in *Citizen Kane* to heighten audience awareness of dramatic changes in power relationships.

Lenses of longer focal length, 135mm, for example, will enlarge their images, decrease the area covered, and cut down the distance of relative focus so that eventually it becomes a very narrow band in the distance. These we commonly call telephoto lenses.

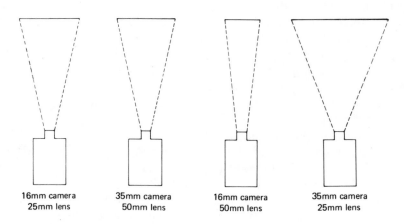

| 16mm camera | 35mm camera | 16mm camera | 35mm camera |
| 25mm lens | 50mm lens | 50mm lens | 25mm lens |

Each lens has its particular characteristics operative under the conditions of movie production: sensitivity to the color spectrum, general sharpness of focus, requirements for refocusing when the camera is moving, durability, behavior on the peripheries of its vision, shape of objects in motion, representations of horizontal and vertical patterns, and so forth. Such qualities are affected not only by the various focal lengths but by the lens apertures as well—that is, the amount of light admitted from the outside. Quality also varies among different makes of lenses.

For example, cameramen tended to approach the early CinemaScope lenses as if they were land mines, not only because the new picture ratio (relation of height to length) was unattractive to them, but because the lenses constituted a setback in terms of performance. Horizons curved upward as 'Scope lenses of diminished focal length were fastened to the 'Scope cameras. General definition (the overall sharpness of lens vision) was poor. Color quality deteriorated; focus was shallow. Close-ups were avoided not only because the faces would be gigantic on the huge new screens anyway, but also because with these lenses faces flattened out and broadened like pies. The equipment of Panavision, another lens-and-projection system, was much preferred and was eventually adopted by many studios, partly under pressure from cameramen.

A cameraman is particularly concerned with each shot's composition, both in depth and as a two-dimensional projection—the paradox of the moving picture. In theory it is the director's prerogative to stipulate what spatial organization he is after with each camera setup. In practice a director may or may not consistently exercise his compositional judgments. Either way the organization within the frame, particularly as it is revealed by light, must be executed by the cameraman. He may draw on a favorite painter for help, as Lee Garmes adapted Rembrandt's low-keyed, unhighlighted north light, or Leon Shamroy tried to evoke Rousseau and Gauguin when filming *South Pacific* (1958). Yet every shot will present its special problems, in terms of not only surface and lighting but screen dimensions as well. Arthur C. Miller illustrated the potential for integration of picture composition and narrative purpose when speaking of a Lewis Milestone film he did for Twentieth Century-Fox in 1944, *The Purple Heart.*

These fellows were shot down in Japan, six or seven of them, and tried in a Japanese court. In back of the three judges was a Japanese flag. I had it made loose, so I could raise it a little, lower it a little, or turn it a little. Because when I'd get one judge, I could balance him off with the composition of the red ball on the flag; if I had two judges and the ball came over his eye, I could always move it over a little and get composition. Now sometimes when I'd want to emphasize this thing, above the importance of the judge, I'd put on a long-focus lens, get back farther, and make the flag predominant. If I want to emphasize the judge, I'd get closer, use a wide-angled lens—I'd still have the flag, but it would be smaller in the background. And you'd use this with your actors—you make one more important than another by the focal length of the lens you use.[7]

Of course, lighting, color, and movement will also play one figure more importantly than another in the shot.

The advent of wider screens occurred in the fifties when movies tried competitively to regain their wartime audiences from TV by developing qualities unique to theater-viewing and unavailable on the smaller screen. This was a battle rivaling the combined war scenes of *The Birth of a Nation* and *War and Peace,* and the cameraman-director was presented with a kind of compositional nightmare.

Wide screens had no precedent but wall murals. The older screen dimensions, 3:4 (or 1:1.33), are more like what we find in picture frames. Such a rectangle serves to reinforce horizontals, and the sense of gravity this produces fits the realistic, representational inclinations of cinematography. At the same time, the 3:4 ratio is so nearly square that a photographer is able to relate his image compositionally to the screen edges with moderate ease.

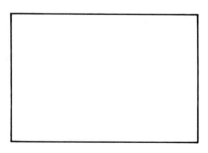

The newer ratios differ, but CinemaScope, for example, is 1:2.66 (for comparison to 3:4, the newer ratio could be expressed as 3:8).

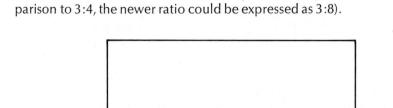

The photographer is harder-pressed to relate his images to the sides of such a frame because they are so far apart. Top and bottom are in reasonable proximity, but left and right could only be related by inverting the rectangle, a possibility that has fortunately not occurred to movie executives. In consequence, the narrative picture was thrown back to a theatrical proscenium kind of organization, lining actors up like prisoners of war waiting execution, until new methods were investigated to fit the new format.

Since everything was included in each magnified, long-shot composition and abrupt angle shifts were thought jarring, cuts became appreciably fewer in any wide-screen feature. As Charles Barr points out in an interesting study of CinemaScope,[8] the ensuing deep-focused, many-detailed compositions asked a viewer to attend to significant relationships between different elements *within* the shot. In consequence, relationships were less likely to be forced upon the audience as was true in earlier, more heavily edited sequences, like Eisenstein's boots and peacock or strikers and cattle slaughter. Thus wide-angle film tends to escape the sort of situation in which single-subject shots may be equated with nouns and the relationships between shots with verbal syntax—for example, Eisenstein's disposition toward metaphor.

As Barr says, film "suggests the essence by showing the substance." Where relationships between elements are to be drawn, the wider expanses of new aspect ratios can organize complexities into one shot, hence each element is simultaneously rather than sequentially available to the viewer, and he is encouraged to draw his own conclusions about their conjunction rather than depend on the intervening "interpretive" presence of the editor.

Wider screens, too, because they are more spectator-engrossing, are less inclined to place him in a "figuring things out" relation to his experience. They elicit a more emotionally involved, "tripping" response, more wordless and closer to time's flow.

At the same time, because of the ambition of all films, wide screen included, to spend their old age on the Late Show, the cameraman must realize that his movie image will be brutally treated by the little television screen. If it is not shown in full width by blacking out top and bottom of the small screen (a technique infrequently used because it diminishes the image's size as well as creating a second border within the picture tube border), the picture edges will be chopped away, left and right. Some networks have experimented with a scanning kind of telecine projector (a movie projector adapted to the TV camera and its scanning differential —30 fps as against 24 fps), in which the television camera passes across the wide-screen image, picking out its significant spots, but composition is changed and borders are cut just the same.

Faced with such a probability, as well as the fact that many theater screens themselves cut off picture borders, the cameraman may elect to work essentially within an image much closer to the earlier 1:1.33 ratio, filling the picture edges with nonessential visual matter.

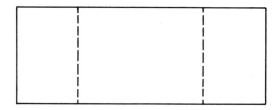

Thus he gives token obeisance to technology while retaining what compositional integrity can be managed for the several lives of his image.

We should not think of "substances" shown on film exclusively as people or even as objects or props. Everything photographed has texture as well, and, given supportive lighting, color film is particularly sensitive to surface differences. The contrasts of surfaces can sometimes effect comparisons far more dramatically than either speech or movement, as in La Notte (1960), where Jeanne Moreau's despairing presence is played against flaking, devastated city walls while the emotionally sterile Marcello Mastroianni is shot against hospital corridors, glass, and polished steel.

The cinematographer's manipulation of light will define composition, texture, "look," and performance quality as well. Light was first provided by the sun, and there are cameramen—Raoul Coutard, for example—who still elect natural, flat illumination where possible. At the turn of the century, Edison's black-walled studio, called the Black Maria, was constructed so that it might be revolved on tracks to follow outdoor illumination. The history of early moviemaking is dominated by the quest for effective, dependable sunlight. When productions became studio-bound, the cameramen developed increasingly involved needs for artificial lighting, so much so that the choice, location, and control of arc and vapor lights came to dominate his job. In Britain, the chief cameraman devotes himself exclusively to lighting, rarely if ever actually handling the camera.

Lighting needs changed with camera lenses, emulsions, sound, technological development, and the dimensions of the sets. Particular cameramen developed reputations that allied them, accurately or not, with special kinds of lighting effects and picture "look." These accomplishments helped to define the appearance of different studio products. For instance, James Wong Howe says he was hired by Jack Warner for the way he photographed Hedy Lamarr in *Algiers* (1938), and was advised to concentrate on low-key lighting as a studio trademark. Further, many photographers gained reputations and studio contracts on the basis of their capacities to glamorize women in general or some particular actress. (Howe darkened the pupils of an early twenties cutie named Mary Miles Minter by reflecting them off a black velvet frame mounted around his camera.)

Much of the praise that surrounds the silent films made in the late twenties rests properly on the cameraman. He was a fantasizing magician living among beautiful women. Each was backlit ("hit" from behind with a focused spot) to create an iridescent halo, key-lit (touched with a tiny spot of strong intensity) to highlight her bone structure, and soft-focused through gauze or a diffusing lens to produce a sort of dreamlike haze. (Later, soft focus was used more selectively to render wrinkles less visible

Greta Garbo.

Marlene Dietrich.

on the studios' aging investments.) Garbo became associated at M-G-M with cinematographer William Daniels, who translated his understanding of her visual best into long shots and close-ups (fewer medium shots), movement, reclining or seated postures rather than erect, a high-placed key to shadow the long eyelashes onto her cheeks.

In this respect, a performer might be not so much an acting talent or the result of a particular story type as a screen presence, created by one or more arbiters of movement and painting with light. "One or more" points up the relation of cinematographer to director. Marlene Dietrich is a case in point. She first came to international attention in the role of a shoddy, seductive, long-legged entertainer, singing "Falling in Love Again" in *The Blue Angel*. On the basis of this performance (she had been unspectacular in a few earlier roles), both she and director Josef von Sternberg received Hollywood contracts. Von Sternberg, who viewed the screen Dietrich as his creation, the way a painter might distinguish his portrait from a model, considered himself a cinematographer-director.

There are some directors, among whom I am numbered, who can photograph their own films. Personally I have often preferred to work without a photographer, and where I have worked with one he has used light and position of camera with precise instructions from me, even when he afterward accepted "Academy honours." I find it wastes time to instruct in something which I can equal with little effort, and therefore have combined the technical function of director and cameraman to the intense disgust of the companies I have worked for, who have repeatedly challenged me to stop "fooling" with the camera. This "fooling" with the camera saves time and energy, as otherwise a director and cameraman must outguess each other and waste valuable effort in synchronizing their work.[9]

Likely as not, von Sternberg refers to Lee Garmes, who filmed *Dishonored* (1931) and *Shanghai Express* (1932). Remembering his first studio tests of Dietrich, Garmes says:

I had seen *The Blue Angel,* and, based on that, I lit her with a sidelight, a half-tone, so that one half of her face was bright and the other half was in shadow. I looked at the first day's work, and I thought, "My God, I can't do this, it's exactly what Bill Daniels is doing with Garbo." We couldn't, of course, have two Garbos! So without saying anything to Jo, I changed to the north-light effect. He had no suggestions for changes, he went ahead and let me do what I wanted. The Dietrich face was my creation. . . .

I had a favorite shot of Marlene Dietrich when she pulled the door closed and leant her head against the wall and looked up: I just had an inky-dinky spot directly over her head, that's all. And I used that again when she stood at the back of the train. Things like that won me the Oscar.[10] [He refers to *Shanghai Express.*]

The relative contributions of von Sternberg, Garmes, and Dietrich could probably not be sorted out even by von Sternberg, Garmes, and Dietrich themselves. Dietrich either learned or instinctively understood how to play to the key. She was said to measure studio light intensity by wetting her finger. More important is the broader issue of relative contributions by a cameraman and his director to the picture seen by an audience.

Just as the scriptwriter has a special responsibility for the core of structure to a movie story, the cinematographer must account for a picture's overall look: the consistent visual character of its entire footage. That look will originate in different fashions. It may come from a general choice of lenses, as these define depth of field and how distant the objects within a shot will remain in focus. (Old cameramen like to argue about who used deep focus before Gregg Toland in *Citizen Kane*.) It may center on the special character of camera movement or the color qualities of a picture. For example, George Roy Hill screened a number of westerns and then concluded that Conrad Hall photographed the best exteriors. For Hill's *Butch Cassidy and the Sundance Kid,* Hall overexposed by as much as two stops, shot into the sun, and obscured his images with dust and smoke pots to secure the washed-out quality that was sought. Certainly different cameramen working with the same director will give distinctive casts to his work—lyric, harsh, humane, epic, intimate. Words are inaccurate guides to those qualities that can be evoked by lighting, composition, and camera movement.

The personality of the cameraman himself may hold special qualities that will adapt to a film story or perhaps conflict with it. Stanley Cortez, for instance, strikes the chords of expressionism when he says, "Even though a thing might be technically wrong, to me that thing can be *dramatically* right. To hell with all this caution! To hell with this 'academic approach'! You must *distort* color, play around with it, make it work for you, intentionally throw it off balance. You can mirror emotions in color. There are times when nature is dull: change it."[11]

Talking specifically about one of his films, *Smashup* (1947), in which Susan Hayward played a drunk, Cortez explained how he evoked the actress's experience.

I went to my doctor to ask what happens in a person's mind when he is drunk. He told me about the flashing lights across the brain, and I had lights actually inside the lens; and I conducted a kind of symphony of light over her. As she reached a pitch of distress I raised the lights to the highest pitch possible. Susan Hayward helped by actually getting drunk to play the part! I didn't want to do the cliché thing and show her distorted impressions, but rather convey her thoughts with abstract play of lights alone. It was fantastic.[12]

One can as easily imagine such a personality in conflict with another directorial temperament. In fact, cameraman stories always have their quota of walkouts and directors who were "impossible to work with."

The more complicated the shot, the more planning and teamwork will be necessary to bring it off. Some of director Max Ophuls's awesome moving-camera shots took days to design, organize, and execute. A cameraman is sometimes inspired by the notion of "wouldn't it be a great thing if we could do all of that in one shot?" One impressive instance of this happened in *The Magnificent Ambersons* in a tour through the great Amberson mansion. Since each setting posed its own problems of lighting and camera movement, the shot became an intricate ballet of coordinated teamwork in which the camera operator was directed by his boss, Stanley Cortez, on RKO's Stage Three up a staircase and through rooms in barefoot, choreographed progression while lights moved, walls were pulled aside, and mirrors drawn back on hinges to avoid reflections, then replaced on cue, so that every enclosure seemed to have four visible walls.

The cameraman in many ways encapsulates the dramatic "high" in film production because it is through his hands that all the preliminary investment, planning, and performance are finally captured on the little rectangles of cellulose acetate. At best he may claim partial credit for the quality of those images. At worst he shrugs and tells anyone interested that under the circumstances it was remarkable that anything decent came out at all.

11 ▪ Performance

Like everything else in moviedom, the broad concept "acting" seems to cover a range of performance. Much of what may pass for acting in film would be laughed off the stage, but this is as much a testament to what happens to human beings on screen as it is to their talents. The medium of film created screen acting, after all. Knowing how the screen belittles stage projection, we can carry the Kuleshov experiment to a reasonable conclusion: If a talented actor can gaze off camera with ambiguous expression and have his performance lauded, not because of its intrinsic merit, but in consequence of an editor's imaginative design, why then does he need to be a talented actor?

Such a situation, dividing as it does the unity of any actor's performance into most of the movie-production stages (conceptualization, directing, shooting, editing), equally splits up the responsibility and credit for effective screen presence. Certainly the Kuleshov evidence holds up as long as performance depends on what is really a mimed relation to story, the melodramatic tradition in film. Under these conditions, an actor is asked less to become than to be. He does not need stage techniques for communicating interior states, like posture, speech, and facial expressions. Instead "he" consists of a certain kind of presence, whether riding horses, getting out of bed, or eating a cheeseburger. The unequipped actor or actress is in danger of overextending himself when exposed to script requirements that outline a kind of individualization that is contrary to his personal disposition. This is the demarcation that has distinguished the "authentic" from the simulated personality onscreen since film's early period.

Mae Marsh expresses shy anticipation by plucking at her dress.

Griffith, for example, was inclined to people his simple stories with character types rather than individuals and then to cast accordingly. In *The Birth of a Nation* even the names testify to this generalizing. The brother was The Little Colonel; his little sister, The Pet Sister. Acting skill, the individualization of performances, is marked by little details like Mae Marsh as Flora picking at the cotton with which she has lined the homecoming costume she wears to greet her brother, back from the war.

Eisenstein, working to make heroes or villains of groups rather than individuals (Kerensky was an exception), tended to cast his parts by reference to physiognomy, a practice he called "typage." It operates out of the caricaturist's eye for significant visual detail, and works effectively in the measure that narrative requires a director's rather than an actor's employment of faces. Thus a banker in actuality might become a revolutionary leader, and a peasant some Czarist bureaucrat.

The traditions of documentary followed something of Eisenstein's silent path with regard to nonprofessional actors; roles were allotted in terms not of face but of class and caste. The underlying philosophy was that a man can do any job in front of the camera that he might perform ordinarily. He is authentic, like the star personality, so long as not required to behave inconsistently or to draw on attitudes and emotions that are foreign to his culturally derived makeup. This approach to acting was taken up by the Italian neorealists, whose stories, for example, Cesare Zavattini's, were disposed to show normal people in ordinary life. The director Vittorio de Sica was lauded for his capacity to uncover "natural actors," like the boy and his father in *The Bicycle Thief* (1948).

Under such conditions, it has often been incumbent on a director (or on his ego) to "draw" a performance out of someone whose training and natural dispositions may be foreign to the dramatic requirements. Erich von Stroheim was famous for such efforts, playing brutal Svengali to untrained actresses. Such work is possible, if time-consuming, not only be-

The fact that neither the father nor the son in the neorealistic *The Bicycle Thief* was a professional actor contributed to the authenticity de Sica strove for.

cause of the capacities of editing to absorb individual behavior into a wider frame of meaning-laden reference, but also because of the very bits and pieces that are used to accomplish that design, especially in silent film. Given budget and time to work, the director may use one or more of many techniques, including catching a player unawares, to capture some fleeting expression or gesture, which by editing can then be made to assume a significance that the audience ascribes to apparent continuity. Long takes and spoken interplay among actors place the greatest demand on individual talents, and in this respect, wide screens have imposed more "acting."

In some cases the actor might fairly be considered more of an *auteur*—that is, an individual presence subject to constant critical reconsiderations picture-to-picture—than is the director. If he is a "name" (if we watch Jeanne Moreau as much or more than we do Catherine in *Jules and Jim* [1961]), then our sensibilities are openly attuned to variation within expectation. We bring certain anticipations to the experience. The actor as personality in film dates back to its early period, when producers responded to audience interest in reseeing particular performers. Executive response was cautious, because the financiers feared that large salaries would eventually threaten profits, but soon "names" were drawing huge sums *and* crowds. The very notoriety of "$10,000 a week" or a "million-dollar contract" encouraged already implanted fantasy. For decades, the entertainment film reinvested its "salaries" into publicity and made more millions.

At first the stars, figures like Charlie Chaplin and Mary Pickford, grew out of direct, pragmatic responses of the audience, as measured in letters and ticket sales. When movie executives in the twenties began to "develop" publicized actresses in the manner of baseball's farm system, we start to experience that element of contrivance that muddles efforts to identify an industry as complicated as the movies with folk art. The star image passes, in McLuhan's phrase, from archetype (an undistorted mirror of audience expectation) to stereotype (a manufactured copy).

Like any business, entertainment film is predicated on profit, and profit sits most comfortably in the world of the predictable, which helps to account for sequels, the purchase of best-sellers, and the development of "another" stars: another Jean Harlow, another Clark Gable, and so on. Sometimes these efforts were successful, particularly when the industry was able to enlist script, lighting, and directing talents whose energies submerged personal imperfections in a haze of audience wish-fulfillment. But when any performer, sometimes for reasons quite beyond conscious volition, hit it big, he tapped some special audience dream. He became one of mass man's secrets writ large.

Usually such stars expose a spectator tension in acceptable form. If the subject was sex, the expression was not simply in terms of libido, but so organized as to resolve what anxieties it released. An easy example is Marilyn Monroe, who combined the traditional availability of the big-breasted, wet-lipped blonde with an element of childish vulnerability. This combination, when recognized, was exploited by Twentieth Century-Fox. The minor comedienne of *How to Marry a Millionaire* (1953) and *Gentlemen Prefer Blondes* (1953) had been worked out of an earlier stereotyped dumb blonde, who made sexy entrances as George San-

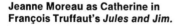

Jeanne Moreau as Catherine in François Truffaut's *Jules and Jim*.

ders's protégée in *All About Eve* (1950) and Louis Calhern's mistress in *The Asphalt Jungle* (1950), then developed in *We're Not Married* and *Monkey Business* (both 1952). Momentarily she strayed into the unhappy, overambitious dramatic byways of *Niagara* (1952) and *River of No Return* (1954). Vehicles like *The Seven Year Itch* (1955) and *Bus Stop* (1956) were ideal for Marilyn Monroe because they exploited both her sex and the "little talent" (which one wanted to protect and defend) within a range of real if circumscribed acting ability. She played the ukelele and sang an entire song with an all-girl orchestra in *Some Like It Hot* (1959), and she practiced for days with the ping-pong paddle for *The Misfits* (1961).

Many male stars successfully project tensions that supply running motivation through each story while setting up the basis for eventual emotional resolution. Such a tension may often be repressed violence, as in the careers of James Cagney and Humphrey Bogart, more recently Clint Eastwood. In more updated versions of the rebellious anarchist, the violence may be turned inward (James Dean, Montgomery Clift).

Certain directors may recognize an actor's under-the-surface image

John Wayne in Howard Hawks's *Rio Bravo*. *(Credit: Warner Brothers)*

and capitalize on what has been passed over by others. Howard Hawks's western *Red River* (1948), for instance, made use of John Wayne's strengths and incipient violence in ways that seem less apparent in the same actor's performances in John Ford's *Stagecoach* (1939), *She Wore a Yellow Ribbon* (1949), and *Rio Grande* (1950), although Ford burlesques something of it in *The Quiet Man* (1952).

We ought not to demean movie stars or diminish what may be special kinds of performing talents because their fortunes seem to rest so often with studio flacks, directors, and key lights. Much apparent narcissism, neurotic temperament, and self-doubt rise out of a constant quest on the part of some Norma Jean Baker or Rodolpho d'Antonguolla themselves to locate Marilyn Monroe or Rudolph Valentino, and then to manipulate that presence so that it continues to work for them. A star combines the recognizable personal inflections (Cagney's jabbing finger and high-pitched chuckle that melds joviality, energy, and threat) with variation from picture to picture. A star is never *really* always the same, although it may take a discerning eye to locate variations on the theme. Cagney's is a versatile talent, his range extending from a bouncing, stiff-legged, strutting George M. Cohan in *Yankee Doodle Dandy* (1942) to the psychopath of Raoul Walsh's *White Heat* (1949). Unlike many male stars, Cagney's masculinity was not subverted in violence, despite the fact that shoving a grapefruit in Mae Clarke's face "made him" (*The Public Enemy* [1931]).

Screen performance may combine the most intense self-consciousness with minimal behavior, or else that consciousness may be altogether pointed outward. Frederic March's comment after being admonished for overprojecting ("Oh yes, this isn't a play. I'm not supposed to act") is modified by Spencer Tracy's gruff advice to young hopefuls ("Learn your lines and don't bump into the furniture"). The actor is often described as a reactor, partly because his performance, like the Russian Mozhukin, is always a part of an enveloping context, partly because minimal response can develop useful ambiguities, or as Howard Hawks said to John Wayne, one "won't offend the audience."

Like the musician who tape-records for study purpose, a movie actor has a special, sometimes frightening opportunity to view himself externalized, a view no mirror can give him. He studies himself, supremely sophisticated in his body image. Perhaps this quality accounts for the success of many performers who do not overintellectualize their work. There is always that danger which Alexandre Dumas recounted in *Twenty Years After* and Godard recalled in *My Life to Live* (1962): Porthos, the unthinking one of the Three Musketeers, set a bomb, lit it, and, while fleeing, commenced for the first time in his life to consider the act of running. He asked himself how anyone could raise a leg, press it forward, and set it down in front of the other one. As he thought, Porthos began to question. In doubt, he stopped. Stopping, he died in the explosion.

Watch how actors move their legs, arms, and torsos. It is surprising how often, on reflection, we find that we associate minuscule muscle behavior with some particular screen personality. Of course each of our friends has characteristic gestures and visual patterns, but rarely are these nurtured and refined as on the screen. It is a kind of choreography. We may equate, without strain, Cary Grant's erect, high-necked, shoulders-back posture under stress (even when he is not doing an open-mouthed double-take) with a typical Ginger Rogers movement, head bent back and over her shoulder while kicking up a foot behind her and dancing the Piccolino, the Yam, or the Carioca with Fred Astaire (né Frederick Austerlitz).

It is interesting to follow, by watching old movies on television, an actor like Humphrey Bogart becoming himself before our eyes. In the early films like *A Devil with Women* (1930), he is not Bogie at all, but rather some smooth-faced Broadway player, almost juvenile. After his performance as Duke Mantee in *The Petrified Forest* (1936), we begin to see the mannerisms develop, refine, and work themselves into a composite, manufactured image, whose naturalness is testament to the performer's abilities. This happens through the Warner Brothers period, when Bogart played subordinate to James Cagney and Edward G. Robinson (*The Amazing Dr. Clitterhouse* [1938]; *Angels with Dirty Faces* [1938]; *The Roaring Twenties* [1939]). He is far more neurotic and one-dimensional in *Dead End* (1937) than as the fleeing outlaw of *High Sierra* (1941). By *The Maltese Falcon,* Bogie is complete.

Movie critics are often prone to ignore such skills until an actor dons heavy makeup and perhaps grows old, hair turning blue. Lon Chaney in *The Hunchback of Notre Dame* (1923): Now, there's acting! When the movie star steps out of his "typical" role, often when he releases more open emotionality, which is associated with "acting," he is the more likely to receive an Academy Award, as Bogart did as grizzled, drunken foil for Katharine Hepburn in *The African Queen* (1951), or the eye-patched John Wayne in *True Grit* (1969). Similarly, Elizabeth Taylor's acting talents are regarded as touching some level of grandeur the more she seems to be neurotic and to raise her voice (*Butterfield 8* [1960]; *Who's Afraid of Virginia Woolf?* [1966]).

Equally important as stars to the narrative film idiom are the supporting actors and actresses. Many, of course, are talented, versatile performers, but other minor players profit from playing one-dimensional roles that carry from picture to picture—the sort of player whom movie buffs gleefully identify in obscure films on the Late Late Show, Jerome Cowan, say, or Franklin Pangborn. Since most movie plots can hardly support more than three or four fleshed-out major characterizations, the bit players supply a sort of animated, talking background against which the name figures may operate. As an old story has it, the life of a bit player can be told in four stages, each expressed in orders from Central Casting: (1) Who is Chill Wills? (2) Get me Chill Wills! (3) Get me a Chill Wills type. (4) Who is Chill Wills?

Faced with procedures of motion picture production, the stage actor is frustrated in his efforts to build a part, even to carry his performance from Point A to Point B with a modicum of consistency, if not development. The manner in which a film is made has much to do with the movies' tendency to keep its characters on a rather flat pitch of performance throughout. An actor may find himself doing scenes early and late in the story in two consecutive days, particularly if they use the same sets, which is often the case. The chronology is not only askew, but each setup (the positioning of camera, lights, and set) is short, its moment fragmented and isolated from any dramatic matrix. And most production time is not working but waiting. In consequence, an actor who seems to change with his experience, particularly without makeup alterations, is impressive: Alec Guinness in *Tunes of Glory* (1960) or Laurence Olivier in *The Entertainer* (1960), which undoubtedly profited from his experience in the stage version.

Enlightened views of foreign actors depend, too, on our knowledge of the culture. To evaluate an Anna Magnani part, we need either to know her milieu well enough to distinguish Magnani from the dialect and gestures, or else we must have seen her in enough roles that the skills may be distinguished from one another.

An actress may find herself playing a love scene not to a bed partner, but rather to the cinematographer, grips, juicer (electrician), director, and script girl. An ability to play to the camera, often without a glance in its direction, is *the* essential movie skill and a basis of great competition among performers who are not without aggressive instinct. Sometimes an actor's relation to the camera is a never-ending, passionate love affair, even including those diplomatic lies that the camera will tell as years go by. For other performers, the camera is a kind of psychic cannibal. When it is said of Robert Redford that the camera "eats him up," what is described is a relentless, uncompromising, inescapable examination that not only ferrets out the most minuscule eye movement but consumes his every effort toward variation of style. If the cinematographer thinks himself a visual magician, the actor may often view him as implacably demanding, giving little in return.

Just as a spectator may enjoy camera movement or color control or editing pyrotechnics for their own sakes, he may isolate performance skill from its celluloid context. There is always the temptation to admire an actor's tour de force independent of the narrative itself, although of all the movie production talents, it is one most requiring integration.

Olivier, for example, in *Sleuth* (1972) was not simply pitting a detective-fiction English gentleman against Michael Caine's hard-boiled, first-generation, swinging Briton. Each of the two accomplished actors was

Michael Caine and Lawrence Olivier in *Sleuth*.

also competing with the other's acting style with great precision and mutual respect—now working in support of the other's solo, now dominant, now interwoven. Ensemble playing on the screen, especially the wide screen, is something like Dixieland jazz music. We are reasonably confident that the melodic lines will hold few surprises, and direct our attention instead at timing and dynamics, as horn players compete in the choruses.

12 ■ Editing

Most young people, when they study motion picture production, take especially to editing. It is their first opportunity to deal in direct terms with the little photographic images on which so much time, money, and effort have been expended. Unlike writing a screenplay, which only formulates a strategy of attack, or shooting footage, about whose results you are never altogether certain at the time, editing allows one room to experiment, to rethink one's ideas, and to solve problems. It is a practical occupation. Different from many other aspects of the production process, editing is essentially a one-man operation, although the cutter will usually work under some guidance from the director. After working on his film for weeks, the student editor may not remain as pleased and dedicated as when he began. After all, the human qualities of patience, organization, exacting memory for the smallest visual detail, and tolerance for cell-like confinement were never distributed equally among mankind.

The editor lives in a little cubicle of accumulating memories as each set of rushes gathers around him. The procedures of his work are geared first to the needs of ongoing production, then to an organization of all the footage toward maximum total effect. Each day's rushes return from the laboratory in a form appropriate to projection—that is, positive "work prints." These are synchronized with accompanying sound as necessary. (This is the reason for the clapboard identification that precedes each camera take, identifying it and supplying a visual referent against which the cutter may relate his sound.)

The day's work is then viewed by editor's and director's selective eye toward determining the best of several versions recording each scene. Decisions on what to keep must balance technical factors (picture and sound quality) against performance. The editor culls the "out takes" and files both these and what remain for easy access.

When enough material has been accumulated, he will mount the shots sequentially on larger reels, progressing from broad, overlong assemblages (the "rough cut") to a final version that meets both dramatic and time requirements (the "fine cut"). In its last version, the picture track will contain appropriate directions to the laboratory regarding optical effects (fades, dissolves, and such) so that the work print amounts to a linear message of coded signals that accompanies the original footage, which itself has been cut to correct specifications for printing. The soundtrack will serve as a guide to whatever postsynchronization is necessary: music, effects, additional dialogue, perhaps narration.

Sound editing will occupy as much attention as picture. Faced with the best visual on Take 7, which has dialogue problems, and a good soundtrack on Take 3, the editor may spend a restless night trying to decide how to coordinate best picture with best sound. Should he intercut another shot at the point where some faulty synchronization would be apparent? Or edit two or more soundtracks together? Or both?

Soundtracks are built out of every necessary component (effects,

A film editor working with a moviola chooses the best from a series of takes.

speech, music), each timed and adjusted for volume. A composer may be commissioned to write so many minutes of music, each segment broken down to an exact measurement in seconds. He may be assigned themes or particular effects. Probably foolishly, he may be asked to contribute a song to accompany the production credits so that the picture may be more effectively exploited. His music scored and copied, the composer will assemble an orchestra and record against a projected work print to assure time synchronization. Or some material may be taped "wild" for discretionary use.

MARKING WORKPRINTS FOR OPTICAL EFFECTS

When marking workprint, use white grease pencil. Be sure to indicate desired effects at all splices, **including** straight-cuts. Be sure grease pencil markings are on the **same** side of the workprint as the edge-numbers. These "rules-of-thumb" in marking workprint will ease the conforming operation and greatly reduce the chance of error.

TAIL	FADE-IN	SPLICE	SPLICE	FADE-OUT	HEAD

Marked by two straight lines forming a long "V". The lines run diagonally for the length of the effect, starting at the center of the frame at the scene change. (We will accept a mark of "FI" at the point where the fade-in is to start plus length in frames.)

The reverse of the fade-in marking, with the diagonal lines running for the length of the effect and meeting at the center of the frame where the screen will be totally dark. (We will accept a mark of "FO" for fade-out plus length in frames.)

DISSOLVE

A fade-in of one scene superimposed over a fade-out of another scene, as the markings indicate. The midpoint of the marking occurs at the splice in the workprint, and extends an equal

distance into both scenes. (We will accept a mark of "D" at the splice indicating the center of the dissolve plus length in frames.)

SPLICE	UNINTENTIONAL SPLICES	SPLICE

Splices in the workprint which are to be disregarded in matching are indicated by drawing two short paralleled lines through

the splice. This shows the editor the scene is **not** to be cut at that point.

DOUBLE EXPOSURE

Double exposures, superimposed titles, etc., are indicated by cutting a few inches of the superimposed scene into the background scene to indicate where the double exposure begins. Several inches of the superimposed scene are cut in to indi-

cate the end of the double exposure. These two pieces are then connected by a wavy grease pencil line. To insure proper matching, it is essential that one of the two pieces of workprint be edge-numbered or otherwise identified.

EXTENDED SCENE

Mark extended scenes (indicated in the workprint by leader) with a long arrow, the shaft of which is drawn through the

leader and the head of which comes up to the last frame of the leader to indicate the length of the extension.

Editors mark workprints with optical effects instructions for film laboratories. *(Credit: Calvin Productions)*

Sounds completed and organized, they will be mixed (blended on one composite track), a reel at a time, by one or more technicians, seated at control boards and twisting dials to raise or lower each separate track where needed as they watch the projected picture. Finally the full sound will be united in the laboratory to completed picture in a composite print appropriate to theatrical projection.

As the editor assembles his picture, he joins each shot to its companion, guided by various principles. Like Eisenstein, he may choose to collide his images, not necessarily to create a dialectical synthesis but perhaps just to startle his viewers or to force relationships that are not inherent in the separate takes. He may, on the other hand, strive for the invisible cut, the one that is never noticed by a viewer because it maintains some continuity of sound, picture, or both that overrides the transition.

To accomplish the latter, the editor may carefully locate that moment at the end of Shot 1 where his viewer's eye is centered on a screen location that coincides with the point of interest in Shot 2 (matching screen position). He may keep a movement continuous by picking it up on Shot 2 just where it leaves off in Shot 1 (matching action). He may match two images that are altogether different except in the similarity of their shapes, like a globe and a bald head, or the apeman bone cast upward to become a spaceship in *2001: A Space Odyssey.*

The viewer's tendency to preserve a sense of constancy while watching movement and shape allows the editor to smooth his transitions from one camera angle to another. In fact, if there is not a shift of some distance, as from medium shot to close shot, the continuity will likely appear interrupted, so that a walking figure, for example, will inexplicably jerk at the cut (*jump cut*). Should he so wish, the editor may even effect the most complete shifts in time and place while maintaining a constant motion. This phenomenon, which the French have termed *faux raccord,* carries a special quality of the surreal because of the dislocations that it may effect. In a short, personal film made in 1943, *Meshes of the Afternoon,* Maya Deren unites three altogether different locations with a rhythmic pace of feet as they walk from one ground to the next.

Resnais, who was once an editor, used the technique often in *Last Year at Marienbad,* for it clouds his time and place switches with ambiguity. Delphine Seyrig, her elbow characteristically bent, forearm across breast, hand curled against her neck like a wounded bird, swings her torso in Location 1 to complete the action in Location 2, arm shifted and dressed in a new costume. Giorgio Albertazzi asks Delphine Seyrig, "May I?" as they stand in a large hall. "With pleasure," she replies, only now they are dancing, elsewhere, perhaps at another, remembered time.

Constantly the editor's decisions are affected by time. If he is a TV movie butcher, he must both cut in commercials at appropriate intervals

One step, three locales, a *faux raccord* from Maya Deren's *Meshes of the Afternoon.*

and fit the entire feature on the Procrustean bed of station programming —usually ninety minutes or two hours—in which case a subplot may disappear altogether except for some unexplained presence in a shot that contained part of the main action.

Apparent time (Time II) is dealt with by the editor in ways we considered earlier, smoothing ellipses by matching movement and composition. Sensed time (Time III) is especially important to the editor. He must account not only for the measurable duration of any shot, but also for its tempo, how it reads, how many *beats* it has. The beat is a kind of essence that every shot carries in any given context, and if one cuts too quickly or holds an extra beat, a scene may change its meaning as it puzzles or frustrates the viewer. The rhythm of a shot grows from its visual composition and length, the type of camera movement used, and the kind of motion or activity captured in the footage. Each has its own characteristics. In combination, they will impart a distinctiveness to every shot. The editor may wish to parallel interior rhythms and those between conjoining shots or to oppose them, just as he manipulates screen direction (the direction of movement within a shot). He may cut his material literally or figuratively to a musical beat. (Most American and European films seem to me to move almost exclusively in duple rhythms: 2/4, 4/4.) Stanley Cortez says he visually composed Shelley Winters's death scene, triangularly designed, in *Night of the Hunter* (1955) to the music of *Valse Triste,* played in his head. The spatial rhythms of screen composition can be played with or against the linear rhythms of movement and film length. Of course each sound element will add its further variants.

In addition to his rhythm, movement, and shape continuities, the editor must maintain control over picture tone—the gray scale or color quality that characterizes each shot. Within minor limits these may be "fixed" in laboratory processing, although most such responsibility rests with the cinematographer.

The editor may use sound to ease transitions, a technique that often introduces the sounds of Shot 2 while we still view a remaining moment of Shot 1. Such a device may simply smooth a cut, like matching screen action, or it may be used to anticipate later events (the dissolves, noted previously, in *The Naked Night* and *A Place in the Sun*).

For example, there is a typical moment in Arthur Penn's *Bonnie and Clyde* that marks the farewell between Bonnie and her old mother. They are standing in a field with Clyde, who has been trying, in his foolish but awkwardly friendly way, to reassure Mrs. Parker that the danger he and Bonnie are in has been exaggerated, that they will give up robbing banks as soon as times get better, perhaps even settle down near her. Bonnie is disconsolate at leaving her mother (clearly for the last time), eager to reassure her, mutely asking for some kind of parental wisdom, and herself anxious of what will come.

After listening to Clyde's speech, the mother says, "You'd best keep runnin', Clyde Barrow, and you know it," in flat, matter-of-fact language that seems to belie her message. Then, " 'Bye, honey."

The shots and sound are assembled in the following fashion.

1. CLOSE-UP. MOTHER
   MOTHER: "You'd best keep runnin', Clyde Barrow . . ."
2. CLOSE-UP. CLYDE (REACTION SHOT)
   MOTHER (CONTINUED OFF SCREEN): ". . . and you know it."
3. CLOSE-UP. BONNIE. (REACTION SHOT)
   SOUND: CAR MOTORS STARTING. VOLUME RISES.
4. CLOSE-UP. MOTHER
   MOTHER: " 'Bye, honey." AGAINST MOTORS.
5. LONG SHOT. CARS IN FIELD
   CARS start to depart.

As played, the relation of sound and picture develops emotions that would be different if the images had been organized otherwise. The synchronous identification of Mrs. Parker and her speech in Shot 1 awards her the first dramatic emphasis. Having listened to Clyde and seen her daughter (she too knows that it is for the last time), the mother passes on her last advice like a final blessing.

Shot 2 allows Warren Beatty to respond in silence to what he has heard, and emphasizes with sound his own awareness by the words themselves: ". . . and you know it." Clyde's expression really doesn't change, maintaining a kind of happy, innocent, foolish grin, his eyes squinting slightly in the midwestern sun.

Bonnie's reaction is then picked up (Shot 3). Her mother's parting words are over, spoken for her but directed to Clyde because he is a man. Now she faces the inevitabilities without the pretense of optimism. She is leaving her mother. She knows the end is imminent for all of them, herself perhaps first. A mounting anxiety is not so much betrayed by Faye Dunaway's expression, which carries something of Beatty's placidity although more somber, as it is by the soundtrack. The sound of the automobiles (Shot 4) is functionally planted (other members of the party are preparing to leave), a kind of ominous, mechanical undertone expressed in the stutter of old Model A mufflers, and a premonition of the place where Bonnie and Clyde will soon die—the automobile (Shot 5). The last words of Bonnie's mother are drowned in the automobile engines.

After the departure but before the final death scene, Bonnie is wounded in a skirmish (Clyde, too, but seemingly less seriously). Here music is used to increase our sense of foreboding. Until now, the dominant sounds have been an exuberant, raggy banjo-picking, which enlists an almost Keystone Cop effect of jocularity whenever the old cars race across the midwestern plains as our thieves make a getaway. Their adventures seem like games to Bonnie and Clyde, and somewhat to the audience as well, like Hitchcock's technique of seducing our sympathies for the criminals. From the moment Bonnie is wounded, a lively country fiddle is added to the banjo music, equally gay in tone but insistently and increasingly out of tune with the other strings.

Finally, Bonnie and Clyde are sitting in a field as she concludes a reading of her "Ballad of Bonnie and Clyde," which has been printed in the newspaper. The poem is a pathetically childish effort to impart some kind of epic dimension to their escapades, but it is deeply meaningful to Clyde, who thinks that it explains his motives and somehow vindicates the murder and theft in his own mind. Revealed finally not as a criminal but some kind of romantic, rebellious figure, Clyde is at last able sexually to consummate his love for Bonnie, to "become a man" in full.

Warren Beatty's line is, "You made me somebody to remember," delivered in medium long shot as he bends over the recumbent Bonnie. Wind effects are brought up, the newspaper is blown screen right, and camera pans right to follow, thus rationalizing its shift from the bodies. The roar of wind is faded into the reappearing banjo music, only now, the music has a new, threatening meaning, for it connotes Bonnie and Clyde's fresh vulnerability. Until this time Clyde has expressed his masculinity with a pistol, an image almost overbearingly underlined early in the picture. (It's an Arthur Penn proclivity and permeates *The Left Handed Gun* [1958] as well.) Now, while the couple make love, they are being betrayed by C. W. Moss's father, the event to which we cut from the shot of the newspaper.

As well as knowing when to cut, the editor must equally consider when not to. In a sense, this decision is out of the cutter's realm, for it may be preordained by script and shooting. However, shot duration is really a disclosing function, like editing. The long take may be even more effective as a technique of joining images, as we considered earlier. The wise editor will even reject alternate close-ups and cutaways if he realizes the master shot plays more effectively. Just as the long take requires a certain skill of actor performance, an abundance of short shots in an editor's bin is actor-centered in its own way. The editor is encouraged to pick the most impressive performance from a selection of alternative shots that have equal technical quality.

The power of montage is at its greatest in the assemblage sort of film, cut out of old newsreels and stock footage to create new impressions like an artist's collage, but editing is really a skill that permeates the entire filmmaking process. Each job is in some way editorial. Nevertheless, only the solitary figure crouched over his flickering Moviola* feels that special, direct contact with film that is like a sculptor's with his stone.

* A machine for viewing and editing film footage. With it one can stop the film at any frame and hold it or reverse it. It features a numbered guide to the footage length, like the counter of a tape recorder, and a small viewing screen. Some also have sound replay.

13 ▪ Special Effects

The notion of special effects runs from the legerdemain of shooting (models, mattes in camera, and other kinds of trickery) to laboratory processing—printing and developing, often combined with "optical effects." Photographic effects date from film's earliest days by way of Georges Méliès, who was a professional magician and adapted many of his stage routines to the camera lens in a little movie studio outside Paris. Other of his accomplishments are said to have originated by accident, as when his camera jammed momentarily, so that when he viewed the developed footage Méliès saw a bus disappear inexplicably from view.

Camera trickery, like editing, takes advantage of the fact that interruptions and readjustments may be performed while a film is being shot (or edited), since nothing unphotographed will ever be seen and our perceptions of the projected image remain constant. If film, as Godard once said, is truth at twenty-four frames per second, it is equally lies at the same speed.

Because audiences were amused by high divers leaping from the water back to their boards and slowed or speeded motion (Truffaut pays homage to both in his first film, *The Mischief Makers* [1957]), such techniques were indulged in until they palled. The actual size of a projected image will also be disguised unless the same screen gives us some perspective referent. This phenomenon encouraged exploratory use of models to film certain scenes. Battles between prehistoric monsters, for example, might be manufactured with flexible figures whose positions could be minutely altered between each frame exposure like animation pictures to give the final impression of size and life. I remember visiting the property department of RKO studios years ago and seeing a little, doll-like King Kong perched high on a shelf, like a character out of *Winnie-the-Pooh*.

Special effects were also used in high-budgeted feature films to save expense by creating the impression of huge sets and great crowds. A common practice of the twenties silents was the glass shot, which obscured a portion of the regularly exposed scene by a meticulously painted simulation of the remainder of the composition. Sometimes a crowd scene might be filmed in the lower half of a camera frame, then the same actors moved to the unexposed top to reperform while the identical footage was run through again. In such cases, it was vital that members of the top crowd not descend below designated boundaries, or they would disappear in the middle of the screen.

The advent of sound encouraged a renewed interest in special effects, for the requirements of microphones and accoustics restricted filmmaking to studio floor space. Since the settings could not remain constantly indoors, technicians worked at new illusionary tactics to give the impressions of other worlds, hence the development of devices like rear-screen projection, in which slides or motion-picture film were projected on translucent screens behind the performers in order to simulate different locations. The quality of such illusion varies. It must answer problems of perspective, focus, picture quality (and color if required), movement, and relative distances. Sometimes the deception is extraordinary, aided by intermediate props and stage dressing that blends set to screen as in nineteenth-century dioramas and panoramas. Sometimes it is woefully inadequate. Watch cars through rear automobile windows in terms of the driver's steering. Sometimes projected presences may be fun, as when we identify the jungle of King Kong's Skull Island in the background of a picnic scene in *Citizen Kane*. And, of course, a filmmaker may make use of the visual deception itself, like Hitchcock's fake-looking rear-screen

W. C. Fields goes out to milk the rear-screen projected elk in *The Fatal Glass of Beer.*

projection behind Marnie's horseback ride, or W. C. Fields, when he goes out to milk the elk in *The Fatal Glass of Beer* (1931).

Rear-screen projection and props may be used to create giants and midgets, such as in *Doctor Cyclops* (1940) and *The Incredible Shrinking Man* (1953). They can suggest great expanses of forest, desert, and architecture. Other devices, water tanks and movable stages, also appeared as plots demanded their use. The thirties films were a time of great catastrophes, like earthquake (*San Francisco* [1936]) and fire (*In Old Chicago* [1938]).

The transformation scene, another hoary theater trick, also lent itself to movie fantasy: man into subman, or wolf, or vampire, or cat, or fly, or vegetable, or inches-high homunculus. The very idea of a double self echoes another of mass man's secrets, the scandalous knowledge that we are not what we seem and are emotionally very different from our public posture. Makeup and camera interruption could contribute to such changes. Another helpful agent was color. Because the sensitivity of black-and-white film to different spectrum ranges was subject to control, it could be manipulated by lighting, the placement of makeup, and an interjection then removal of filters to block out the greasepaint. Hence such transformations as that of Dr. Jekyll to Mr. Hyde "before our very eyes."

At first those camera trickeries that had to do with exposure were accomplished by the cameraman. If he needed to film an actor shaking hands with himself, the cameraman obscured one side of the image, photographed the performer once, rewound the film, and matched his other side by the most accurate of registrations. When something as simple as a dissolve was called for, a cameraman was required to fade out the first image, rewind his film, and fade in the next scene on cue. The success of such ventures depended not only on the accuracy of his judgment, but the adequacy of what was photographed. On occasion, a single reel of film might call for as many as eight such maneuvers. If one of them went wrong, the entire undertaking collapsed, and the situation was known to drive photographers to nervous breakdown.

Similarly, fade-ins and fade-outs were sometimes controlled in the developing baths by allowing an emulsion's latent image to develop frame by frame. The emergence of the motion-picture laboratory as an agency of strict technical controls and varied accomplishments is Hollywood's great technological achievement.

Processing might affect how the image looked; printing determined what it could be. First, contact printers were developed so that an original might be reproduced in great quantity, its exposures regulated as necessary, and visuals effected by running material through more than once. This allowed the printer to expose previously obscured sections of the new film so as to hide editing splices. By overlapping shots, their exposure controlled, he could create dissolves and superimpositions of any length. Tedious as such work was, operations could be standardized, and experiments reattempted, so that success was possible as long as the original images were acceptable.

Even those images, created by the cinematographer, were subject to change with the development of the optical printer. Where the contact printer ran picture against unexposed raw stock at a one-to-one speed and a common magnification, the optical printer permitted variation by exposing picture to raw stock with greater variation. The new film is exposed to the old not by contact, but like another movie camera. In consequence, what it photographs can be modified in terms of size, masking, and speed. If the original image is held stationary while the new picture exposes at regular speed, for instance, a freeze-frame is accomplished, like the last moment of *The 400 Blows* (1959) or *Butch Cassidy and the Sundance Kid* (1969).

Opaque mattes may even be interjected between the two images to mask out designated portions of the exposed stock. Such masks can

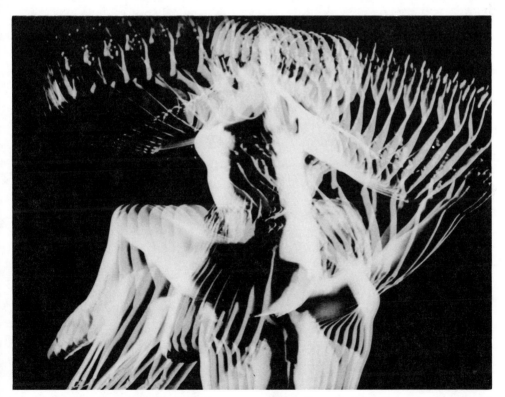

Multiple images in *Pas de Deux* were created by the optical printer. *(Credit: National Film Board of Canada)*

themselves be composed of motion-picture film, and hence move. If their reverse image is introduced on a second run, calibrated exactly to the first, what was shown is obscured, what was hidden, exposed. By such techniques the most varied of optical effects are accomplished, from the whirling-newspaper montage shot to wipes, pinwheels, and super-heroes flying through space.

Because laboratory work itself is only an execution of orders from people who presumably know what they want (lab technicians have their own opinions about the quality of the films they work on), optical effects are neutral with reference to stylization and the naturalness of a final image. One way to achieve an overall film look is through color control. Color filters may be interposed into printing so as to desaturate the original image for atypical effect, as in *Reflections in a Golden Eye* (1967) and *Tell Them Willie Boy Is Here* (1969). But a laboratory may work with equal dedication to soup up an image exposed under the most adverse lighting conditions so that it gives a semblance of naturalism. Technicians may seek to correct exposures by compensating in developing and printing; within one or two lens stops in either direction, this is often possible. It is even possible to recompose an original shot by enlarging part of it, although the factors of grain and picture quality will be introduced into such effects.

Laboratories have always been a prideful bastion of illusion-making for the film industry, because they embody a situation of skilled technicians working privately to effect the miraculous. Yet they are no more responsible, ultimately, for the sound and images of a movie than the magnetic tape that passes below recording heads, or the film emulsion in front of the camera lens.

14 ▪ Production

The role of producer developed with the industry, although writers, editors, photographers, directors, and actors are sometimes hard put to understand quite what it is producers do. As filmmaking became technically more complicated, each venture calling for greater investment, it was inevitable that the money demanded overseeing. The character of producers was defined, too, by a developing situation of high-priced stars and well-paid directors and writers whose creativity was not always obvious and whose working methods seemed at times dilatory at best. The producer was created by the studios to keep an eye on productions, to bring them in on schedule, hold the reins on expenditure, and supply a continuity among assembly-line artisans so that the workers' relation to any film more closely paralleled bolt-tightening in an automobile plant. At Paramount, for example, B. P. Schulberg was expert at firing writers the moment they finished an assignment.

Because its skills are not easily defined and its job description not technical, producing was unfortunately open to misuse and disparagement. In many studios producers got their positions through nepotism, which nurtured cynicism on the part of production crews. "The son-in-law also rises."

But the job of the producer was clear in the producer's mind if not in others'. He watched the money, tried to get the money on the screen, and sought, through cajolery, threat, and diplomacy, to realize the project as it had been understood by *his* superiors. He was a field officer. When schisms developed between director and producer, lower-level agents for each, assistant directors and associate producers, were created to resolve and negotiate.

Depending on the interests of a director and on his contract, the producer devotes his early attentions to set design and costume—two areas where investment is most visibly apparent to the audience. Such arrangements are clearly dependent on a firm script and shooting schedule, control over which is sometimes disputed terrain between director and producer. For such reasons, he may be particularly interested in locking up a satisfactory script as early as possible as well as in hiring actors and actresses for whom dress may be thoughtfully, individually designed.

The idea of a wise, skilled, creative producer is attractive to ordered minds, for it suggests an agent of the financiers who is directly operative, *in charge* of what may otherwise seem to be chaos. Perhaps this explains the charisma of a figure like Irving Thalberg, who rose from minor secretary under Carl Laemmle at the New York office of Universal to production head at Universal City by the age of twenty. When Metro-Goldwyn-Mayer consolidated, Thalberg assumed control of its production offices, where he remained until losing power in 1933. The last three of his thirty-seven years were spent with M-G-M as an independent producer.

Thalberg supervised enough successful pictures that his abilities were tangibly evident on screen: for example, *The Big Parade* (1925); *Ben-Hur* (1926); *The Crowd* (1928); *Broadway Melody* (1929); *Anna Christie*

Irving Thalberg.

(1930); *Trader Horn* (1931); *Grand Hotel* (1932). Such titles display a variety of material, all well financed. In fact, one of Thalberg's talents was the ability to define not how to save money on a costly production but where to locate its insufficiencies and shore these up with more investment. For all his personal interest in income, Thalberg was never parsimonious where money was useful to the company.

His credits, too, trace the abilities of M-G-M to weather change and technical innovation with some imaginative resilience. *Ben-Hur* was a mighty spectacle, saved from early, disastrous overseas shooting. *The Crowd* was a King Vidor statement on conformity, which was regarded as dangerously experimental in its day. The *Broadway Melody*'s in the thirties, like the *Footlight Parade*'s and *Big Broadcast*'s, were Hollywood's solution to synchronous sound—music, dance, and fast wisecracks with offstage plots in which crisis strikes on opening night.

Anna Christie introduced Garbo as a speaking star ("Garbo Talks!") and successfully accomplished the transition for Swedish Greta Gustafsson, whereas performers like John Gilbert (her silent costar) and Douglas Fairbanks failed when they had to open their mouths. (Her introductory lines, were "Gimme a Visky. Ginger ale on the side."—*The Waiter leaves*—"And don't be stingy, ba-bee.") Thus a major investment was preserved.

Trader Horn was the first major sound feature venture into location shooting, and although its White Goddess and superstitious natives chanting "oogabooga-oogabooga-oogabooga" were as hokey as Rider Haggard's novels *King Solomon's Mines* or *She,* the African settings were real. *Grand Hotel* joined together a roster of M-G-M contract stars to set off their skills (and the studio's payroll) in an adaptation of Vicki Baum's novel, which might otherwise have drawn a smaller audience.

The contrary aspect of the producer and of Irving Thalberg's reputation rests in his relation with Erich von Stroheim. It was Thalberg who fired von Stroheim from *Merry-Go-Round* (1923) and who ordered *Greed* (1923) cut from the director's forty reels down to its present fractional version.

In the eyes of Hollywood money, von Stroheim was the egomaniacal director run amuck, ordering embroidered underwear for his palace guard extras and insisting on real bells at the end of prop bell pulls. Thalberg's designated function was to earn his company money, not to throw it away, and such a confrontation was inevitable. The failure of its resolution (not that others didn't discharge von Stroheim too) may be seen as an underlying motif to the entertainment film. It must make money; it must be good. Hollywood-Pinewood-Mosfilm-Cinecittà is a business and an art.

The transitional figure between Thalberg and today's producers is perhaps David O. Selznick, who learned the business from his father, moved through the big Hollywood studios, and from the mid-thirties into the sixties headed his own units, first within M-G-M, then culminating in Selznick International. Selznick, who organized his productions as an orchestra leader might, brought to his pictures extraordinary enthusiasm and energy, particularly at the writing stages. As each progressed, his near-maniacal attention to detail was sometimes the cause of firings, resignations, and anguish. *Gone With the Wind* (1939) is the great example. Selznick worried about the crease on Gable's pants, Tara's walkway, Vivien Leigh's breasts, and the accent of a bit player in the bazaar scene. He demanded daily reports on the progress of Max Steiner's musical score. One reason for the discharge of George Cukor, *Gone With the Wind*'s first director, was Cukor's displeasure with Selznick's daily dialogue changes.

Then there are minor producers such as Val Lewton—men who were in fact the creative, organizational, directorial centers of their films, working with writers, directors, and set designers toward maximum effect. Perhaps Gottfried Reinhardt tried to be another. You can read of his moral and artistic adventures in *Picture*,[13] by Lillian Ross, which documents the history of one film, *The Red Badge of Courage* (1951), with far more candor than the participants realized at the time, an occasion when Louis B. Mayer and Dore Schary were vying for studio power. Such producers, who divorce themselves from the charge of employers and associate their function rather with the interests and will of the production unit, are rare turncoats.

In some measure, the role of the producer has shifted with the demise of major studios. Because fewer features are made, and since each one demands a more independent organization, the producer's job has become more like that of other production workers. The contemporary producer is likely to be closer to a film's financing. Functioning as a packager, he is more inclined also to share in discussions and preliminary negotiations with a production's creative personnel. Since his commitment is firmer than that of the old studio-contracted figure, the producer is more inclined to engage personal interests in a script and to seek out appropriate actors, directors, perhaps rewriters.

On the other hand, from a director's viewpoint the replacement of major studios by conglomerates may work to his disadvantage. According to John Schlesinger (*Midnight Cowboy* [1969]; *Sunday, Bloody Sunday* [1971]), the single, tough studio head against whom he would once have been pitted has now been replaced with "middlemen who are constantly looking over their shoulder."

Because of their relation to so many facets of a film's progress, particularly the least-familiar part, the inception of the work, the producer figure carries with him a behind-the-scenes aura, a little like that of a *Broadway Melody* plot. Novelist Irwin Shaw uses a producer as his protagonist in *Evening in Byzantium,* as he employed a director in *Two Weeks in An-*

other Town. Even if his allegiances are predictable, the producer is an interesting figure, like other power brokers, when he is close to top authority. F. Scott Fitzgerald, less than successful as a Hollywood writer, used a producer as the subject of his final, incomplete novel, *The Last Tycoon*, based in part on a rather idealized version of Irving Thalberg.

A common practice is the alliance between producer, actor, and sometimes director or financier—for example, Newman-Foreman. In such arrangements each figure maintains his own interest while sharing in the talents of others. The venture is attractive to the star because he is assured of work and maintains script approval over as many properties as he chooses to consider. The producer is assured of the appeal and talents of his star, and the money men know their partners are as committed to profit as they. Something of an analogous situation exists on the part of the double functionary writer/producer, like Stirling Silliphant and Dore Schary. Some directors will produce their own films. In these cases the burden is not necessarily doubled at all, because each man commands the power to hire and to supervise however many underlings are necessary to carry out the day-to-day matters under negotiations. Rather, the director/producer is assured that these issues will be worked out in his favor, that if there is serious difference, it must be resolved between his own two heads, not himself and a single, tough studio boss.

One of the last old studio power bases has been at Paramount, where Robert Evans is production chief and Frank Yablans was, until early in 1975, president. In the old tradition, Evans requires that the option of final cut be his whoever the director may be, as for example with *The Godfather*. Although Evans and Yablans decided to "avoid the old Louis B. Mayer versus Irving Thalberg battle for power," each seemed desperately committed to achieving maximum personal credit for any film's financial success, always a risky business with stakes so high. A case in point is *The Great Gatsby* (1974), which easily offset its $6.4 million cost by requiring prerelease commitments from exhibitors. Given *Gatsby's* cool critical reception, such strategy was undoubtedly wise. In the same season other films released through Paramount (*Chinatown* [1974], *The Parallax View* [1974]) cost much less and were doing a far livelier business.

In 1972 George C. Scott directed his first film, *Rage*, for Warner Brothers, who to his mind cut and altered the final version beyond endurance. In *The Savage Is Loose* (1974) Scott produced, directed, performed, and heavily financed the venture for his own Campbell-Devon Productions. Then, rather than passing release prints on to a distributor for 35 or 40 per cent of the gross receipts, Scott sold the prints to theater chains outright. Avoiding the middleman, he guarantees production costs, collects about a million dollars for his own services, and foresees later profits in foreign sales, 16mm distribution, and airline rentals—these to finance further ventures over which he may again exercise total control.

Since production (the securing and employment of filmmaking money) and distribution (the strategy of designating film exhibition toward maximum financial gain) are so closely affiliated in our society, today's obvious debilitation of heavyweight production companies augurs serious change. Spectaculars will probably be done much more cheaply. Predictable types of genre are under constant reexamination (nostalgia films, youth films, porno films). More imaginatively, the enterprising filmmaker, like George C. Scott, will revert to merchandising his own product—harking back to D. W. Griffith's own roadshowing of the first great American feature, *The Birth of a Nation*.

RECOMMENDED READING

■ Interviews with twelve practicing Hollywood writers will be found in William Froug, *The Screenwriter Looks at the Screenwriter* (New York: Macmillan, 1972). A. J. Reynertson, *The Work of the Film Director* (New York: Hastings House, 1970) is the best book on direction. The reader might also see Don Livingston, *Film and the Director* (New York: G. P. Putnam's Sons, 1953). Raymond Chandler speaks of his Hollywood years in *Raymond Chandler Speaking* (London: H. Hamilton, 1962). Studies of several American stars and of Jean-Pierre Léaud will be found in *The Velvet Light Trap* no. 7.

■ On Marilyn Monroe, see the speculations of Norman Mailer, *Marilyn* (New York: Grosset & Dunlap, 1973) as well as Fred Guiles, *Norma Jean* (New York: McGraw-Hill, 1969) and Maurice Zolotow, *Marilyn Monroe* (New York: Harcourt Brace Jovanovich, 1960). The first book is inclined to develop factual material which may be found in the other volumes. See also Joseph Morella and Edward Z. Epstein, *Rebels: The Rebel Hero in Film* (New York: Citadel Press, 1971).

■ The definitive study of editing is Karel Reisz and Gavin Miller, *The Technique of Film Editing*, 2d rev. ed. (New York: Amphoto, 1968). For a clear rundown on 16mm editing mechanics, see Hugh Churchill, *Editing Handbook* (Belmont: Wadsworth, 1972).

■ F. Scott Fitzgerald's novel *The Last Tycoon* (New York: Charles Scribner's Sons, 1941) and Irwin Shaw's *Evening in Byzantium* (New York: Delacorte Press, 1973) and *Two Weeks in Another Town* (New York: Random House, 1960) tell tales of Hollywood.

The reader interested in pursuing various aspects of film production might consult:

■ John Alton, *Painting With Light* (New York: Macmillan, 1949)
■ Edward Carrick (Edward Anthony Craig), *Designing for Films* (New York: Studio, 1949)
■ Hans Eisler, *Composing for the Films* (New York: Oxford University Press, 1947)
■ Raymond Fielding, *The Technique of Special Effects in Cinematography* (New York: Focal, 1972)
■ Lenny Lipton, *Independent Filmmaking* (San Francisco: Straight Arrow, 1972)
■ Kurt London, *Film Music* (London: Faber and Faber, 1936)
■ Roger Manville and John Huntley, *The Technique of Film Music* (New York: Hastings House, 1957)

■ Vladimir Nilssen, *The Cinema as a Graphic Art* (London: Newnes, 1937)
■ Raymond Spottiswoode, *Film and Its Techniques* (Berkeley: University of California Press, 1951)

NOTES

1. Ingmar Bergman, Introduction to *Four Screenplays of Ingmar Bergman* (New York: Simon & Schuster, 1960).
2. Peter Bogdanovich, *Allan Dwan: The Last Pioneer* (New York: Praeger, 1971), p. 39.
3. Quoted in Stephen Farber, "The Writer in American Films," *Film Quarterly* 21 (Summer 1968) p. 7. Reprinted in A. J. Reynertson, *The Work of the Film Director* (New York: Hastings House, 1970), p. 234.
4. Quoted in Louis Marcolles, "A Conversation with Jean Renoir," *Sight and Sound* 31 (Spring 1962), p. 82. Reprinted in Reynertson, *Film Director*, p. 230.
5. Quoted in C. G. Crisp, *François Truffaut* (New York: Praeger, 1972).
6. Most of the cinematography references and anecdotes appear in Charles Higham, *Hollywood Cameramen* (Bloomington: Indiana University Press, 1970) and in Leonard Maltin, *Behind the Screen* (New York: Signet, 1971). Interviews with Leon Shamroy, Lee Garmes, William Daniels, James Wong Howe and Stanley Cortez appear in Higham. Arthur C. Miller is in both books, and Hal Mohr in Maltin.
7. Maltin, *Behind the Screen*, p. 79.
8. Charles Barr, "CinemaScope: Before and After," *Film Quarterly* 16, no. 4 (Summer 1963). Reprinted in Richard Dyer MacCann, *Film: A Montage of Theories* (New York: E. P. Dutton, 1966), pp. 318–28 and in Gerald Mast and Marshall Cohen, eds., *Film Theory and Criticism* (New York: Oxford University Press, 1974), pp. 120–46.
9. Josef von Sternberg, "More Light," *Sight and Sound* 25 (Autumn 1955) p. 72. Quoted in Reynertson, *Film Director*, p. 101.
10. Quoted in Higham, *Hollywood Cameramen*, pp. 40, 42.
11. *Ibid.*, p. 98.
12. *Ibid.*, pp. 109–10.
13. Lillian Ross, *Picture* (New York: Rinehart, 1952).

Part IV

**Film Theory
and Criticism**

15 ■ Reviewers and Critics

The popular success of the motion picture encouraged a journalistic response which came to exert increasing influence as more and more newspaper readers began going to the movies. The development of the feature film, with its increased costs, required longer theater runs and, in consequence, promotion. Promotion might be purchased through advertising or manipulated through public relations, such as press coverage of the antics of "stars." A prime ingredient in the major cities where films opened soon became "critical" enthusiasm.

REVIEWERS

Film criticism originated in periodicals, a routine journalist's assignment. After the first vigorous growth of film, it was considered, when appraised at all, either through the vocabularies and value judgments of the other arts or else as a noisy offspring among what came to be known as the "popular arts," and as such subject to standards of criticism different from those used to evaluate more traditional forms. The first position was epitomized by the poet Vachel Lindsay, who had been trained as an artist. In his book aptly titled *The Art of the Motion Picture,* published in 1915, Lindsay used examples from English prose and great painters in his consideration of the silent screen. His judgments on movie experience were fired with enthusiasm, tending toward broad responses and fanlike supports of favorite actresses, a position that is not far from some of today's newspaper writers.

Movies were "discovered" by the intellectual essayists of the twenties, such men as Edmund Wilson and Gilbert Seldes, and regarded as pristine, innocent, ebullient, qualities they associated with the comic strip, popular dance, vaudeville, and jazz. Jazz they understood to be Paul Whiteman's symphonic band playing the "Livery Stable Blues," and film was about equally well comprehended. Charlie Chaplin was particularly praised for combining music-hall traditions with the new art in a theatrical format that could be easily understood by everyone.

Major "criticism" of the film tended, in the thirties and forties, to be associated with successful reviewer-columnists, people like James Agee, who wrote for *Time, Life,* and *The Nation;* Otis Ferguson, a *New Republic* reviewer who covered other aspects of popular culture too; and Manny Farber, a painter who brought a keen eye for formal organization and visual detail to his columns in *The Nation* and *Cavalier,* and who continues to do so in, most recently, *Artforum.* Pauline Kael and Penelope Gilliat follow in their tradition at *The New Yorker.* Such writers all boast a concise, fluent journalist's style, which tends to be adjectival, personal, and image-evoking. Their function is to communicate an impression of recently viewed new films and to share their enthusiasm or repugnance in terms of our past experience—other films we all ought to have seen as well as the residue of books, plays, and sometimes paintings that make up our common heritage. Their attitudes toward a particular film are inclined to be expressed in vivid metaphors. Farber is especially talented at picture-evoking similes; Kael, at how a movie made her feel. Like other columnists, they seem to maintain fairly consistent rhetorical postures: Dwight MacDonald dwells on how much more humane and insightful were earlier filmmakers; John Simon, on the effrontery of most films to intrude themselves on his considered sensibility; Kael, righteously indignant either at the filmmakers or at the critics who have misunderstood the filmmakers.

Weekly or monthly columnists operate on the premise that we, the readers, have yet to see the film they advise us about. In this respect they carry the burdens of the daily newspaper reviewer and have to tell us enough about each film that their own evaluations make sense. We can decide whether we ourselves want to see a film by considering what reaction it provoked from the reviewer, whose past performances give his taste predictability within minor variation, like the expectations we would bring to a star's performance. It isn't necessary for us to agree with a writer in order to use him this way. As a matter of fact, many film buffs know that a new movie that raises the hackles of some particular reviewer will be just to their liking. To find your own benchmarks, it would be instructive to reread a number of critiques on a motion picture that you yourself have recently seen.

When we undertake such a project, we are often struck both by inaccuracies and by agreements among many reviewers. Since film critics surely bring no less acute an eye and mind to the viewing experience than the rest of mankind, it must be concluded that these errors serve as further reinforcement to the difficulties of retention, on single viewing, of many, many details. Writers must work too under the pressure of deadlines and length, although any good stylist will always give an unhurried appearance to his work. As sportswriter Red Smith once said, it's easy to write a column. You just sit down at the typewriter, open your wrist, and bleed.

The curious recurrence, in the different reviews, of certain phrases and factual details having to do with a production's history is testament to the practice of handing out throwaways—the pressbooks, information sheets, and performer-director-writer biographies that are distributed at special screenings for potential distributors and favored journalists. The extent to which many writers (Farber, MacDonald, Kael, Simon, and Gilliat are not among them) will make use of this material is less interesting to us as evidence of a critic's sloth than it is witness to a lack of individuality among the opinions we receive.

Another less attractive aspect of newspaper and periodical reviewing is the extent to which advertising may color a film's critical reception. Journalism schools, like film schools, have not successfully introduced ethical standards into the businesses they teach. It is sadly evident that advertising and editorial functions are not separated from one another in many magazines and newspapers. In this respect, the integrity of *The New Yorker* is an extraordinary exception to the rule. "Little magazines" and small-circulation journals are freer, too, from such corruptions, not through the inherent honesty of their editorial staffs but because they have no great block of advertising copy and revenue to seduce their ethics. At the opposite extreme, the *New York Times* is large and prestigious enough that advertisers can hardly afford not to display their wares there, and although power and prestige bring their own temptations, the rights of reviewers are somewhat safe.

Otherwise one is left with a vast wilderness of copy, the enthusiasms of which often bear curious parallels to the amount of advertising taken out for any particular new release. From the standpoint of money, it's hard to weigh what one man thinks against a full-page ad. Editorial confrontations are not charged with melodrama, like Ibsen's *The Master Builder* or Ayn Rand's *The Fountainhead*. Rather many publications, in the long run, will simply ease out the acerbic, independent critic, perhaps reassigning him to art or obituaries, where there are fewer advertisers. In his place is assigned a gusher, some film enthusiast who, like a radio or TV "critic," likes everything he sees, probably in all honesty. This way everyone is served: integrities intact, advertiser happy, publisher righteous. The old reviewer may even come to like obituaries or to learn something about art.

In today's world, the interrelationship of advertising and film is even further complicated by the corporate ownership of film production and distribution agencies. Just to cite two examples out of many, Paramount at this writing is no longer merely Paramount Pictures, but Paramount: A Gulf & Western Company. United Artists is United Artists Entertainment for Transamerica Corporation. Films are involved with vast conglomerates of automobile companies, book publishers, parking lots, distilleries, you name it. How reasonable it is, then, for a film to display prominently the identification of an airline when the heroine arrives at La Guardia, the label of a beer can in the kitchen or a soup can in a spaceship. The tie-ins have become as countless as pages of four-color ads in homemaking magazines, and a film producer can always plead that such brand identifications reinforce his film's authenticity. But you will not find these labels so often in the older movies, nor will they be remarked by most contemporary reviewers.

CRITICS

Another echelon of film evaluation is the small, specialized magazine, the circulation of which never passes twelve to fifteen thousand movie students, teachers, and enthusiasts (sometimes these categories are mutually exclusive, sometimes not). Such magazines operate on the presumption that a reader has seen not only a director's most recent film but *all* of his films—within the past two weeks. If Manny Farber may draw on a shared cultural inheritance of, say, Krazy Kat, Fats Waller, and The Band, the small film magazine is confident that our exposure to all of film history is boundless and encyclopedic.

Film-journal articles also direct their attentions toward broader issues than do reviews: retrospective considerations of director, actor, or studio; interviews; genre studies; historical research; technical developments; and sometimes aesthetic and theoretical issues. If a journal survives (no film magazine is immortal and many fail to reach adolescence), it will likely specialize its attentions, an editorial choice reflected first in the table of contents, then by way of advertising, if any. Thus, *Film Quarterly*, for example, which has tended toward general consideration of European and American commercial film since it was reincarnated from the old *Hollywood Quarterly*, now gives increasing attention to politically committed films and to the output of underdeveloped countries and continents. It has many book ads. *Film Society Review* directs itself to the kinds of movies that are useful to college and university film series programming and carries the advertising of 16mm film distributors. *Film Comment*, once a bastion of sociopolitical motion-picture issues, has turned increasingly toward contributions from abroad and structuralist approaches from the schools. *Film Culture*, which appears infrequently, may be dedicated either to the American underground or to Hollywood history, depending on who is editing a particular issue. And so on.

Most film evaluation by Americans tends to focus on the literary and theatrical aspects of the experience, whether in newspapers or journals. Even writers who would argue that the movies are a unique and distinctive art form may be found in practice to talk about them with very little reference to principles of formal organization or to qualities that might not be duplicated among the other arts. Just take any piece of writing on film, black out the titular and personal references, and read it as though it might be describing a current book or play. Usually the piece not only fits into such a category but does a creditable job of it. Of course, most writers on film, and movie reviewers for radio and TV, will give token recognition to the medium by a passing reference to the direction (which might apply equally well to theater), photography, and perhaps editing. These notices are usually composed of pat phrases. The photography is "static" or "fluid." Editing is either "smooth" or "frantic." If frantic, it's "self-conscious." For some reason, reviewers and critics like to say "jump cut" and "overacted." Such approaches irritate partisan movie enthusiasts and make film students gnash their teeth.

What one confronts in most reviews is an approach to the film as a narrative experience common to several media and in some respects equally accessible by each. At least, some part of the narrative is centrally basic as far as it may be described and organized in summary language. To this extent, what passes for criticism or reviewing (individual evaluative talents aside) is not simply a shadow of older forms but rather a kind of first, cautionary step toward verbalizing what goes on in a movie.

16 ▪ Getting at the Film Experience

At this point, we need to divide our attention between two aspects of film: what the narrative essence is, and how the critic may perceive it. The idea that narrative is common to several media is viable only as long as we allow it a sort of theoretical, corporeal independence, but narrative in film is not "visualized" oral stories, or books and plays "translated" into some different scheme for communicating them, like water poured into differently shaped pails—not so, at least, if we allow film its integrity and do not relegate it to a subordinate and merely derivative role. Film experience is somehow different. To locate this difference we are well advised to investigate the relationship between screen and story.

For example, Scott Bartlett is a successful, independent and experimental Bay Area filmmaker. His films (*Metanomen, Off/On, Lovemaking, Moon 69*) are short, intense collections of images, tending toward overlaid, partial abstractions and accompanied by insistent soundtracks, using electronic music or ragas. Where the films are effective with audiences, the reception may be quite powerful; one can literally hear the spectators moving through the experience—the quiet rustle and the absence of other sound that a filmmaker learns happily to identify when his movie is working.

I once told Bartlett that the films reminded me of Alfred Hitchcock, by reason of both filmmakers' abilities to lead the audience, by the nose, as it were, through a variety of feelings, some reassuring, some anxious, into a resolution. Bartlett tends to agree with everything one says to him but seemed genuinely to enjoy the likeness because it touched on a certain truth with respect to his unstoried work.

If images such as these, divorced from the usual handles we put on film, like "character" and "narrative," can evoke a sequential experience, then it must follow that film calls up and controls our feelings with something of the urgency of the storyteller at the campfire, without necessarily falling back on his words. (Other "nonnarrative" examples of the same capacity are Michael Snow's *Wavelength* [1966–67] and Bruce Conner's *A Movie* [1958].) Although "experimental" films are beyond the range of this book, they do point up the potential power and character of movie images existing plotless in time. Susan Sontag, referring to Ingmar Bergman in her essay "Against Interpretation," describes good film as "transparent." Her intention is to reject an inclination to read "meanings" into the movie images by gluing literary or psychological associations onto their appearance. The images resist interpretation because they are anarchically, stubbornly, intractably themselves, like Popeye the Sailor ("I yam what I yam") or e. e. cummings's snow, which doesn't give a soft, white damn where it falls.

Triggered by the issue of image *and* narrative, the movie-in-time *and* the movie-flat-on-a-screen, we encounter an even broader significance: the disparity between the conjunction of the thing represented (by the photographic propensities of the medium) and the way the thing represents itself (by film's linear organizational principles), which is a disparity in film's essence. In that melodramatic confrontation, which nobody ever really wins (for in this respect art is truly like life), there emerges a kind of theoretical seesaw. On it teeter sets of one-dimensional continua between certain polarities. These polarities measure the presence or absence of qualities usually associated with the entertainment film, and they interact as any given production tries to find its own particular balance between the extremes indicated here:

Story ——————————————————— No story
Audience ——————————————————— No audience
Depth illusion ——————————————————— No depth illusion
Time II ——————————————————— No Time II
Subject movement ——————————————————— No subject movement
Cuts ——————————————————— No cuts
Aggression ——————————————————— No aggression
Subject oriented ——————————————————— Not subject oriented
Formally oriented ——————————————————— Not formally oriented
Auteur presence ——————————————————— No *auteur* presence
Point of view ——————————————————— No point of view
Point of reference ——————————————————— No point of reference
Shared rhythms ——————————————————— No shared rhythms

Getting at the Film Experience ▪ **189**

Continuity ————————————————	No continuity
Use of tradition ———————————	Rejection of tradition
Camera movement ———————————	No camera movement
Real space ————————————————	Invented space
Transparency ————————————————	Referentiality
Determinist ————————————————	Aleatory

Purposely, these polarities have been arranged in no particular order. In fact, they *have* no sequence, for each set operates some way in any narrative film. They mark certain decisions made willfully or by default by the filmmaker. Repeated interrelation of any two or more will begin to establish intentions and uniqueness among different filmmakers, different schools of filmmaking, and different cultural traditions.

In the history of narrative film, some of these parameters have borne greater emphasis than others, but all are present. Many have been the subject of experimental projects based less on an interest in narrative than on the investigation of the formal limits of the film.

Most of the terms are self-explanatory, if not covered elsewhere in this volume. Of the rest, "aggression" refers to the filmmaker's attitude toward his audience (as discussed in Noël Burch's *Theory of Film Practice*[1]), whether his intentions are to attack his viewers with sound and image, to unsettle their preoccupations more obliquely, or perhaps to pat them on the psyche and reassure suspicions. Aggression is subject to the passage of time, like the author's presence discussed in Chapter 2. When Buñuel and Dali slit the girl's eyeball in *Un Chien Andalou* (1928), they regarded their image as a direct, primitive assault on the audience in the tradition of *épater les bourgeois*. Buñuel's action (it is he stropping the razor) still draws a gasp from viewers, one mixing rage, indignation and abhorrence, but it quickly becomes assimilated into our industrial-age sensibility of "kicks," just as department stores hired Dali to dress their Fifth Avenue windows in the Depression years. Now even Buñuel has mellowed. Today he believes our problems are not overpoweringly sex, religion, class, and inhibitions of feeling but the population explosion and ecology.

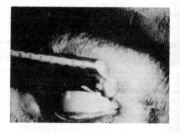

Even as frightful a sequence as this from *Un Chien Andalou* may evoke different audience responses in different eras.

The idea of "point of reference" is ambiguous. It may refer to a stable referential point in time (lacking in *Marienbad*), in space (partially obscured in the "Odessa Steps" sequence), or in credibility (absent in the films of Alain Robbe-Grillet). "Shared rhythms" refers to a relation of the editorial intelligence to its audience: whether images are maintained at a pace that corroborates or denies the expectations of the viewer.

An example of a film with "continuity" is *Lady Sings the Blues* (1972), despite the facts that it alternates stills and moving pictures, sepia tone and color and that it shows scenes of Billie Holiday (Diana Ross) singing in Carnegie Hall intercut with flashbacks of her as a child and flashforwards to newspaper clippings of her final arrest and death. Despite, too, that Billie Holiday was not in fact accompanied at Carnegie Hall by a large, silly orchestra, that she was never attacked by the Ku Klux Klan, that she knew many men who mistreated her, and that she wrote "God Bless the Child" with a white composer. (Note how easily one can slip into talking about films as if they were simply human events.)

"Use of tradition" refers to the way a filmmaker brings history to bear upon his films—both the human history we all share and the history of the movies. *The Birth of a Nation,* for example, presents an aggressively Southern view of the Civil War and Reconstruction. At the same time it was a seminal influence in the history of movies' narrative exposition. *Wind from the East* violently attacks the Griffith story and consequent film traditions while maintaining deeply felt convictions toward Marxism and revolution.

"Transparency" recalls the Susan Sontag proposition of the image seen only as itself. Its polarity would be a situation in which everything we experience has other meanings as well as its own, in which everything is a symbol, as in an orthodox Freudian interpretation of dreams. In fact, where this unhappy phenomenon occurs, it is apt to enlist Freudian images, sprung on the spectator like leering winks or elbows in the ribs.

A "determinist" film would be one in which every element has been preordained; "aleatory," one evolving out of uncertainty, chance, luck, or contingency. (Humor often rests on the meeting between improvisation and the inevitable, as suggested in Freud's essay on wit, or Bergson's on comedy.) In the broadest sense, no film can be completely subject to a filmmaker's control. Even the proverbial one-man film must adapt itself to a variety of audiences and viewing conditions. By the same token, no film is altogether open to the operations of chance, for some organizational principles will manage to insinuate themselves into its design at the viewing stage, if not earlier. In one respect, the ultimate formal polarities of film are light——dark; sound——no sound, as in "flicker" films, in which flashing screens play only on these variables.

The student may find these polarities helpful in furthering his personal access to "difficult" films as well as expanding his awareness of the more ordinary product. The value of the table rests in its neutrality. Neither

Getting at the Film Experience ▪ 191

the presence nor the absence of cuts, for example, is in itself "good" or "bad." More to the point is why either phenomenon takes place in a given production, how it furthers the apparent intentions of the film-maker, and whether its usefulness meshes successfully with other polarities. For instance, we associate heavily edited film with a strong formal impulse (Eisenstein). Long, unedited camera runs often give the impression of far less control over what happens on the screen. Yet the film-maker's manipulation of events may take place equally well *within* a shot —through subject movement, camera movement, and composition. In these respects he may have merely substituted one form of control for another. Understanding that no polarity exists independent of other considerations, the student may yet find profit in singling out two or three particular aspects of a given film the better to find his way into other, hidden passageways.

17 ▪ Theorists

Another way in which films may be considered consciously enlists philosophic and psychological concepts. These define just which polarities shall receive special attention and where, on the scale of each, a film "ought" to be located. The ontological issue is basic. Where does reality originate, inside the head or out? If outside (realism), the photographic commitments of motion pictures are reinforced. Doctrines of Siegfried Kracauer hold sway: matter over mind, or more explicitly, substance over form. The materiality of the world's surfaces sustains a pre-eminence that will resolve questions of order and organization in film, as elsewhere, without our imposition of design.

Realism is rooted in a kind of spiritual faith in the environment. Because a Marxist aesthetic, as it finally developed in the twentieth century, equates realism with apparent commitments to proletarian values (socialist realism), we find that a Marxist film theorist like Béla Balázs[2] rejects formal techniques of evoking interior states (like impressionist distortion and interior monologues) in favor of photographic realities. Equally suspect are any visibly stylized devices that deny the evidence of our senses by supplying what cannot be known through observation. By such a measure, the greatest subject is the human face, which may serve as an emotional map that registers what can be known—what ought to be known—about our feelings.

The commitment to the world also bars the use of highly involved and manipulative editing techniques, such as Eisenstein's; for these breaches of realism he was attacked as a "formalist" before the Soviet Central

Committee. The whole period of Russian silent film is interesting in this respect, for it was a time when many aesthetic issues, including more nonillusionistic, expressionist, and artificial techniques fought and lost on a political-aesthetic battlefield.

When one reads Kracauer's book *The Theory of Film*,[3] one may be surprised by examples the author cites in support of realist principles, not so much because the film sequences he commends are lacking in formal organization but rather because this design is disguised to the eye. Realist films, markedly those of Italian neorealism, do not ignore the formal aspects we have reviewed earlier—subject movement and camera movement, for instance. Rather, the Italians have chosen so to conceal their presence and function from the viewer that he is not distracted from his sympathetic absorption in issues of the stories. Filmmakers like Vittorio de Sica (*Shoe Shine* [1946]; *Umberto D* [1952]) and the early Luchino Visconti (*La Terra Trema* [1948]; *Bellissima* [1951]) never threw up inchoate gobs of photographed *realia* to our perception. Instead, they organized dramas in such ways that we overlook the formalities of organization because our attention is so held by the subject.

We are affected by Jean Renoir in a somewhat similar fashion. The movements of his camera and actors have the appearance of spontaneity and fortuity, particularly performers' entrances into and exits from the frame. In fact, closer examination of such movement—for example, the mobile camera shots cited from *The Rules of the Game*—reveals that the shots are very carefully timed, placed, and executed for dramatic purpose. He maintains the *appearance* of integrity in the space outside the frame. (An interesting experience is to run such involved shots backward on the projector. Entrances and exits, camera and subject movements become strikingly apparent, whereas, seen projected normally, they appear to happen quite casually, almost as if by chance, and one would tend to take them for granted.)

Another example would be certain films by Roberto Rossellini, particularly *Paisan* (1946) and *The Little Flowers of St. Francis* (1950). Here, particularly, Rossellini desaturated his plots of their emotional conventions and concentrated, episodically, on more subdued occasions of greater significance, a technique Antonioni carried further in the fifties: nondramatic moments of life that carry a subtler drama. Italian filmmakers seem to veer between two other poles: the restrained, nonheightened moment and Grand Opera.

The opposite of realism is idealism, the doctrine that what we know we only know by way of the mental life. Since the organs and techniques of perception are located in our heads, the extreme form of this notion, nominalism, argues that there are no universals, no general images outside the mind—a philosophy that leaves the photographer confined to his darkroom and the painter enclosed in a windowless studio, as far as relating their formal impulses to the world.

Rudolf Arnheim seeks to break through this enclosure by emphasizing those organizational principles in the subject matter of film that assume their form from the nature of the medium. In Arnheim's measure,[4] film's strengths lie in its limitations: the artificialities that lenses substitute for depth and perspective, the gray-scale equivalents to actual color, the flatness of a projected image, and the conditions of viewing. Such a position points up the visual, two-dimensional aspects of our screen experience, its likenesses to painting, which is really Arnheim's greater enthusiasm.

By calling attention to the formal attributes of film as these are organized and understood by eyes and ears—composition, for instance—Arnheim locates principles of design at the forefront of his attention, rather than what piece of material reality is being reproduced. Yet Arnheim is not a "formalist," for he places form in the service of illusionistic narrative exposition. What is interesting to him is how the flat, graphic movie elements may contribute to story by way of their design principles. For example, he cites an early moment in *Variety* (1925) when Emil Jannings appears as a prisoner. The bulk of his shoulder obscures our perception, its mass overpowering the screen composition, which includes a warden facing him across a desk. While we see the warden's face, Jannings is further depersonalized by his prison number, which looms on the back of the uniform.

Arnheim's early film interest developed in the time of silent German cinema. Because his examples are often drawn from these classics, and since synchronous sound seemed to him to deny the graphic elements on which movies thrived aesthetically, we are inclined to associate *Film as Art* with the German traditions, particularly expressionism; the maker of silent films was no more bound than any painter to the integrity of surface reality. Although Arnheim's principles apply with equal validity to other film styles (see his remarks on *Red Desert* quoted earlier), the confrontation between him and Kracauer in terms of each's movie enthusiasms serves to underline certain tendencies of the two philosophic positions, realism and idealism, with reference to locations on our several polarities.

Arnheim once said that he used to argue with Kracauer, who was an old friend, about how we understood the screen image. Kracauer maintained that if we saw a cat on the screen, it was a cat, pure and simple: unique, vivid, literal, and useful to the story in the way that it was treated—kicked, petted, or ignored. Arnheim, however, emphasized the catness of the cat. This quality was immediately perceptible to a viewer because, in Arnheim's terms, our eyes are but an outpost of the brain and perform its conceptual functions at the instant of perception. By this token, although all images are vivid and tangibly real, the viewer is not committed only to their illusionary moment (Time II), as if the screen were life itself; simultaneously he generalizes, calling on his sensory-mental resources to integrate each visual experience into a matrix of meaning in terms of the image's gestalt: its principles of design and order, its "meaning as a whole." To put it in other terms, when a child lives in a room with a photo of the Parthenon on the wall, he responds not to the Parthenon but to the photo.

This disagreement evokes again our melodramatic confrontations between polarities—what we called the conjunction of thing represented (the photographic propensities of the medium) and the way the thing represents itself (its organizational principles). Every artist must adopt a strategy satisfactory to himself by which he may impose formalist skills on the raw materials of reality; if he is a film artist, the possibilities of affecting these raw materials are modulated by the characteristics of photography and of motion-picture film.

André Bazin differs from Siegfried Kracauer and Rudolf Arnheim in that he is interested in grounding his assertions less on a realist/idealist continuum than on film and theater history and, to some extent, Catholicism. Yet like Kracauer, Bazin is attracted to the "epidermis of reality" aspects of the film experience. Like Arnheim, he is interested in formal elements and the circumstances of film's perception. His broad and deep film background is that of a serious, enthusiastic critic and is enriched by his humanity, his nationality, his experience outside the moviehouse.

Bazin argues that movies have historically evolved in the direction of their earliest conception: a simulation of reality. Wide-screen, colored, stereophonic images only more closely approximate what movies have always sought. He traces screen development in terms of two traditions: that of the cut (Griffith, Eisenstein) and the long take (von Stroheim, Murnau). By this measure, the advent of sound, with its effects on film editing, did not destroy a tradition but simply nudged film onto an alternative path: that of the continuous, sometimes moving camera. Since his sympathies lie toward noninterrupted, photographic illusion, Bazin finds that this juncture was not destructive; in fact he believes it salutory.

In Bazin's mind, film that approached the dramatic conditions of live theater was particularly interesting. Griffith's tradition of editing, he said, had imposed rigidly doctrinaire dramatic perceptions on the spectator. The director-editor told us what to see and how long to watch it. He pointed out details. If two or more actors were in conversation, the camera-angle changes from one to another gave us little latitude in deciding for ourselves what moments, faces, and movements might be singled out for personal attention.

This condition was not true on the stage, where although a director might use his own skills to shape audience perception (as with set design, actors' movement, and lighting, a condition especially evident at the Comédie Française), still a viewer enjoyed freedoms of perception that were inhibited only by his distance from the actors. Sound films, particularly those that emphasized the long, deep shot facilitated by lighting in depth and wide-angle lenses, combined the freedoms of a proscenium with visual acuities that came from the greatly enlarged image. Here the spectator was free to engage himself in the dramatic conditions, and the very ambiguities that encouraged his involvement tended to "modernize" the film aesthetic by including audience in the performance, somewhat in the manner of contemporary theater and music.

As the long, narrow screen aspect ratios of the fifties lost their novelty and became more subject to experimentation, they came to be seen to reinforce Bazin's earlier enthusiasm for depth staging. As we noted before, each type of screen ratio imposes particular limitations on the cameraman. In addition, the wide screen field of view creates too sharp and dysfunctional an edited jounce as we move from farther to nearer space; close-ups particularly, since they usually single out solitary objects for consideration, are difficult to compose, except for women lying down.

This condition has diminished the number of shots, hence cuts, in most wide-screen films. It has also affected the character of space movements, except those accomplished by mobile cameras, the motion of which is continuous rather than produced by cutting. In compensation, photographers have often composed shots so that we may enjoy close-up and long shot, or sometimes even more complicated combinations of actors and objects, in a single composition, by locating people nearer to and farther from the lens. (A common design these days is the old medium shot so composed that one face is close-up on screen left, the other backed away at screen right.) Such techniques allow us to enjoy several angles in one while yet maintaining the Bazinian freedom of selection. Citing a moment on the older 3:4 screen, Bazin emphasizes this narrative scheme at the end of William Wyler's version of *The Little Foxes* (1941), originally a Broadway play. In the background, Herbert Marshall is struggling up the stairs to get his heart medicine after the onset of an attack. In the foreground sits his wife, Bette Davis, motionless. She faces the camera so that we may watch her expression—vicious yet torn by conflict.

As we have noted before, the technique of foreground-background composition is common to theatrical staging; it also appears in the work of such turn-of-the-century illustrators as Charles Dana Gibson. It also works well in film. Nonetheless, the composition remains spatially staid, however its participants may move. (Poor Herbert Marshall falls down the stairs.) And most camera shifts in such an ordering have become rather conventionalized too: tracking past close-up faces that slip off the side of the frame looking carefully away from the camera, for example.

However, some directors have cut the wide-angle, wide-screen shot more uninhibitedly. In *Theory of Film Practice,* Noël Burch uses the example of Alain Resnais in *Last Year at Marienbad.* During an evening scene where Delphine Seyrig and Giorgio Albertazzi are standing at a long bar, Resnais repeatedly intercuts another shot—one of Delphine Seyrig alone in her bedroom. The bedroom scene is very white, accentuated by costume, decor, and exposure, and it is metrically flashed before us in shots of carefully measured duration, first 9 frames, then 8, 8, 8, 16, 24, 26, 24, 24, 24, 24, 72. The experience is somewhat like viewing a flicker film with slight variations, but complicated by images dense in visual information.

What is interesting and special about Resnais's sequence is his decision about what shall be varied, what held constant. In orthodox joinings of two shots by a cut, either we move in space (as from long to medium shot) or else we break one sequence and go on to the next, in which case dramatic tempo is conjoined with the images. Here, Resnais maintains a constancy of spatial perspective (the bedroom scene is somewhat closer, but both are filmed straight on) while varying exposure, length (Time I), and (in the context of his story) meaning. As Burch says, Resnais's control over his bedroom flashes is tantalizing. At first they are very rapid, then increased in duration, in a sort of emotion-flecked progression.

Our response mingles an energetic effort to *read* the second image (for it doesn't stay on screen long enough to betray all its secrets) with a simultaneous attempt to account for the bedroom's appearing at all. The editing is not explained by narrative context or by dialogue. Resnais concentrates our attention by maintaining silence just as he holds distance constant, intensifying his intention by diminishing the screen variables. Is the character played by Delphine Seyrig hallucinating? (She never has seemed very stable.) Is it a kind of flicker-flashback? Do the two moments exist somehow side by side? Is Albertazzi silently imposing the bedroom image on her consciousness in the bar? All these possibilities occur as the moment passes us. In this particular movie, they are all equally true, for *Last Year at Marienbad* is far to the right on the point-of-reference continuum. The sequence concludes with Albertazzi inhabiting Seyrig's bedroom shot, and Seyrig screaming, then dropping a glass in the bar.

Another way in which wide screen may affect spatial understandings is through manipulations of our visual points of reference. We judge perspective by some specific image within any greater composition, as Arnheim notes. This serves as a measure against which to presume distance and relative size. A director may, for example, show us a self-enclosed world and then introduce an altogether different perspective by moving it, thus revealing that we had been looking at the scene reflected in a mirror on hinges, say. Or he may begin with a close-up: a truck, for instance, and then drive it away, providing us with an altogether different vantage. Such tactics may simply substitute object movement for the cut, but in the measure that they jar our perceptions by the recognition of our spatial misconception, the maneuvers can serve additional purposes.

One of these is to reinforce special formal aspects of the large image. Another is to supply purpose to the visual event, giving it a kind of propulsive meaning, as can be done with a cut.

Such moments show decisions on the filmmaker's part, the kind of decisions to which Truffaut referred in his definition of the complete director. In such cases, the decisions define an attitude toward narrative in terms of shots and cuts, space and time. They meet many ulterior designs of the sophisticated filmmaker and of the theorists we have cited. As with Eisenstein, there is a dislocation of audience perceptions and understandings. (It may be elicited in other ways, too, like maneuvering our expectations of where a cut will match or a screen position reappear.) As in Griffith's films, our perceptions are controlled. Yet in satisfaction of Kracauer, the exterior world remains intact. For Bazin, the narrative scheme reflects a theatrical point of view, and Arnheim's formalities of perception are maintained.

18 ■ *Auteur* Criticism

A critical position that originated among the French and has found an ideological haven in American classrooms with reference to American film history may further illuminate earlier mentions of "directorial presence." This approach uses the concept of *auteur,* French for author, although the French conceive authorship in broader fashion than we.

Perhaps the reader has noticed that on many occasions we employed the vaguer word *filmmaker* when *director* might have been used. Our intention was explicated in a previous chapter—namely, that each film is uniquely defined by some particular vision, which may or may not be located in the sensibilities of its director. By our measure, every film enjoys authorship—good or poor, complete or partial, coherent or fragmented, personal or anonymous—but who the author is will vary with a crew's different production skills, and authorship will always extend somewhat from the director out to other personnel.

François Truffaut was responsible for the origins of the *auteur* notion as a critical premise. A violently opinionated and ardent film critic before becoming a director, Truffaut published a piece for the young *Cahiers du Cinéma* called "A Certain Tendency of French Cinema," in January, 1954.[5] In it, he called scornful attention to the domination by scriptwriters with literary inclinations of his country's "tradition of quality," a derogatory term he used to describe films with presumptuous ambition.

Film, argued Truffaut, is diminished in the measure that its shooting is subordinated to production scripts that only invoke what are essentially prose and theater techniques, forcing the final film into a mold that fossilizes its vitalities and deadens any stylistic verve. For Truffaut, the "tradition of quality" was a film inheritance that placed the literary work in a position of unreasonable pre-eminence, making film servant to another form.

With these dispositions, Truffaut criticized studio-bound productions, adaptations, conventional acting techniques, certain writer-director teams, and a kind of stultifying atmosphere, which, he felt, compared poorly with the energies and innovations of Italian neorealism and the vitalities of the American film. In consequence, he called for location shooting free of the restrictions imposed by studio interiors, more original scripts to serve as story bases, a looser approach to acting and directing, directors who originated their own material, and the opportunity for new talents to emerge. The old guard he despised were respected figures like René Clair, Jean Delannoy, Yves Allégret, René Clément, and Claude Autant-Lara. He applauded individual, innovative talents such as Jean Renoir, Jacques Becker, and Jean Cocteau.

Truffaut's barrage had several eventual effects. It helped to codify an editorial position on the part of *Cahiers du Cinéma,* which had been recently founded by André Bazin and Doniol-Valcroze. It was an early fusillade in the underground skirmishes of criticism and production preparations out of which the French New Wave finally erupted late in the fifties. And it initiated what developed into a critical ideology about film authorship.

Truffaut's strategy was mostly polemic. He wanted to replace certain highly regarded French cinema figures with others, and he related true quality to an individuality both of personality and the overseeing of a film's production. The loathed "tradition of quality" figures were those who, first, shared their responsibilities like factory workers and, second, let a shooting script so dominate later production stages, where it was in the hands of personnel unknown even to the scriptwriter, that the fresh air of imagination might never touch a production at the very time when it could most creatively be affected: while the film was being made.

By the end of the fifties, *auterism* (Truffaut's term, which emphasized his polemic intentions, was *la politique des auteurs*) had developed into lists of names, and the lists reflected enthusiasms of the young French critics, colored by their access to the Cinémathèque Française. This exceptional film archive and theater offered the Parisian film buff a utopian program of constantly changing features, many American, which had been unavailable to the French all during World War II and were greedily absorbed by Europe after the Armistice.

Cahiers writers organized the Truffaut enthusiasm into a basis for critical adjudication. His proposition that the director ought to be writer as well was translated into a prototypical director who was central, authorial agency to his film, a concept that has always been honored in word if not in deed and is clearly true of most first-class filmmakers.

Cahiers' judgments became exercises in appreciation, essays of enthusiasm. Writers directed their attentions to personally favorite directors. By extension, the new product of any favorite director became a favorite film, since the director was the central object of interest. Writing critically of the ideology, Bazin said that in the equation

$$\text{Author} + \text{Subject} = \text{Work}$$

the *Cahiers* critics were omitting "Subject."[6]

Where did the presence of the director lie in his material? Critics found it necessary to distinguish the visibility of personal style from: (a) other picture credits; (b) stylization imposed on the film by period and place ("thirties," "Paramount"); (c) the stylizations (iconography, dialogue, plot) of genre. As one became more familiar with a particular personality, his accumulated work assumed a kind of pattern, each film taking on the resonances of earlier work. As Jean Renoir was quoted as saying, a filmmaker made the same movie again and again. The statement was hardly an admission of imaginative dearth but rather testimony to the coherence of a filmmaker's private vision and the variable strategies he used to reassert his values. It was another way of expressing something his own father had told him. Pierre Auguste Renoir, the great impressionist painter, once said he wished he had been permitted to paint the same picture over and over again, all his life.

Such a position, while it does not derogate subject matter, places it in a certain subordination to formal organization. While hardly unique to France, the affirmation is especially Gallic in the measure that it stresses how a thing is accomplished, distinguishing precisely between life (the subject) and art (its treatment). All life well conducted has style, but style *becomes* the subject matter as life is used by the painter, novelist, filmmaker, and poet. In the measure that he defines his work uniquely, the style expresses the man.

In the crest of Truffaut's first polemic wave, the applications of *auteurism* led to rankings, another passion of the French. A writer, Michael Wilmington, has compiled a summary of the *Cahiers* enthusiasms between 1954 and 1968. It is based on the magazine's "ten-best" proclamations, an annual event through 1968, chosen each year from films that enjoyed a general release in Paris during each preceding year (hence some low grades for certain directors—like Renoir—because they were less active or less available during the period). Wilmington also qualified the consistency of his notations in terms of changes among the magazine's staff itself over a fourteen-year period, variance in popularity of a particular director, momentary enthusiasms, and his own occasional subjectivity in the compilation. Here is his list:[7]

La *Politique des Auteurs* (1954–68)

1. Max Ophuls
2. Jean-Luc Godard
3. Robert Bresson
4. Carl Dreyer
5. Luis Buñuel
6. Orson Welles
7. Kenji Mizoguchi
8. Howard Hawks
9. Alfred Hitchcock
10. Ingmar Bergman
11. Alain Resnais
12. Jacques Tati
13. Charles Chaplin
14. Jean Renoir
15. Roberto Rossellini
16. Jacques Rivette
17. François Truffaut
18. Luchino Visconti
19. Jean Rouch
20. Michelangelo Antonioni
21. Alexandre Astruc
22. Jacques Becker
23. Federico Fellini
24. Fritz Lang
25. Jerry Lewis
26. Nicholas Ray
27. John Ford
28. Jacques Demy
29. Elia Kazan
30. Otto Preminger
31. Agnès Varda
32. Samuel Fuller
33. Robert Aldrich
34. Eric Rohmer
35. Joseph Losey

What is one to make of this list? The names are about equally English-American and French (some directors are vagabonds; it is difficult and perhaps foolish to categorize them by country), followed by a contingent of Italians. The early notations are arguably apt or understandable in terms of *Cahiers*'s critics-turned-directors. But Howard Hawks nineteen places above John Ford? Charles Chaplin a greater director than Antonioni? Max Ophuls the best of them all? Visconti ahead of Fritz Lang? What is Jerry Lewis doing there? And Elia Kazan. Samuel Fuller?

During the mid-sixties, *Cahiers,* like other magazines and film itself, was politicized. Its own situation was accentuated by its essentially apolitical posture traditionally and its feuds with a Marxist film journal, *Positif.* In recent years it has abandoned earlier designations of *auteur,* while conferring the title on figures from the past like Dziga Vertov, as well as printing the scientifically oriented analytic investigations of Christian Metz (see pp. 220–22). François Truffaut resigned his by-then-figurehead position on the editorial masthead, explaining:

It was not a disagreement. My name no longer represented the basic tenets of the magazine. When I worked on *Cahiers,* it was another era. We spoke of films only from the angle of their relative beauty. Today at *Cahiers,* they do a Marxist-Leninist analysis of films. Readership of the magazine is limited to university graduates. As for me, I have never read a single line of Marx.[8]

The film critic Andrew Sarris was responsible, more than any other figure, in popularizing the premises of *auteur* criticism in this country. In retrospect, his seems almost a Reformation, its bibles first *Film Culture*

Jerry Lewis seen from the French perspective, not as a slapstick spastic, but as a notable director of comedies touched with surrealism.

and the *Village Voice,* then a book, *American Cinema,*[9] which constituted a personal ranking of the country's directing personalities accompanied by evaluative filmographies for each.

Traditionally, the French have been especially enthusiastic of things American, responding earlier than we to this country's arts and popular culture, and often with special insights. They were keenly interested in the American wilderness and the opening of the West. Recall the popularity of the Arizona Jim (pronounced *Arezona zsheem*) pulp series in Renoir's *The Crime of Monsieur Lange* (1935). It was the French, led by Hughes Panassié, who understood that American jazz was not ephemeral, speakeasy entertainment but a serious, complicated, and original music. Panassié began to make lists. The French regarded Faulkner's *Sanctuary* as a serious work of art in the thirties when it was seen here as commercial sensationalism. The French understood the link of American slapstick and the Marx Brothers with surrealism. André Gide was enthusiastic about the work of Dashiell Hammett. And so forth.

If, then, one is confronted with names such as Jerry Lewis, Nicholas Ray, Elia Kazan, Samuel Fuller, and Robert Aldrich, plus special ranking for Alfred Hitchcock, the matter bears special investigation, which Sarris undertook. It was not only the critical premises of *la politique des auteurs* that might be examined but their particular enthusiasms too.

Just as Truffaut had argued that the "tradition of quality" in French film had nothing at all to do with noteworthy accomplishment, despite its pompous literary values, American styles became subject to re-examination. We have, since the advent of sound, often called on the reputable vehicles of stage and prose for subject matter in movies: "good" books, "important" plays. The directors of such adaptations often enjoyed special esteem, in part because of a presumed ability to reconcile sensibilities between two different worlds.

Now it was suggested that the merits of a film might not lie in story as judged from the perspectives of other idioms. Instead, the less ambitious, less script-bound, often less heavily financed film could merit greater concern. Manny Farber,[10] in fact, had argued for years that movies were most truly movies in moments of mimed action, which we were most likely to find among raunchy genre pieces: detective films, comedies, westerns, and gangster thrillers. The understanding is implicit, too, in Pauline Kael's enthusiasm for the unpretentious, entertaining Hollywood film, regardless of her outrage at the extremes of *auteurism*. In this respect, Sarris's "movement" only accelerated dispositions of insightful American criticism, just as its best writers had always identified and described the more interesting if little-known directors: James Agee writing about Val Lewton, for example, or Manny Farber about Preston Sturges.

The Hollywood director's personal imprint on a studio product differed from that of foreign directors. The circumstances were unlike. More often, the man in Los Angeles was assigned a script and production crew and was likely to be pulled off and committed to another project as soon as shooting was completed, particularly true as one worked back into the first two decades of the sound era, when the studios were in their heyday and contracted directors at their most docile. How, then, was the director who didn't write his script and couldn't affect its editing and didn't hire its stars to be isolated from his work and identified as a personality? Sarris confronted this quandary by establishing a new premise in the application of *auteurism* to America. The director's presence was often to be understood in tensions between his material and himself—as if an improvising musician of special talent were given a piece of particularly unmalleable music, like an aria out of *Naughty Marietta,* and told, "Here, man, cut this."

Such a critical posture tended to emphasize those aspects of a production that presented themselves to the director-when-in-charge—namely, camera angle, screen composition, control of acting performance, the pacing of a shot (how it reads before, rather than after, it is edited), the interpolation of special props or dialogue, or mannerisms, and any singular tone that might be located throughout.

When a director impresses himself upon a *given* body of material, he is more inclined to express attitudes toward the material rather than through it. Goethe observed that imitation is the lowest stage of art. Manner arises when the artist expresses himself. Style is beyond imitation and subjective manner.

Such distinctions ask us to separate the notion of directorial presence from that of stylistic presence in a film, to reintroduce Film in Bazin's equation, at least if we find a film more interesting than its maker. One of the problems of personality-prone *auteurism* in practice has proved to be personality. In recent years, I have worked with a graduate seminar to apply tenets of *auteur* theory to minor works by such directors as Samuel Fuller, Budd Boetticher, and Don Siegel. Clearly it was possible to identify personally held attitudes toward genre—how, for example, Indians or Mafia figures are treated. After viewing as much of a director's total output as was available and familiarizing ourselves with some biographical facts, we sought to construct a pattern of consistencies common to the different film titles—Howard Hawks's treatment of women, for instance. Thus, it is argued, the personality of the *auteur* emerges: a portrait written by way of the values implicit in his attitudes and the manner of their expression. But the possibilities of such personality construction as a critical tool must at some point confront the question of how one feels about different personalities. This may well prove to be a matter of taste somewhat independent of formal film aesthetics. Some personalities are just more agreeable than others.

Consider Alfred Hitchcock. While he has been highly applauded, there remain some critics who hold strong reservations about Hitchcock's attitudes while retaining respect for his work. Each of us must sometimes make distinctions between how a movie affects us and how we feel about being affected that way. How the effect is achieved will often resolve into considerations of style. Some stylists delight in calling attention to their own skills. Hitchcock enjoys poking fun at his techniques. Other men operate more secretly, reducing the visibility of their presence for the sake of a kind of submerged intention buried in the interstices of the material.

In this respect, it may be interesting to investigate some ways a director will use his material, openly or not, to express values we would not experience unless we saw the film, just as learning something about any piece of music will not take the place of hearing the music itself.

The earliest filmmakers enjoyed the advantages of primitivism. When we view a film by Thomas Ince or Mack Sennett, its character is defined in large measure by naïve autonomy. It refers back to little beyond itself, and certainly not with any sophistication. Like a painting by Grandma Moses, it gives the impression (sometimes with more skill than is immediately evident) of having spontaneously created the form it inhabits.

The polar extreme to this kind of filmmaker would be Jean-Luc Godard at the tail end of his "bourgeois" period, when he was erupting against an entire tradition of film history while operating within its regimen. *Pierrot le Fou*, for instance, is not just a substructured detective story. It is laden with references to earlier films and filmmakers, the way that T. S. Eliot quotes or paraphrases Webster, Shakespeare, Pound, and Ovid in *The Waste Land*.

Ferdinand (Jean-Paul Belmondo) faces the audience and tells them that he has thought up a plot for a novel which would describe, not peoples' lives, but life itself, what exists between peoples' lives: space, sound, colors. When he is saying this, Ferdinand imitates Michel Simon, thus paying a small homage to the actor, referring to *La Chienne* (the Renoir film of which Ferdinand has just told the story) and drawing a parallel between Simon's story there and the story of Ferdinand and Marianne (Anna Karina): a man drawn by a girl into an odd adventure. In addition, Ferdinand's words not only express his wish to know reality more completely, but show, with allusion to Joyce, the problems of literature and Cinema as a means of expression, and stress a general tendency in Godard's style, revealing at the same time one of the most direct and immediate meanings of *Pierrot le Fou*. This enormous accumulation of references in a single static shot which lasts no more than thirty seconds exemplifies the structure of the film and its multiplicity of resonances.[11]

In one scene, Samuel Fuller (playing himself) appears at a Parisian party attended by Ferdinand and explains his own understanding of cinema: "The film is like a battleground: love, hate, action, violence, death . . . In one word, emotion." The little love song that Marianne sings to Ferdinand in her apartment may be likened to Catherine singing to Jules and Jim in Truffaut's film, only Godard implies that Marianne has just killed a man in the next room, stabbing him in the neck with a pair of scissors.

Similarly, in *Weekend,* Godard throws in an "Arizona Jules" caption, referring simultaneously to Renoir's *The Crime of Monsieur Lange* and *Jules and Jim* while asking us to connect the family/community spirit of those films with his own exposé intentions. There is an effort at communication represented as "Battleship Potemkin calling The Searchers," the latter a reference to a John Ford film of the fifties and suggesting Godard's ironic vision of reconciliation between two cultures. Other names pass in fleeting evocation: Johnny Guitar (a favorite film by Nicholas Ray), Gosta Berling (Mauritz Stiller's 1924 vehicle for Greta Garbo).

Godard is like a churning battleground of old images and names, always presuming that film is the agency of reconceiving the past for future effect. In *Breathless* (1959), when Belmondo studies a movie poster of Humphrey Bogart, then wipes his mouth in a Gallic version of a Bogie grimace, we are witnessing no facile tribute to a favorite genre but are party to the impossibility of a young man's translating movies into life or surviving long on their characterizations. Jean Seberg "picks up" the gesture from Belmondo when he dies.

Godard's attitude-striking is particularly visible. His essays (often written under the name "Hans Lucas" as one of the first *Cahiers du Cinéma* critics) identify similar dispositions on the part of other directors, amidst a barrage of puns, triple entendres, and literary allusions. He sees, for example, the relation of camera to subject not so much as an expository technique as a moral issue. In fact, he makes no distinction between the two. Commenting on a popular film by Claude Chabrol, *The Cousins* (1959), Godard writes:

Almost constantly in pursuit of the characters, Chabrol's big studio camera hunts the actors down, with both cruelty and tenderness, in all four corners of Bernard Evein's astonishing decor. Like some great beast it suspends an invisible menace over Juliette Mayniel's pretty head, forces Jean-Claude Brialy to unmask the great game, or imprisons Gérard Blain under double key with a fantastic circular movement of the camera. When I say that Chabrol gives me the impression of having invented the pan—as Alain Resnais invented the track, Griffith the close-up and Ophuls reframing—I can speak no greater praise.[12]

In a similar vein, Godard connects a director's relation with his camera to his sense of script, world, and causality:

Broadly speaking, there are two kinds of filmmakers. Those who walk along the streets with their heads down, and those who walk with their heads up. In order to see what is going on around them, the former are obliged to raise their heads suddenly and often, turning to the left and then the right, embracing the field of vision in a series of glances. They *see*. The latter see nothing, they *look*, fixing their attention on the precise point which interests them. When the former are shooting, their framing is roomy and fluid (Rossellini), whereas with the latter it is narrowed down to the last millimetre (Hitchcock). With the former (Welles), one

**Jean-Paul Belmondo
in Godard's *Breathless*.**

finds a script construction which may be loose, but is remarkably open to the temptations of chance; with the latter (Lang), camera movement not only of incredible precision in the set, but possessing their own abstract value as movements in space. Bergman, on the whole, belongs to the first group, to the cinema of freedom; Visconti to the second, the cinema of rigor.[13]

Such attitudes ask us to revise our understanding that "the style is the man" to include deeper levels of characterization, for Godard is not speaking about "Look ma, no hands" pyrotechnics but the essential, subconscious layers of human nature. In his own case, moral fervor led Godard to break sharply with the entire heritage of entertainment film and, in doing so, with all of his intellectual allusions and image references. The double and triple meanings have been replaced by more concentrated references to media characteristics, like color and movement, and to a didactic dialectic.

It is often possible to find the director's presence in a film by thinking in terms of two or more elements operating either sympathetically or at odds (but always intentionally so) at any given moment. Sometimes these elements may be made up of two or more of our parameters, sometimes variations on one, but a director often defines himself and shapes his material through comparison and contrast.

Previously we have considered such techniques as derived from literary syntax—Kerensky and the peacock as a simile, for example. Even these cases are not without their novelistic equivalents. A famous scene in Erich von Stroheim's *Greed*, for example, is the wedding. A young couple pledge their vows in the living room of the bride's family, while through the window we view the hearse and mourners of a passing funeral. But the image is taken directly out of *Greed*'s source, *McTeague*, by Frank Norris. Stroheim was extremely faithful in his adaptation.

John Ford is a good example of the studio director who defined himself over a long career by way of story and performance. It is possible to speak of a kind of Fordian world, just as we may think of a world of Preston Sturges or, vulgarly, the world of Walt Disney. Each is peopled by a repertory group of players, etched sharply by face, speech, and mannerism, although in every case, the actors bring certain consistencies of behavior from picture to picture. They carry their motives in their makeup kit.

In Ford's case, the sound films were inhabited by John Wayne, Ward Bond (different from his policeman's role for Huston in *The Maltese Falcon*), Victor McLaglen, Maureen O'Hara, Woody Strode. His is an interesting director's career to look at, because it has many of the qualities we associate with a sharing of credits for creative work. Many of his films were done with one writer, Dudley Nichols, in the thirties—*The Lost Patrol* (1933), *The Informer* (1935), and *The Long Voyage Home* (1940) among them. He had excellent cameramen, whose distinctive visual tem-

John Wayne, a star in John Ford's stock company, in *The Man Who Shot Liberty Valance*, one of Ford's many Westerns. *(Credit: Paramount)*

peraments certainly cast individual auras over different films. Compare Arthur Miller (*Tobacco Road* [1941]) with Gregg Toland (*The Long Voyage Home*).

His films were cast with stars. (Henry Fonda is another Ford player.) Also the Ford stories fall into certain categories. His Irish proclivities appear in titles like *The Informer, The Quiet Man* (1952), and *The Plough and the Stars* (1936). "When in doubt," Ford said, "make a western": *Stagecoach* (1939); *My Darling Clementine* (1946); *Fort Apache* (1948). Sometimes the western material merges with elements of American history, as in *The Man Who Shot Liberty Valance* (1962). Ford was interested in culturally and historically defined human relations, like the persecution of the American Indian in *Cheyenne Autumn* (1964). Sometimes more storybook history was treated: *Young Mr. Lincoln* (1939); the Civil War sequence in *How the West Was Won* (1962). Ford also adapted best-selling novels to film, like *The Grapes of Wrath* (1940), *How Green Was My Valley* (1941), and *The Last Hurrah* (1958).

210 ■ Film Theory and Criticism

Through much of this material, Ford seems to play variations on those simplifications of moral issues that accompany war, the frontier, and economic strife. A man's behavior may range from John Wayne's as the Ringo Kid in *Stagecoach*, avenging personal code in a typical shoot-out, to Victor McLaglen's as the tormented Gypo in *The Informer* who has betrayed his friend and the Cause through ignorance and drink. In the elaborated Ford moral code, a figure is required to behave in some fashion prescribed by his experience of old traditions slipping away, like Wayne in *The Man Who Shot Liberty Valance*, or again as Colonel Marlow in *The Horse Soldiers* (1959). Under these conditions, a character will freely acknowledge the inherent, anomalous absurdity of his actions, which likely will bring disaster upon himself and even others, and might better be avoided. But to act otherwise would deny the integrity of the past; that is unthinkable.

Working with such material, Ford must often tread a fine line between convention and personal conviction. Referring back to our use-of-tradition——rejection-of-tradition polarity, we might say that he interplays the two vantages: history and genre. Ford poses one against the other in the setting of some passing life-style. It would be false to ignore the sentimentality that has characterized many of Ford's narratives, particularly their resolutions. At a time when Ford's nationalism and historical perspectives are not enjoyed by everyone, however, we must be careful to identify his talent. (But what of Dudley Nichols? Or Gregg Toland?) Ford is credited with a special capacity to recompose his shots through actor's movements as the camera runs; yet he was said not to bother to look through the viewfinder or to see his rushes.

To cite a very different director, we might consider Federico Fellini along one of the same polarities. Fellini entered filmmaking as a scriptwriter for Roberto Rossellini, and parts of his early films, especially *I Vitelloni* (1953), carry autobiographical flavor: the young man from Rimini who ran off to join the circus at age twelve and finally migrated to Rome when he was seventeen. (The boy with his suitcase looking for a place to stay in *Roma* [1972].)

Fellini's work with Rossellini (he collaborated on *Open City* and *Paisan*, and wrote *The Miracle* [1947], in which he played the itinerant who seduces Anna Magnani) introduced him to the tenets of neorealism, and it seems almost as if this social-aesthetic view explains Fellini to himself until he becomes a film director. Yet even in the early films like *Variety Lights* (1950) and *La Strada* (1954) we begin to encounter special motifs, which reappear later in increasingly garish costume. There is a melancholic irony, often in the characters played by his wife, Giulietta Masina, which overpowers the hard-eyed proletarian faiths and optimisms.

In *La Strada*, these other attributes of the Fellini presence come out.

One is an elliptical cut that betrays our expectations even as it forces us to re-examine them. For instance, Giulietta Masina as Gelsomina joins a circus troupe, where she finds acceptance and adventure. It is a world into which she fits, more so than Anthony Quinn, who plays Zampano, a wandering strongman with an act too crude for the subtleties of the circus. Gelsomina, as she shifts from one level of artifice to the next (she had been traveling with Zampano from town to town while he broke metal chains with his chest in the village squares), is puzzled about where she "belongs," where the meaning of her own existence can be explained by something greater than herself. She feels vague, metaphysical urgings. The circus troupe is in transit. Gelsomina never knows where they are going, because she has never been anywhere. On the road, she points to a distant building and asks what the dome is. "That's St. Peter's in the Vatican," she is told. "We're coming to Rome."

The nature of the conversation with its accompanying pointing leads us to anticipate next some kind of a motivated cut to what is mentioned, St. Peter's famous dome. Instead, the next shot is an interior of the circus tent being thrown up. Its own shape is enough like a cathedral dome to fulfill something of our expectation while at the same time disappointing us. If we are alert to the juxtaposition with its similarities of shape, we may then draw certain parallels between the circus and religion—the former as secular equivalent of the latter. Both deal with great audiences, particularly when our comparison is with Italian Roman Catholicism. Both deal in mysteries. Both use drama to intensify their ritual. Both are deep in the past of the country. Both have costumes. Without a great stretch of the imagination, it could even be said that the balancing acts so characteristic of circus performance have their metaphysical equivalent in the Church's idea of spirituality, according to which each human being walks a kind of fine line of reconciliation between sacred and profane.

In terms of story, Gelsomina never sees the Vatican. Her life is now the circus. She becomes increasingly comfortable and adapted to its ways. Finally, it is violence between Zampano and a clown, played by Richard Basehart, that forces her to leave. While Zampano is animal-brute, Basehart more closely answers Gelsomina's questioning needs for *something*. In one scene, he even tells her about purpose in life by likening her to a pebble. But Zampano kills the clown, and Gelsomina finally dies, quite alone, leaving him alone too.

There is another aspect to Fellini, illustrated by a shot in *La Strada*. Zampano has abandoned Gelsomina for a village prostitute to whom he is momentarily attracted. He locks Gelsomina out of the motorcycle-wagon in which they travel. She sits disconsolate at the curb. When a dissolve brings us to the following morning, we find Giulietta Masina in the same sad position, but, standing beside her in the street for no apparent reason is a large, pure-white horse. The horse seems surreal. Its starkness and incongruity have the quality of interjecting into the rural setting, the textures of which are rough and coarse, something that looks almost pasted on, like a collage, but there the horse stands, implacable, as unconcerned with Gelsomina as she with it. One has some vague impression that the horse somehow has to do (it doesn't *symbolize*, it doesn't *mean*, it just has to do) with something *else* about Gelsomina, something always present and rarely visible. Then it wanders off, and Gelsomina returns to her life with Zampano.

At such moments, we might consider Fellini in terms of what we termed transparency——referentiality and, too, use-of-tradition——rejection-of-tradition. He draws on other traditions than our own, circuses and Italian Catholicism. (Each appears with increasing frequency in his work. *Fellini Satyricon* seems almost a desperate plunge into the pagan in order to escape Catholicism and keep the circus.)

He thrives increasingly on the quality of the screen image, rejecting stratified connotation and preserving an air of mystery. As the cycle of Fellini films progresses, we find that the pressures of his sacred and secular impulses appear increasingly to require that he invent entire *mise-en-scènes* (people in settings all of which, together, serve narrative effect) that may be able to maintain their element of mystery while at the same time he organizes inhabitable worlds that can resolve psychic pressures on himself.

Such a place becomes increasingly vast: his own imagination in *8½*, his wife's in *Juliet of the Spirits* (1965), a created past in *Clowns* (1970), a created Rome in *Roma*. As new films emerge, they seem increasingly to depart from tradition-bound styles, like surrealism and psychoanalysis, becoming more grotesque and more wildly dense. If, for example, we compare the traffic jam in *8½* with the one in *Roma*, the difference is apparent. In the early moments of *8½* Marcello Mastroianni is stuck in his car, experiencing what may be a heart attack in a jammed tunnel. Through the closed windows, a juxtaposition of chaotic noise and silence is developed by Fellini into dreamlike effect as the actor grows bigger and lighter, finally floating out of the car and escaping the confusion like some inflated, Thanksgiving Day parade balloon figure.

By the time of *Roma*, Fellini has created a scene that grows gradually from an emotional but credible traffic jam into a kind of protean horror that is finally comical. Our point of reference is a camera truck on which cranes are recording the events as we and they experience them. The silence is gone, and there is no balloon escape. That, in retrospect, has the quality of a man on the couch telling his analyst how he cleverly outwitted an impossible situation in last night's dream. Now Fellini seems to take manic delight in his self-constructed, insane gasoline alley. The car wrecks, honking, blinding headlights, rain, whistling traffic police, shouting passengers and unworldly metal-concrete images receive loving attention, mixing near-insanity with an accepting exuberance.

We can view many films and filmmakers in terms of such relationships:

within shots, between shots, between film and director, among imposed polarities. What is necessary is to distinguish clearly between what is created, what either given or borrowed, and what we ourselves may be inventing. And we must strike an attitude toward Goethe's dictum.

Auteur criticism has not been without its pitfalls. For one, it diminishes the director whose approach varies from film to film, who is inclined to subvert himself in the material, allowing it to take the shape it requires rather than imposing personal, Promethean rigor onto whatever he meets. In this respect, *auteurism* is a kind of movie-fan romanticism, looking for more "greats." It is reducible to competitive recall, with experts sitting over beers and matching names and reputations like poker chips. In the process, a director like Huston, whose career has fluctuated erratically, is passed over, his better works dismissed as "actors' films," in favor of others who are more consistent, even if mundane. Not that Huston's work has never been mundane; at times, including recently, it has been known to be less than profound.

The *auteurist* is inclined to remark the moments that stand out in a certain *sort* of film when one *kind* of director calls attention to his own sleights of hand. The consistencies in a director's work are often tightly scripted by others—recalling Truffaut's "tradition of quality" complaint—or else may lie in minor idiosyncrasies, like Hitchcock's aversion to fried eggs. The tendency is to applaud personality for its visibility, not for its nature. In consequence, a kind of proneness to solo virtuosity develops—the performer plays for applause. Truffaut said, "In my day we discovered *auteurs*. Now they invent them."

Sometimes the result is commendation of the slick, polished small endeavor. Yet, as Pauline Kael has noted, there are other approaches: great, bulky, overcrowded, ponderous, ambitious conceptions, films that perhaps try to do too much, but should in no case be critically diminished because they did not attempt what was too easy. There are movie equivalents to big, nonstylist novelists like Dreiser.

Too much concentration on plot and character and their realization in performance tends to return film to the aesthetic of theater and fiction. Critics' arguments tend to increase as the subject matter becomes less important. Time and attention are squandered on American studio directors who are very minor indeed. Disagreement often devolves not on questions of style but on cultural values—for example, heroism in Samuel Fuller versus heroism in Michael Curtiz.

At some time, too, one has to come to terms with Jerry Lewis, for English-language critics have adopted the enthusiasms of the French along with their techniques. Jerry Lewis proves a rite of passage, like swallowing raw eggs in a fraternity initiation. While his qualities as a comedian can at least be argued, I, for one, find difficulty in locating the extraordinary in Lewis's directing abilities. Perhaps the French are inclined to see

Jerry Lewis's greatness largely in terms of explicit criticisms of American mores. By the same token, they regarded Fernandel as rather an elemental music-hall comedian in their own country.

Finally, the image of director as personality quickly becomes one of director as star. As a result, he is as open to publicity (and prone to exploitation) as any tooth-capped beauty. Theaters and film distributors vulgarize *auteurism* with puffery designed to renew audience interest in what had been old movie reels gathering dust in the warehouses. Even the new filmmakers are subject to the kind of buildup that had previously been only afforded performers. The writer-director John Milius is a case in point. He gained some reputation as the author of *Dirty Harry* (1971), *Jeremiah Johnson* (1972), and *The Life and Times of Judge Roy Bean* (1972), the last a well-financed picture with microphone booms visible in its corners. Milius's stories tend toward the revengeful-bloody. That image is compounded in newspaper pieces and magazine profiles that emphasize his fascination with guns and hunting, his heraldry of war ("the ultimate cosmic riddle"). In his first directing assignment, *Dillinger* (1973), Milius's gangster figure is more lifted from *Bonnie and Clyde* than it is Godardian homage. Amidst the bloodshed, Dillinger slaps his women about and is relentlessly tracked down by a self-justifying G-man, Melvin Purvis. And Milius is photographed for further interviews with a revolver in his hand.

All this said, *auteurism* in America facilitated radical, thoughtful readjustments in our sense of critical reputation, particularly in our evaluation of many early sound careers that had been locked into old footnotes. It has organized and publicized great areas of film history buried in television film libraries for the Late Show. And it reminds us that a subject develops significance from its treatment, not the reverse. Artists create meaning as they create singular images.

19 ▪ Structuralism and Semiology

Thus far, our considerations of moviegoing, production, theory, and criticism have centered on what actually occurred in the evolution of filmmaking, systematized as growth demanded organization or as personal artistry designed some body of work or as cultures contributed their traditional orderings. We would, however, be remiss not to note a developing effort on the part of scholars to define and quantify aspects of film study in order to undertake the kind of analysis that would parallel the close studies of literature done in the past half-century.

During the past ten years an energetic surge of interest in analytic principles has grown out of earlier studies of language. Under the general name of linguistics, the character, function, and meaning dimensions of speech, its linear organizations and psychic origins, constitute one of the fertile research areas of this century.

During World War I, an approach that came to be known as Russian formalism evolved from discussions in St. Petersburg and Moscow between students of literature and linguistics. (Here lie causal relations between Eisenstein and formalism. He collaborated with the poet-essayist-theoretician Victor Shklovsky. Both fell from grace in 1929 with the triumph of socialist realism.)

Growing in part from the Russians' work, the Prague Circle of Linguists, led by Roman Jakobson and N. S. Trubetsky, continued to elaborate analytic techniques by which means language might be quantified and understood not through its history (its etymology) but by analysis of its structure. Scholars centered attention on questions about fundamental meaning units and the kinds of organization among these units that develop meaning complexes. How much, they asked, can we take away from speech while yet retaining elemental denotation?

An example might be drawn from phonetics. We can distinguish between two *p* sounds: one as in *pot,* another as in *top.* Both are unvoiced bilabials—that is, they are produced without teeth by the two lips and lack any action of the larynx, whose expression would change the sound to *b.* English makes no meaning distinction between *p* as in pot and *p* as in top, although the former example releases air by lip action (*explosive*) and the latter arrests air movement (*implosive*). In contrast, a native of India would make a meaning distinction between the two sounds, each denoting something different. The linguists term a minimal sound that carries distinctive meaning a *phoneme.*

More important, the Prague Circle asked one another what kinds of organization among meaning units develop meaning complexes? *Pot* and *top* obviously differ because of phonemic position. In terms of word ordering, we can say *The boy stood on the burning deck* and *On the burning deck stood the boy* without affecting sense, but what is meant by *Burning the deck the boy stood on?* Structuralism, it was concluded, removes language from considerations of historical change, proposing instead that we view it from the perspective of fundamental design relationships, which are independent of syntax or the passage of time.

Language is inextricably related to human culture, and linguistic techniques soon became insinuated into the social sciences. A prime example is the work of Claude Lévi-Strauss. Lévi-Strauss has devoted years of study to oral materials collected from various Brazilian Indian tribes, much of it deriving out of societies far up the Amazon River. The French anthropologist analyzed these peoples' mythic materials, spoken and musical, and identified their characteristic patterns. These he has expressed through the use of a few conceptual polarities. By learning, at least in part, how these elements operate, Lévi-Strauss has located evidence of how the Indians accounted for the discovery of fire, the cooking of meat, how edible and inedible animals were created, why there are stars in the sky, how to explain the celestial and terrestrial realms.

To understand how such material has come to be applied to film study, it is useful to distinguish at this point between two overlapping yet diverging approaches, structuralism and semiology. Structuralism in film analysis has operated more or less according to the methodology and principles of Lévi-Strauss. It presumes that a given body of material, because it is an expression of human culture, like myth, is coterminous with observed "reality." Lévi-Strauss proposes, too, that *any* society's thinking differs little from our own, since all share the same underlying patterns, and so any "new" expression becomes comprehensible if we can only locate the first conceptions out of which its causal and associative connections have extended.

Why, then, might film not be subjected to structuralist analysis, as oral tales and folk music have been? In fact, this has been done with film, if still cursorily. In particular, the English have tried to apply structuralist principles to such *auteurs* as Luchino Visconti, Howard Hawks, and John Ford. Studying the entire body of a given director's work, writers have tried to identify significant themes, motifs, plot organizations, and ideological premises by which the artist may be better understood.

Thus, in some ways the approach would seem to extend earlier *auteur* criticism into systematized technique. Rather than an idiosyncratic hit-or-miss consideration of John Ford, say, the writer Peter Wollen may, through narrative analysis of each film, its themes and images, locate such a polarity as "the wilderness and the garden" as a central core underlying the work. In the measure that Wollen has accurately assessed his material, the same conclusion will be reached by any other analyst, just as one physicist may replicate the work of another. Further, the scholastic legitimacy of such an operation is buttressed by reference to other academic sources—a historical study, for instance, that explicates the director's personal values in terms of communal beliefs about the places from which man originated (the garden) and to which he has been condemned (the wilderness). Wollen did this by citing Henry Nash Smith, *The Virgin Land*. Another critic, Jim Kitses, likewise used Smith to formalize a dichotomy between civilization and wilderness in his study of several directors of westerns.[14]

What is interesting about the Lévi-Strauss approach and less common among his disciples is a constant awareness that myth really has no subjects but only relationships. Thus a hero-figure's physical appearance in one tale may clothe villainy in the next. Pivotal figures are defined altogether in terms of how they act toward other pivotal figures. Such understanding allows the researcher to account for radical shifts in behavior.

Thus far, structuralist approaches to the underlying premises in motion pictures have tended to sacrifice musical form to speech, though movies, quite as thoroughly as myth, embody both principles. In his study *The Raw and the Cooked*, Lévi-Strauss devotes equal attention to language relationships and the connections that define pattern in music. "Mythology occupies an intermediary position between two diametrically opposed types of sign systems—musical language on the one hand and articulate speech on the other; to be understood it has to be studied from both angles."[15]

Structural organizing principles in film study are based, too, on certain presumptions that have not always been defended or necessarily even recognized. One is the parallel drawn between anonymous, oral materials (often inflected through years of repetition and undergoing changes, which cultural anthropologists use to date the age of a tale) and movies. There is some contradiction between positing a body of shared myth on the one hand and examining the singular *auteur* vision on the other.

Either the shared element in fact accounts for most aspects of a director's imaginative genesis, which really denies his singularity, or else he is somehow unaware of what he is doing, in which case how much ought we to make of his "vision"?

The notion that filmmakers and film audiences respond to bases of appeal that nobody consciously knows about certainly poses obstacles. If one proposes to a painter, a novelist, a poet, or a composer that he is ignorant of his own organizational scheme, his response may be less than enthusiastic. Writers, especially, are more likely to admit mental sluggishness to explain repetitions and ritualized patterns in their work. Writers have writers' block because they know too much about what they're doing, not too little. On the other hand, the very popularity of commercial film somehow argues for the existence of a kind of deep-seated communication, which may contain otherwise inexplicable narrative appeals. In such cases, though, a critic might better examine *Billboard*'s Top Ten than the work of an *auteur*. Just as it might be questioned whether, once an *auteurist* has located a director's personality, that discovery is all to the good, the structuralist may be asked if his discovery of underlying structure really measures aesthetic value.

Another aspect of structuralist study that should be noted is the duality of its patterns, in large measure a Hegelian inheritance. On reflection, the reader may note that the language of the structuralists, and sometimes our own, has thrived on opposites. We have called on polarities, linear continuities, antinomies, dichotomies, and parameters. Although the last term is hardly limited to two-ness, it has been so employed here, and one wonders at the convenience of reality to display itself so two-dimensionally for our delectation. Lévi-Strauss commonly speaks of "grids," which may be designed in any pattern, but his own distinctions tend toward bundles of polarities. When he has a triad, like cooked/raw/rotten it is quickly resolved to dualities: Cooked——Raw, Rotten——Fresh. However, Lévi-Strauss refers to extremely fundamental human distinctions —the sort of metaphysical conceptualizations that everywhere repeat their two-ness: in religion, logic, and associative magic. If one were to trace *auteurs'* or genres' underlying structures to a similar stage, he would perhaps follow John Wayne all the way back to the mouth of the Amazon River, a film the "Duke" never made.

Last, it should be noted that access to films for purposes of intensive analysis poses real problems. Many movies, particularly good ones, do not even begin to yield their secrets before half a dozen viewings. If one were to organize a structuralist study of many films, perhaps the life work of a prolific director, he might well have a life's work of his own. The years that Lévi-Strauss has devoted to his studies of a small group of myths and notated music would perhaps not even equal the amount of time necessary to study the total output of just one director.

Structuralism and Semiology ▪ 219

The other branch of language-based film study today is semiology, or semiotics (to distinguish it from an earlier use of semiology which describes the identification of medical symptoms through a patient's behavior). The root is the Greek word *semeion* (sign). Semiology operates from the premise that any aspect of human culture can be studied, hence better understood, in terms of consistent sign systems: the semiology, for example, of traffic signals, the semiology of book bindings, the semiology of automobile seats.

Developed by such figures as Edmund Husserl, Ferdinand de Saussure, and Roland Barthes, semiology has created special vocabularies in order to make necessary, descriptive, often bipolar, distinctions so that the ways by which meaning is communicated may be accurately delineated and the ways that meaning is elaborated may be analyzed.

De Saussure, for example, emphasized the arbitrariness of any sign: the thing "standing for" something in the signifier/signified relationship, such as red, white, and blue "meaning" patriotism. Barthes elaborated de Saussure's notion of *langue/parole* to identify the totality of possibilities in any sign system (*langue*) and their personalized, choice-laden expression, selected from the alternatives (*parole*)—for example, the difference between clothing and fashion.

The application of semiology to movies has been diligently pursued by Christian Metz in a series of essays in *Cahiers du Cinéma*, recently collected together and published as a book.[16] Metz directs his attention toward film narrative and systematically develops an analytical scheme for classifying the common elements among all narrative films and the devices used to develop narrative structure.

A central problem for Metz is the film characteristic to which we have repeatedly returned: the movies' relationship to the surface of reality. The semiologists account for this in some measure by the terms "first articulation" and "second articulation." A meaning unit is said to have second articulation when it breaks through and becomes a sign—in de Saussure's language, something arbitrary relative to what it signifies. The film image is neither arbitrary nor quite equatable with what it corresponds to in "real life." A horse on the screen is clearly both a horse and not a horse. André Bazin likened photography to a fingerprint, but unless we altogether share Bazin's commitment to a very particular form of film naturalism, the analogy holds only for that one style. In any case, film does not have second articulation, and for this reason, Metz has difficulty locating its minimal meaning unit—the equivalent to the linguist's "phoneme," which Metz calls (for film study) a "taxeme."

The taxeme, Metz decides, is what filmmakers call the shot, and yet each shot clearly contains interior "significances" that cannot be effectively isolated. He then proceeds to develop a system to describe the techniques by which narrative meaning is extended through relationships between such film segments. These relationships Metz describes as "syntagmas." Syntagm and paradigm are the two levels of relations between linguistic terms. Syntagmatic sign combinations create units whose meanings are dependent on the order of their appearance. For example, Kuleshov's experiment with Mozhukhin (see page 85) derived its meanings from the relations of the actor's face to the pieces of film that preceded and followed it. Paradigmatic meaning is associative, requiring the viewer to call in frames of reference outside the system in which it occurs; thus, when we see a dissolve in a film of a given era, we know how to interpret it. While Metz fears that film semiotics may develop too strictly along syntagmatic, rather than paradigmatic, lines (all narrative is both syntagmatic and paradigmatic), he finds syntagmatic considerations central to the problems of filmic denotation.

The attractions of semiotics to film study are those of close, unemotional, repeatable textual analysis, working with a vocabulary that translates the functional language of the industry (intercutting, parallel editing, reaction shots) into exactingly descriptive terms. With the reservation that this form of study is very new and currently most enthusiastically supported in academia, we should, nonetheless point out certain current limitations on its employment.

Metz's syntagmatic categories, as elaborated thus far, appear largely to explicate the visual aspects of film language. They account less successfully for those meaning-laden relationships which may be effected by sound of any sort. The syntagmas do not seem at all to encompass variations in point of view, especially the subjective, "conditional tense" of such filmmakers as Resnais and Robbe-Grillet. (In his defense, it should be noted that Metz himself points up certain limitations to his analyses vis-à-vis recent films).[17] Likewise, the syntagmatic categories may be hard pressed to account for radical manipulations of time. *The Birth of a Nation* falls easily within its scheme, but *Intolerance* is less facilely accounted for. Furthermore, the approach is, by Metz's own stern admonition, limited to a particular aspect of film—that is, narrative exposition, independent of time, place, and, largely, authorship. Since semiology proposes not one but a myriad of sign systems, film is particularly open to other significations, especially in the measure that it is committed to photographic fidelity toward the world. In each case, as one abstracts any code from its context he runs the danger of destroying some interior relationships for the sake of highlighting others.

Finally, the very ambition of defining a visual-aural experience with the reductive exactitudes of language creates other problems. We may study language effectively with language, but how effectively can we apply language to film? Even speech, as we have seen, may be changed so as to adapt it to the exigencies of the image. An actor's words are not the same as ordinary oral communication. Semiotics is an exciting, challenging new weapon in the arsenal of film study, but the number of problems it has yet to face is enough to make the semioticist wring his metonymies in despair.

RECOMMENDED READING

■ Vachel Lindsay, *The Art of the Moving Picture,* has been reprinted (New York: Liveright) with an introduction by Stanley Kauffmann. It appeared originally in 1915. A good example of the twenties views on film is Gilbert Seldes, *The Seven Lively Arts* (New York: Harper, 1924). For thirties, forties, and fifties criticism, see: James Agee, *Agee on Film* vol. 1 (New York: McDowell, Obolensky, 1958–60); Manny Farber, *Negative Space* (New York: Praeger, 1971)—really fifties and sixties; Otis Ferguson, *The Film Criticism of Otis Ferguson,* ed. Robert Wilson (Philadelphia: Temple University Press, 1971); and four by Pauline Kael— *I Lost It at the Movies* (Boston: Little, Brown, 1965), *Kiss Kiss, Bang Bang* (Boston: Little, Brown, 1968), *Going Steady* (Boston: Little, Brown, 1971), and *Deeper into Movies* (Boston: Little, Brown, 1973). An interesting anthology of responses to feature films at the time of their release may be found in Stanley Kauffmann, ed., *American Film Criticism* (New York: Liveright, 1972). Film journals will be noted in the Appendix.

■ The title essay of Susan Sontag, *Against Interpretation* (New York: Farrar, Straus and Giroux, 1966) contains her discussion of the film image. Other aspects of film are considered elsewhere in the book.

■ The reader may follow salient points and some face slapping with regard to the *auteur* controversy by reading, in order: Andrew Sarris, "The American Cinema," *Film Culture* 28 (Spring 1963); Pauline Kael, "Circles and Squares," *Film Quarterly* 16, no. 3 (Spring 1963); Andrew Sarris, "The Auteur Theory," *Film Quarterly* 16, no. 4 (Summer 1963); The Editors of *Movie,* "Movie vs. Kael," *Film Quarterly* 17, no. 1 (Fall 1963). Some of Sarris's criticism is collected in *Confessions of a Cultist* (New York: Simon & Schuster, 1972). See also *The Primal Screen* (New York: Simon & Schuster, 1973).

■ Examinations of film in terms of structuralism and semiology are multiplying like the vegetable life in Howard Hawks's *The Thing* (1951). The interested reader might consult the May–June, 1973, issue of *Film Comment,* which contains two useful articles: Charles W. Eckert, "The English Cine-Structuralists," and John C. Hanhardt and Charles H. Harpole, "Linguistics, Structuralism and Semiology." The latter article is followed by an excellent multi-language listing of appropriate references. See also Brian Henderson, "Critique of Cine-Structuralism," *Film Quarterly* 27, no. 1 (Fall 1973) pp. 25–34.

■ The British magazine *Screen* in its issues of March–April, May–June, and August–September, 1972, has published several appropriate essays, including intramural contentious dispute as to which critic structures his structuralism with the greatest precision. Roland Barthes, *Elements of Semiology* is a valuable study (New York: Hill and Wang, 1968). Claude Lévi-Strauss, *The Raw and the Cooked* (New York: Harper & Row, 1969) is the first of a three-part study of Indian myth. An excellent summary and critique of structuralism and formalism as they apply to linguistics may be found in Frederic Jameson, *The Prison of Language* (Princeton, N.J.: Princeton University Press, 1972).

NOTES

1. Noël Burch, *Theory of Film Practice* (New York: Praeger, 1973).
2. Béla Balázs, *Theory of the Film* (New York: Dover, 1970).
3. Siegfried Kracauer, *Theory of Film* (New York: Oxford University Press, 1960).
4. Rudolf Arnheim, *Film As Art* (Berkeley: University of California Press, 1957).
5. François Truffaut, "A Certain Tendency of the French Cinema," *Cahiers du Cinéma in English* no. 1 (January 1966), pp. 31–41.
6. André Bazin, "On the *Politique des Auteurs*," *Cahiers du Cinéma in English* no. 1 (January 1966), pp. 8–18.
7. Michael Wilmington, "Cahier's Favorite Directors," *The Velvet Light Trap* no. 9 (Summer 1973), p. 18.
8. Quoted in Maureen Turim, "The Aesthetic Becomes Political," *The Velvet Light Trap* no. 9 (Summer 1973), pp. 13–17.
9. Andrew Sarris, *American Cinema: Directors and Directions 1929–68* (New York: E. P. Dutton, 1969).
10. Manny Farber, *Negative Space* (New York: Praeger, 1971).
11. Quoted in José Luis Guarner, "Pierrot le Fou," *The Films of Jean-Luc Godard* (New York: Praeger, 1969), p. 94.
12. Tom Milne, translation and commentary, *Godard on Godard* (New York: Viking Press, 1972), pp. 128–29.
13. *Ibid.,* p. 79.
14. See Peter Wollen, *Signs and Meaning in the Cinema* (Bloomington: University of Indiana Press, 1969) and Jim Kitses, *Horizons West* (Bloomington: University of Indiana Press, 1970).
15. Claude Lévi-Strauss, *The Raw and the Cooked* (New York: Harper & Row, 1969), p 15.
16. Christian Metz, *Film Language* (New York: Oxford University Press, 1974).
17. *Ibid.,* chap. 8 "The Modern Cinema and Narrativity," pp. 185–227.

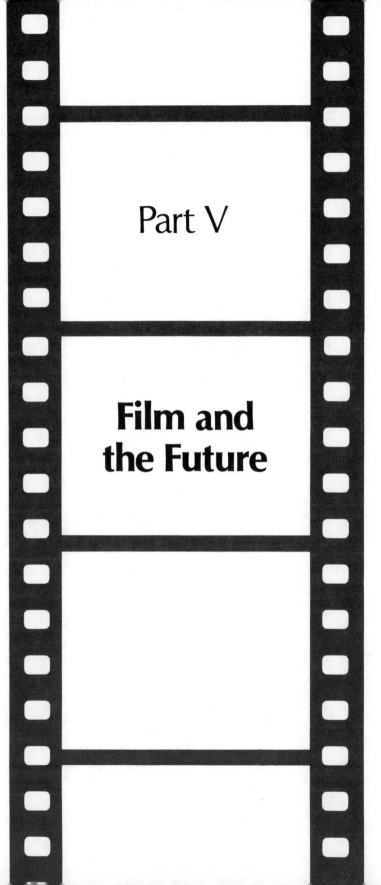

Part V

Film and the Future

20 ∎ The Shape of Films to Come

We cannot realistically investigate the future of the narrative film without considering who its audience will be. If all arts are audience-bound, even should that audience be of one, then the movies are vulgarly so, originating as the entertainment of the urban working class. Their relation to taste was altogether pragmatic: the art's directing intelligences were people *of* the audience. The early production-company presidents had been glove salesmen and furriers and immigrants in New York City.

Commercial films thrived in the twenties and thirties, when they provided cheap, escapist entertainment for the poor and the middle-class family. The industry's crises, from which it never really recovered, were first the post–World War II economic cutbacks and then, in the fifties, television. Profits dipped between 1946 and 1949 from $1,750 million to $1,375 million, punctuated by Great Britain's imposition of a 75 per cent tax on foreign productions and the closing of small independent studios like Liberty and Rainbow. By 1949 Eagle Lion and Selznick had folded up too. A year before, movie-industry employment had fallen 25 per cent below its peak, and half the number of wartime features was being produced.

With the further inroads of television, audiences and production continued to decline, although Hollywood's new role as the manufacturer of network series sometimes blinded the industry to the fate of its theaters. Attendance not only fell, it shifted from families to singles, and today about 75 per cent of the patrons are younger than twenty-nine. Often their escape is less from broader realities of life than from the living-room

TV set. Television cannibalized the Hollywood studio, transforming what had been the B-picture, programmer staple of the industry into *I Love Lucy*'s and *Gunsmoke*'s. In so doing, TV commandeered Hollywood's escapist formulas.

Under such circumstances, film has tried to respond cannily to newer impulses on the audience's part. Some people seem to want to flee broadcast escapism into the even deeper refuge of the wide screen. Others clearly want out, desire something different and more supportive of nonescapist needs, either different subject matter or innovations in form. This chapter deals with each of these impulses by examining both documentary and ongoing experimentation in film.

Underlying these inquiries is one constant issue—financial support to a mass medium. Companies allege that three pictures out of ten make a profit these days, although one shouldn't altogether trust box-office figures. They serve different people different ways. Still, three out of ten isn't very good odds, even if the successful films will often return a profit beyond the wildest dreams of investor avarice. Within the next decade the high-budget feature film as we have know it may even slough off into the history books like the dinosaur, bulk too big for its brains. M-G-M's withdrawal from film producing seems an omen. Even if this should happen, it will not mark the demise of the movies. What must be acknowledged, however, is the possibility of radical change in the circumstances of film consumption as well as the character of its narrative organization.

DISTRIBUTION

Television introduced a whole new concept of film distribution, atomizing audiences into nuclear groups of two or three. Not only does this altogether alter the film experience (see chapter 1), it also gives a different sort of commercial base to producer intention. Television's function is to sell products; filmmaking's function is to sell film.

There *is* a recent technological breakthrough that might link home viewing with the commercial-free independence of theatrical features. The different disc and videotape-cassette "film-through-TV-in-the-home" systems all promise living-room entertainment that may be inexpensively viewed, usually more than once, at a time of one's choice and without interruption. Such schemes seem to suggest a strong potential for film distribution to individuals rather than to massed audiences. In fact, the equipment manufacturers so far remain at loggerheads, arguing over standards of gauge and technology, each fearful that the others may somehow dominate the market.

In the absence of these uninterrupted movies in the home, theater and network differences in commercial strategy remain much in evidence. Advertising operates on a unit-cost basis. The more people exposed to a commercial, undistracted by story, the more effectively exploited that au-

The "sock hop" in *American Graffiti* appeals to the fifties revival among young movie-goers—and the real nostalgia of their parents.

dience has been, and the lower the cost per thousand viewers. Large audiences tend toward product homogeneity. The great studio films, lusting after a box office of equal magnitude, produced entertainment quite as bland as television, except that in the case of the movies, story must be the lure for getting ticket buyers out of the home.

Given the age of today's movie audience, theatrical film has largely given up the over-twenty-nines to middle-aged television reassurements and has instead gone for the children. Yet in one sense, both film and TV spin much the same, stroking tale through different encoding systems. Daddy wants to be told that his work, sacrifice, and suffering has been worth it, hence Carol Burnett, Kung Fu, and the Merv Griffin Show. (Substitute your own popular programs of the year.) Junior wants to be retold that the world is hopelessly corrupt and that he is powerless to affect it. Hence any year's *Easy Rider*. *Electra Glide in Blue* (1973), for instance, replicates *Easy Rider*'s premises like carbon paper with different colored ink.

Another strategy is to attract by "outspoken" material that cannot be

The Shape of Films to Come ▪ 229

duplicated on G-rated (sometimes PG-rated) television. Here we find films like *Happy Days* or *Flesh Gordon* (both 1974), which, in parodying earlier entertainments, seek to cash in on formularized conventional responses while guised in the costume of nakedness. At its most interesting, the X-rated melodrama (a good example is *Last Tango in Paris*) as opposed to the skin flick has undertaken advanced explorations in naturalism, a further extension of nineteenth-century writers like Zola and Balzac, whose aim was to define human psychology by the most minute observations of behavior and surroundings: *cinéma vérité* in the bedroom.

The newer directors depart from older adolescent anxieties like *I Was a Teenage Frankenstein* (1957), instead playing on differences of sensibility between over-twenty-nine and under-twenty-nine—for instance wordless, lyric passages like the slide sequence in *The Parallax View* (1974). Such moments often halt narrative progression to explore a mood or atmosphere. Stanley Kubrick's nonverbal time trips in *2001: A Space Odyssey* happily appealed to both age brackets, but one found differences in where each age-group sat: Youth was considerably closer to the screen.

The 1970 semi-underground success *El Topo* differently served certain coteries of young people to the bewilderment of the older generation. The movie was a violent narrative laden with rape, murder, incest, torture, and assorted agonies, strung together by a "mythic," picaresque narrative. Youth understands and responds to fantasy coated in the garish colors of violence and cruelty. Older people's fantasy tends to require naturalist costume. Hence the tensions triggered by real-pretend blood in films by a director like Sam Peckinpah. In this respect the fantasies of youth (and we must distinguish between fantasy and escape; in our terms, fantasy is but one of several forms of stylization) are more inclined to nonrounded characters, like folk and mythic heroes. Instead, actors each are components of the psyche, broken up like Jungian archetypes into performers who only *seem* to be free agents. They must connect with one another through plot contrivance (rather than the older generation's more motivated plot developments). In such stories, the seemingly real is only surface-deep so as to leave room for exploring through fantasy some ulterior psychological dimension. A good example of this is the British film *Performance* (1970), where identities shifted from scene to scene. To many older people, the experience is incomprehensible, since it doesn't fit the requirements of their own fantasy and thus seems too "unreal." The Germans have a name critical of one-dimensional characters (*eindeutig*), but in films like *El Topo* and *Performance*, the *eindeutig* character is not a weakness but rather a fictional strategy to elicit understandings from the young audience.

Another approach with which today's young film audience sits more comfortably is time-tripping. Because they seem to challenge older story conventions, space/time transitions like those of *Slaughterhouse Five* (1972) are far more difficult for older people to assimilate, although the techniques differ little from earlier flashbacks and flashforwards except that the explanatory cues are less obvious. Many amount to no more than flashy "Look ma, I'm editing" showmanship. In the future, though, it appears likely that more films will investigate the conditional tense, the half-real images like those of Resnais, which cannot so easily be "explained." Here, rather than in characterization, modern ambiguities may rest. It is progressively more characteristic of Bergman films like *Persona* (1966), *Hour of the Wolf* (1968), and *Cries and Whispers* (1972).

Despite their seeming newness, all the above innovations are based in some measure on the mass-audience presumptions that have always characterized feature production. Yet another aspect of industrial-age popular culture has been its openness to diversity, as more specialized audiences are located in larger groupings. There are specialized paperback-book audiences, specialized phonograph-record audiences, specialized hobby groups, and collectors beyond measure. Given a group of adequate if diminished size, film may also adapt itself to more heterogeneous interests. In so doing, it could maintain some of its own traditions while yet expanding the resources of narrative inquiry. This is what occurred in the sixties, when college groups found that experimental film brought variety and unconventional experience to campus programs. It also characterizes social-action groups who must seek out ways both to expose their film material to appropriate audiences and to design a sufficient distribution technique.

Distribution, really, is central to the problems of more independent film production. If not the theaters (which are tied to mass-scale guarantees and promotional commitments), if not the television circuit, then how may audiences be located or developed? Various filmmakers, particularly those melding a kind of documentary-entertainment-feature production, have tried to develop their own distribution systems, thus far with no great success.

At issue here is the relationship between production cost and audience size. Despite the avalanche of short films (less than an hour) that has come out of film schools and a movie-conscious generation, there exists little opportunity for such movies' effective distribution. They do not usually fit commercial television's format or policies. Feature-film distributors cannot make enough money to warrant handling them. Short-film distributors cannot develop a broad enough market to expand their catalogues to any great degree. The main outlet for shorts has been sales to educational units, particularly audio-visual centers if the films pass such muster. The situation is presently discouraging to filmmakers, particularly the ones committed either to experimentation or to social action, who depend on sales or rental revenue to finance future projects.

When the ambitions of a filmmaker have expanded to feature proportions, the outlook proves even grimmer as he departs from theatrical distribution systems. Some young people have entered the skin-flick field seeking windfall profits to finance other sorts of feature ventures and also as a training ground, the way older directors used to gain their apprenticeships on B pictures. A greater number of filmmakers, however, have ventured one way or another into documentary, a field that has shown marked evolution since World War II.

DOCUMENTARY

Documentary films were powerfully affected by television's influence on equipment. Filmmaking (as contrasted with most laboratory) technology has always been archaically slow to change, but with the development of portable tape recorders, faster film emulsions, and lighter, sound-proofed cameras, all largely under the instigation of television newsclip and news-special crews, a freer, more candid approach to shooting has become easier and cheaper. Another influence here is the videotape camera, including so-called PortaPak equipment, which uses smaller-gauge tape and, of course, bypasses the frustrating needs for laboratory processing before one may see what one has got or failed to get. Sophisticated videotape equipment is cheaper to work with than equivalent 35mm equipment, and its sensitivity to light will sometimes give a different quality to focus and space. (For example, the Mothers of Invention leader Frank Zappa recommends videotape based on his experience with directing and composing for *200 Motels* [1971].)[1] More important has been video's effect on accentuating the same disposition as wide screen requires—namely, long, synchronous sound camera runs.

Such a tendency may be traced back to the early sixties, when a British documentary movement called Free Cinema (based on industrial subsidies for film projects) was equated with the cresting French New Wave. The New Wave label grouped very dissimilar talents, but at the time it was understood to be an actualization of Truffaut's battle cry: freer approaches to the circumstances of production, which would defeat the preconceptions and other constraints of shooting scripts. In the same way, documentary committed itself to the structures of reality (hence, philosophically, realism) rather than personal visions.

It is important to remember that this approach gave equal weight to synchronous sound. This is one reason why its adherents may be especially scornful both of other aesthetics that emphasize sound/picture counterpoint and of analysts like Christian Metz, who tend, so far at least, to emphasize the visual image and its continuities, like silent-film purists.

There are various subschools within the larger group, but much documentary operates today under the banner of *cinéma vérité*. Some filmmakers may approach their subject matter by joining it, becoming part of the documented experience, like Jean Rouch (*Moi un Noir* [1958]; *Chronicle of a Summer* [1961]). Such a strategy is honest enough to admit the effect of observation on the thing observed; on the other hand it denies the subject its autonomy. Rouch will thrust different kinds of people together, for example, and then encourage them to improvise their responses to an artificial situation.

A somewhat contrary position in the United States is that of Richard Leacock, Don Pennebaker, and the Maysles brothers, Albert and David. Generally, the premise of their films is that while the presence of the camera and crew undeniably affects subject behavior, there are ways to compensate for the distortion. One is to become so much a part of the scene, à la Robert Flaherty, that familiarity breeds inattention. The Maysles did this with a door-to-door bible salesman in *Salesman* (1969), Don Pennebaker in *Don't Look Back* (1966), which covered a Bob Dylan tour through England. Often an additional tactic, characteristic especially of Richard Leacock, is to choose some subject that will generate its own natural drama: a political campaign (*Primary* [1960]); a high-school football rivalry (*Football* [1961]), a condemned murderer and his lawyer awaiting possible reprieve from execution (*The Chair* [1963]).

Under such circumstances, the filmmaker has two factors working to his particular advantage. One is the subject's awareness threshold, which will increasingly ignore camera presence as life demands more of him. Second, the drama of the event develops its own rhythms and excitements, even though neither subject nor filmmaker knows what directions the plot will take.

Because of the latter circumstance, because life has a plot albeit sometimes tedious, mundane, or melodramatic, we may view *cinéma vérité* as *narrative*. It is another unfictionalized approach to story-by-observation, like Balzac-Bertolucci in the boudoir. But such vision, never knowing when "something will happen" is inclined to continuous, mobile camera runs, shooting far more footage than will ever be used. These shots, although they may well be selected from alternatives, are no more subject to editorial control than those of a studio director like Hitchcock, who leaves his cutter with no choices to make. In consequence, they tend to survive more or less intact in the finished film, supplying their own up-and-down tempo of excitements and dead spots, just as we may relive the curiosities of time past by tape-recording conversations that were unknown to the parties involved.

In some measure, this domination by time is compensated by the cameraman's freedom to locate his own subject of attention and, in the camera movements, or stops and starts, to impose his own rhythms ("cutting in the camera"). However, the very nature of the production denies the kind of articulation of space we associate with editing.

In the Maysles brothers documentary *Gimme Shelter* the Rolling Stones' concert tour is dramatically climaxed by unanticipated violence. *(Credit: Maysles Bros.)*

The matter of how far documentary footage may be manipulated poses moral quandaries on its filmmakers, especially as time is reconstituted. As documentary is approached increasingly as feature production, the line between fiction and fact will be obscured. For example, the Maysles brothers' *Gimme Shelter* (1970) has the Altamont killing mentioned at the beginning, goes back to the Rolling Stones' cross-country tour just as in an old movie flashback, then returns to the violence in conclusion. Here the entertainment values of the structure (subordinating suspense to the more deeply felt question of how and why it all happened) resonate on the filmed performances, themselves complicated by the Stones' put-ons, by Jagger's constant sense of himself as performer in *any* circumstance.

Most such films are too demanding, or "inappropriate," or too long for television unless eventually they can successfully fall into Movie of the Week slots. They must take their chances in the downtown theater marketplaces or else scrounge for attention on 16mm distribution circuits. Frederick Wiseman is an interesting figure who has successfully financed and shown his feature documentaries on television, then put them into the 16mm distribution maelstrom. Because he tends to examine American institutions, Wiseman can also compete for sales to school film libraries: *High School* (1969); *Hospital* (1969); *Basic Training* (1971); *Juvenile Court* (1973).

An interesting intermingling of documentary and fiction is *The Tragic Diary of Zero the Fool* (1969), a film by a Canadian, Morley Markson. Markson worked for months with a group of patients at a mental institution, members of a drama group, who dedicated their movie to Samuel Beckett. Two men and a woman assume their movie personalities from characters in the tarot deck, then invent (or unintentionally reveal) interactions as the actors are placed in different relationships. The result, which combines observable illness, semiskilled performance, and sometimes impassioned attempts at group therapy, is a grueling experience. It poses problems not only of filmmaker responsibility but also of audience responsibility. How much anguished privacy should we violate with our eyes? In the measure that *Zero* evokes the desperate resignations of Beckett, we are led too to ask ourselves how far drama and life really affect one another.

MIXED MEDIA

So far in this book, we have avoided discussing recent experimentation in film because it would have led us too far from the central issue of narrative. Now, however, we shall investigate several film forms subsumed under the term "mixed media"—film/theater collaborations, avant-garde undertakings, multiple images, and wildly varied screen shapes.

Many of these experiments do not fall into the category of film as mass medium. The special projection situations they require or their elaborate combinations of live and filmed performance do not lend themselves to the standardized exhibition techniques on which the movies' huge audiences have traditionally depended. Furthermore, many, though not all, mixed media experiments seem to abandon the cumulative, ongoing exposition of narrative that engrosses and entertains the mass audience.

Given these reservations, we must consider other qualities of today's films and their present and future audiences. For instance, current audiences, particularly younger viewers, suggest by their attendance and enthusiasms that older forms of storytelling are neither required nor necessary. Fed up with the fairy-tale version of naturalism found in TV, this audience may be searching for a larger sort of experience, one that departs from straightforward narrative into more suspended "moments" that demand more complex awareness.

Second, the whole character of an audience's relation to a theatrical event has drastically altered in recent years. The work of a John Cage, Bertolt Brecht, or Andy Warhol asks us to bring all our day-to-day questionings and perplexities to the art experience, requiring it to be more emotionally relevant to ourselves and less informed by tradition. The audience becomes more literally a part of the event. Filmmakers, too, have become interested in overcoming the customary separation of art and audience.

Third, the film medium seems on the verge of a substantial transformation. Whether such change, if it should occur, means that film will depart the mainstream of popular culture for a small-audience aesthetic is a question that may be answered in the next two decades.

These matters prompt us to look to film's future in terms of its experiments; otherwise, looking at what presently surrounds us, we can do little more than re-examine its past.

In theory, there is no reason why any feature film needs to be composed within a single rectangular size. One might, in fact, vary composition borders with the narrative requirements of any given sequence. Griffith experimented with different compositions, particularly in *The Birth*

Note the picture within the picture provided in this scene from *Hallelujah the Hills.*
(Credit: Adolfas Mekas)

236 ▪ Film and the Future

of a Nation and *Intolerance* (1916), by blacking out nonuseful areas and thus recomposing within the limitations of the film frame and projection screen. In *Hallelujah the Hills,* Adolfas Mekas (or perhaps his cameraman Ed Emschwiller) periodically printed rectangular frames of varying ratio within the larger screen image, thus recomposing a second picture for us to enjoy. The result was charming and exciting.

It may be argued that the requirements of narrative are not satisfied by varying screen size when consistent vision is to be maintained. Eisenstein once proposed, perhaps tongue in cheek, that we ought to work within a square frame, since it gave maximum variations by way of its neutrality. But when film is combined with another form such as theater, size and shape assume other functions.

Using film and live performance in combination is hardly new. Joining theater and motion pictures suggests collaborative accomplishment unavailable separately to each. Film has always lacked the live presence and immediacy of theater performance. But movies may distinctively affect the viewer's perceived space, and they have ways to control tempo and the dynamics of discovery that are inaccessible to the stage.

The German Bauhaus school of the twenties experimented in affecting audience perceptions through innovations in projection. Moholy-Nagy, especially, manipulated image magnification and form. If we think about ways these qualities may be inflected, we can separate out five variables:

1. *Image size.* Enlargement of a projected image will depend on the distance of projection source from screen and the focal length of the projection lens. The one may be a consequence of theater architecture, the other dependent on technology and available materials. Another element controlling image magnitude is, of course, the distance of each viewer from a screen.

2. *Image shape.* Our rectangular frame results from the projector mask, which defines this aspect ratio on the projected image, accommodated by a screen of particular size and a film-frame image so photographed that almost all its surface eventually reaches the screen. The anamorphic lens "squeezes" the image when photographed, something like El Greco with astigmatism, then expands it out again in projection.

There is really no technical hindrance to photographing or projecting any other shape, providing it can accurately be represented by the projection system. Certain early films of British-Canadian animator Norman McLaren were simply hand-drawn longitudinally along clear 35mm film. Their rectangular character was defined when masked to that dimension by movie printer and projector. A mask might as easily assume any other mode—a circle, a parabola, an Arp-shaped invention, or whatever. Necessarily any projection surface would have to accommodate its image borders.

3. *Surface.* Screens are constructed so as to maximize the illuminated

intensity of the projected image and to make it fully available to spectators located anywhere in the auditorium. (Light reflections fall off sharply as we view a flat surface from the sides.) But what if we are less interested in image fidelity? The texture of a projected image can be given other qualities by altering the screen surface: stone, concrete, plaster, wood, mirrors, cloth, draperies. An experimental filmmaker named Ben van Meter made an interesting project out of photographing anew the Hindenburg disaster as it was projected on a young woman's bare stomach.

4. *Multi-images.* As soon as we choose to abandon the single projected image, we open a Pandora's box of possibilities. Narrative use of multiple images will be explored in the next section; here we need only note that such images require some definition of their relationships to one another. Each may maintain its own discrete spatial autonomy (as in the Du Pont "World of Chemistry" exhibit at the 1964 New York World's Fair), but more often several images will be overlapped, literally or ideologically or both. When this happens, each gives up the integrities of its own shape and the relation of its borders to the space surrounding it, following the rules of what the psychologists term figure-to-ground relationships.

5. *Production dynamics.* We are accustomed to conceive of all film and most theater as occurring essentially in a static architectural design. This need not be true either. There is no commandment that says, "Thou shalt not move" to performer, audience, or projectionist. In an auditorium situation where the spectator is mobile, relative to performance, he gains the aesthetic choice of selection to a far greater degree than Bazin ever envisioned, more approaching the relation of an audience to architecture or sculpture, except that his art object need not be stable either.

Similarly, the performer may relocate his relationship to projected image and mobile or stationary audience. One of the theaters designed by Herbert Blau for the California Institute of the Arts in Valencia, California, is an effort at providing maximum alternatives in performer-audience relations, from spectators perched on the walls to actors emerging out of the floor.

We do not even need to work with stable projectors, clamped to a sturdy base. Provided that the equipment itself may be moved and a projectionist is strong enough or enterprising enough, the projected image can assume various distances from the screen. Such movements change both image size and relationship to the other elements of performance. In one San Francisco 8mm film festival, participants carried their own films threaded through their own projectors, shining these onto the walls and one another within the limits of their extension cords—perhaps a healthy exercise for venting the aggressions that young filmmakers sometimes harbor.

Given so many variables, it is not startling that mixed-media performance has shown myriad approaches and experienced many successes and failures. One of the most organized and designed film/theater ventures is that of Laterna Magika, created originally for the Czech Pavilion at the 1958 Brussels World's Fair. Laterna Magika integrates live and film actors, live and recorded music, slides, and poetry into what is essentially a theater aesthetic. Its stage designer, Josef Svoboda, has said, "Theater must maintain an artistic space," underlining the subordinate relation of film image to performance. An illustration of the company's theatrical employments was its version of *Tales of Hoffmann,* in which the great part of the stage backdrop was used for projected images of the protagonist's vivid imaginings. Such a technique essentially modernizes the nineteenth-century picture scene, used to visualize an actor's thoughts, which was assimilated into the movies' flashback. On a more ambitious scale, Laterna Magika uses multiple screens, which themselves can be relocated between acts or during performance. These not only accommodate projected images, film or slide, but may also provide far greater control and variation in stage lighting than is practiced in more orthodox theaters.

In New York, Ed Emschwiller has conducted film/dance performances in which the live, leotarded figures moved before audience and projectors. Holding little screens, they cast back reflections of film images of themselves. In the darkness, dancer and dance image meld into a single pattern.

At the Once Again Festival held in Ann Arbor in 1965, an interesting projection/performer production was staged, under the title *Unmarked Interchange.* On top of a parking-lot building, the simulation of a drive-in theater screen was constructed, its surface including panels, louvered openings, a catwalk, and a sort of large drawer. These elements were designed so that they divided the "screen" into smaller rectangles. The old RKO moneymaker *Top Hat* (1935) with Fred Astaire and Ginger Rogers was projected onto the larger surface. While Fred and Ginger did their numbers, an actor in one location read selections from Pauline Réage's pornographic novel, *The Story of O.* An actress walked across the catwalk periodically to throw custard pies in the face of the reader. Elsewhere, a piano player performed. A couple ate dinner on the "drawer." Silhouettes of girls hanging clothes and so forth were thrown against the screen from the rear.

Under such circumstances, an avalanche of ideas and sensations will run through any spectator who is not simply appalled at what has been perpetrated on the Piccolino. Since each live performer has interjected himself between projection source and screen, *Top Hat* will be cast on his figure, at least on that small portion of the screen he obscures. So each live event in the entire performance both melds into the projected image, becomes a part of the RKO production, and asserts its separate identity as far as it remains, too, a visible anomaly. The actor is free to move to any portion of the larger screen and maintains the same surface/off-surface tension, like a kind of live traveling matte. As he becomes, in movement, part of the projected film image, he affects the texture of the screen, affording it an animated, ever-shifting surface pattern.

Each "act" or relationship between acts sets up its own living connection with *Top Hat*. The reading of *The Story of O* requires us to make certain decisions, at least ask ourselves certain questions with relation to pornography, which is heard in contrast to the thirties sensualities of Astaire and Rogers: the outrageous and the ingratiating as contrary approaches to entertainment; the differences between live presentation and filmed dialogue/image. When the girl pitches custard pies into the reader's face, she both evokes an old movie image (the film gets back at its offenses) and expresses one of society's estimations of pornography, especially as imposed on a trapped, unwilling audience. The dining couple contrasts a live imitation of the gracious screen fantasy, where no one is unintentionally rude, and raw edges of ordinary existence are smoothed by dancers' movements. The rear-screen-projected silhouettes inject a more mundane, less imitative reality onto the screen surface. The piano player as film accompaniment predates *Top Hat,* as other acts postdate it.

Further, the superimpositions of images afford an altogether different quality to our sense of exposition. If we equate a single screen ratio with a coherent narrative picture, the mixing up of that composition by means of several other, smaller images, each with its own coherence and a relation to the larger framework, presents something like Picasso's and Braque's early Cubist paintings: several separate perspectives and time scales working both independently and *in toto*. The possibilities of response to such a performance are almost endless.

On reflection, it may be suggested that the integration of projected image and live performance presents at least six new possibilities to narrative exposition:

1. When movies are edited, each shot assumes a collection of meanings in terms of its interrelationships with the surrounding shots (Mozhukin and the food; see page 85). When we juxtapose projected image and performer, the same kind of meaning interplay occurs, only in the latter case it is a continuous relationship rather than bound into the time sequence of movie film's linearity.

2. The projected image escapes flat, distanced qualities characteristic of the usual auditorium-with-screen-on-the-wall. Film enters the total, ambient space of the spectator.

3. The Christian Metz dictum of "time past, image present" is denied in the measure that film has successfully integrated itself into a new performance aesthetic. The celluloid image becomes immediately real by way of its relation to live performance.

4. Movie performance has escaped the always-the-same-when-repeated qualities to which it is condemned in the conventional viewing

situation. Joining the theatrical kind of ritual, as Norman Mailer described it, each performance is subject both to the vagaries of any live execution and to the boundaries of any preconceptualized script.

5. Live and projected images not only have the picture-edited relationships of film but the counterpoint characteristic of movie picture and sound as well. These may amount to no more than clever tricks, like Laterna Magika (a live performer hands an apple to a screen image of himself, who accepts it). But they can be elaborated, too, into very complicated, extended exposition. For example, the double image of a single performer may be developed as central to an entire story, in which his two parts operate as psychic mirrors of a single personality. Such plot devices are traditional to the horror story, but their use in mixed media poses quite different possibilities by way of the very differences between two versions of one reality. (The actor is no more "real" than his photographed self.)

6. Any relationship between film and theater that allows aesthetic parity to each while integrating their functions will present its audience with a multiplicity of choices. Even the most complicated single-screen film story operates within bounded narrative limits that do not apply to mixed media. The spectator is far more fully participant to the experience, less passive, and more subject to demands that his understandings accompany the performance moment to moment on a joint adventure.

MULTIPLE IMAGE

We have watched multiple images on a single movie screen for years. The techniques of optical printing, appearing at their most euphoric in old Previews of Coming Attractions, broke one projected picture into various framed subdivisions. (My generation used to watch the screen divided into five triangles by the first *W* in Paramount's *News of the Week*.) A wipe across the screen, pushing off half the picture to register both parties in a telephone conversation, has been common.

There was a hallucination of James Mason's in *Odd Man Out* (1947), where haunting faces from his past experience appeared in bubbles of spilled beer, their voices mounting into a muddle of warnings. Auto races multiplied in simultaneous contest in *Grand Prix* (1966). More than one Kennedy speech was juxtaposed in *John F. Kennedy, Years of Lightning, Day of Drums* (1964). Performers in *Woodstock* (1970) were shown simultaneously from different angles. Francis Thompson used a prismatic lens to break a single image into countless repetitions in *N.Y., N.Y.* (1958).

All such techniques have tended to call attention to themselves—impressive but little else. Most often aping TV superimpositions, they intensified at best an atmospheric sense of event; Thompson's did underline the sameness of life in New York.

The use of multiple screens for narrative purposes has followed a some-

Multiple images produced by a prismatic lens in Francis Thompson's *N.Y., N.Y.*

what different history. It was first introduced by Abel Gance's triptych *Napoleon* (1927) which sometimes used one image, sometimes three. The outer frames were often reverse images supplying a setting for central narrative events. Gance operated with three projectors. Andy Warhol calls for two in *The Chelsea Girls* (1966), although in his case there is no effort to achieve exact formal synchronization between both screen events. Their relationships are fortuitous, changing from performance to performance.

Recent world's fairs have afforded settings for the most innovative approaches to multiple screen technique. At the New York State Pavilion of the 1964 New York World's Fair, eight fused projectors surrounded the spectator with an unavoidably total storytelling image, a technique also used by the Russians, and repeated in Expo 67 Disney Circle-Vision: 360 degrees of simulated reality, Hollywood or socialist realism. This approach denies the framed Magritte illusion (p. 16) by doing away with the borders.

Separate images, separately framed, have posed more interesting problems and possibilities. The Du Pont "World of Chemistry" at the 1964 fair employed three movable rectangular screens, working sometimes together for one picture, sometimes separated with different events, including interminglings with live actors and dancers. For IBM, Charles Eames designed a theater in which the viewers boarded a traveling tier of seats that lifted the audience to an egg-shaped upper area, where sixteen screens of different forms showed film, slides, and opaque and overhead projections. In one sequence called "Think," various screens represented alternatives to a single problem, thus providing a functional visual embodiment of a conceptual proposition.

The Czech Kino-Automat at Expo had a film event entitled *One Man and His World,* which enlisted audience participation. The movie was ordinary sex-farce, but viewers were invited to participate in its plot by voting, through buttons attached to each seat, which performer they wanted to "follow" at different times. The film provided thirty-two alternative combinations, and spectators were even given the chance to reconsider a decision, reversing the film to an earlier moment, and taking a different course. Thus audience engagement was actively brought about and computerized.

Another Czech exhibition, *Diapolyecran,* used 112 moving screen cubes, perhaps too many at times to keep track of. In the Canadian Pacific–Cominco Pavilion, Francis Thompson (of *N.Y., N.Y.*) and Alexander Hammid (of *Meshes of the Afternoon*) created a show called *We Are Young,* which used six screens and combinations of seven ordinary and two Cinerama projection systems. The screens were used to evoke various celebrations of youth, often creating their strongest visceral reactions by placing contrary screen movements so close in conjunction that the eye was inundated with frenzied, conflicting compositions. For example, motorcycles would leap from screen to screen, their action matched, but angle changed at the borders.

Christopher Chapman did something of the same with *Ontario: A Place to Stand.* In this case, the theme being geographic, he often used image combinations to represent simultaneous events at different places in the province, thus solving the cross-cut problem of time representation, the difficulties of which, for the single-image screen, we considered in chapter 3. *A Place to Stand* is noteworthy too for being executed on a single 70mm print by applying computer programming to optical printing. Chapman's 70mm image could approximate the size of the multiprojector images and still lend itself to ordinary theatrical exhibition. It has since been reduction-printed to 35mm and 16mm gauges, although color quality was lost in the transition.

The most ambitious and interesting of Expo 67's film exhibitions was constructed by the National Film Board of Canada: a building called Labyrinth with two major movie theaters. One juxtaposed a tall, vertical screen with an adjacent floor-length viewing area, experienced by audiences from balconies located above floor level and opposite the vertical screen. Images here were both counterpointed and paralleled. Where they represented the same event from different angles, the illusion evoked was one in which spectators filled in with imagined movement the space shared by both screens, like the gestalt phenomenon in which viewers appear to see a light pass from one spot to another if two blinking lamps are properly timed and distanced. The architecture of Labyrinth was designed so as similarly to engage the spectator in the screen illusions. The other theater consisted of five screens mounted in the shape of a cross. Here, Canadian Film Board personnel developed a production based on the Grecian hero-beast mythic theme of the labyrinth. Through seven different locations around the world, the beast was stalked. The character of this exposition may help us to locate some directions that future multiple-screen narrative might take.

Experience showed Labyrinth's editors that spectator perception shifted with novelty. In order to control effects, it was necessary to minimize the number of events and to arrange them in comprehensible composition and order. For example, an old Japanese man is shown centrally, surrounded by tree reflections in a pond, which seem to elaborate his meditation.

When one reflection is replaced by the portrait of an aging Greek woman, audience consciousness takes on a conceptual, rather than anecdotal turn. The associations made are those of age, transcending race and geography. Thus the matter of growing old could be developed as one of

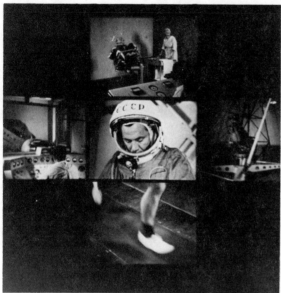

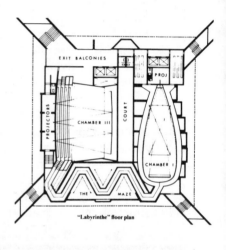

"Labyrinthe" floor plan

Labyrinth, a specially constructed building (above right), provided visitors to Expo 67 with two multiple image experiences, one with five screens (above left) and the other with two viewing areas (right). *(Credit: National Film Board of Canada)*

244 ■ Film and the Future

the monsters, a beast within us. These techniques of transcendent connection are used to equate different events through simultaneous screen appearance, linked to narrative energy. An African canoeing through a dense forest in pursuit of a crocodile can be seen to relate to a middle-aged Caucasian woman staring in the mirror. Fearfully, each confronts the monster.

In Labyrinth we have a serious effort to develop narrative language within a form that must recognize but not accede to the fact that myriad images cannot maintain diversity while yet allowing the spectator to "read" all they say. In McLuhan's terms, the effect is "environmental" rather than full information-imparting. The totally environmental would be film-as-atmosphere—like a light show—denying linear narrative progression for the altogether simultaneous Now. In this respect, Labyrinth, as its very name implies, amounts to a compromise between old and new.

Efforts from the commercial screen to incorporate modern multiple images thus far have been less compromises than they are conservative attempts to dress the old story in new fineries. With The Boston Strangler (1968), for example, Richard Fleischer visualized community terror by showing seven women locking their doors at once. Elsewhere, multiple screens placed unwary victim and murderer on one surface, adapting Griffith's parallel editing to the new technique.

In The Andromeda Strain (1971), Robert Wise adopted additional perspective into the coherent single image by way of two devices. One was the diopter lens, which magnifies a designated portion of the scene clearly while maintaining the rest of the image in more distant focus. Also, Wise hired Douglas Trumball, who had created the Stargate sequence in 2001: A Space Odyssey, to develop the televised views of the Andromeda strain through computerized animation. "Live" television presents a kind of cubist simultaneity; here, its images had something of the effect of the menacing Boston Strangler while more starkly integrating their presence into the sanitized laboratory settings. (A similar, interesting use of TV for multiple perspective is in the Congressional hearing sequence of The Manchurian Candidate [1962] by John Frankenheimer, who also made Grand Prix.) So we find that the old movie forms— The Andromeda Strain is clearly a detective story—seek to reclothe their aging tales in contemporary guise.

The movies continue to operate as an anecdotal, time-bound form in the measure that filmmakers believe their popular base requires linearity. Yet the aesthetic problems of film are not imposed with equal rigor on all the popular media, as we may see by passing reference to comics.

The early comic strips parallel and sometimes antedate the movies' camera angles, narrative sequence (for example, Long Shot to Medium Shot to Close Shot), and continuity bridges (like matching action and cutaways).[2] The comic book maintains and sometimes even elaborates

Panels from *The Spirit*. *(Credit: © 1975, Will Eisner)*

these traditions—so effectively, in fact, that it may resemble an animator's storyboard, which preconceives each shot of a story as well as major alternations within a shot.

Consider a page from *The Spirit,* an innovative adventure series of the forties created by Will Eisner, which has recently been reprinted for a new generation of readers.[3] Panels 1 and 2 appear to constitute one complete low-angled composition of a desk. Alignment of the furniture and skylight confirm this notion, but closer examination advises us that panel 2 is really differently angled when we consider the space between telephone and metronome and the disappearance of the steam radiator. Panel 3 edges slightly closer to the subject. Panel 4 shifts angle as well as employing a new lighting scheme. Note that the metronome casts a shadow while the figure does not. The central four panels proceed from Close Shot to Extreme Close-up. The lower frames alternate a high-angled expressionist composition, lighting, and decor with a last shot in which the face, lettering, and color climax the sequence.[4]

Three samples from the work of another comic book artist, Alex N. Niño, provide even more evidence of complications that can be effected in terms of time and space. In the first panel, Niño locates two sequential images in the same composition without recourse to borders. The central figure is drawn twice, and continuity is maintained by the reader's ordinary progression from left to right on the page.[5] Later in the same story a running figure "moves through" three poses, from Medium to Close Shot within the same panel.[6]

In a last Niño excerpt, a figure walks through wartime rubble (by implication, New York City because of the Statue of Liberty image in the lower right).[7] Taken as a whole, the drawing has the character of a widescreen composition, its action progressing from left to right, but within this larger panel we find two smaller ones: Long and Medium Shots. These precede the final balloon, and yet the ground and broken wreckage of each drawing fit exactly into the larger image. We are faced, then, with a single picture which simultaneously presents time passing and a static encapsulation of accumulated moments. Comic strip time is not film time although the two share sequential imagery.

THE END

What is to be witnessed in today's formally less cautious movies appears at times to be a kind of battle in which investment interests vie with aesthetic impulses in an effort to keep the medium engaging enough to hold a contemporary audience and "straight" enough not to alienate it. One strategy is to exaggerate the already exaggerated violence and sex. Another is to modernize the humor (Mel Brooks for example). Another is the same slowing down of narrative as will be found in theater, art, and comics. Film as event rather than film as parable.

Three samples from the work of Alex N. Niño. *(Credit:
© 1972 National Periodical Publications, Inc.)*

Increasingly visible too is the growing tension between naturalistic appearance and high stylization. Mass audience appeal has always required enough "realism" to sustain empathy. Such audience identification may be on the order of wish-fulfillment, of there-but-for-the-grace-of-God-go-I, or of the lascivious. We may enjoy pretending to be Burt Reynolds or Raquel Welch. We may safely watch Joanne Woodward in *The Three Faces of Eve* (1957) without endangering ourselves to schizophrenia. We may venture in and out from *Behind the Green Door* (1972) and no one will know.

Another commercial problem for the feature film is that of adapting its under-twenty-nine theater audience appeals to the over-twenty-nine TV film cemetery. The financiers are too greedy to wait until the first group ages itself into the second for the same film, carrying their sensibilities across the thirtieth-birthday border. Consequently many movies must somehow accommodate both groups to a reasonable degree. In seeking both audiences, the film will likely serve neither.

Finally, then, we are left with various understandings about the movie audience, which is to say, ourselves, which is to say, where we came in. In the measure that all of us, reader, writer, teacher, and "those other people," maintain a kind of aesthetic stasis, we will preserve commercial filmgoing, but in the process we will stop its formal evolution and give rein to the movies' dinosaur proclivities, film's own beast within itself.

On the other hand, if we opt for film as an experimental hotbed that combines technology with young dreams, we have removed it from mass audience underpinnings—its commercial, vulgar, narrative sustenance—in short, its life.

The alternatives (another polarity, notice) are interesting not only with reference to film (which, after all, is only a part of life) but to our understandings of other arts. More centrally, they pose questions that we might wisely ask of our own relation to the culture: from aesthetic linear stasis to experimental, timeless rootlessness. Where do we settle in between? We *are* the movies (flicks, cinema, film), because we are where their dreams begin.

RECOMMENDED READING

Modern documentary approaches may be studied in:
- Richard M. Barsam, *Non-Fiction Film* (New York: E. P. Dutton, 1973)
- A. William Bluem, *Documentary in American Television* (New York: Hastings House, 1965)
- Louis Jacobs, *Documentary Tradition: From Nanook to Woodstock* (New York: Hopkinson and Blake, 1971)
- G. Roy Levin, *Documentary Explorations* (New York: Doubleday, 1971)
- Louis Marcorelles, *Living Cinema* (New York: Praeger, 1973)

■ Stephen Mamber, *Cinéma Vérité in America: Studies in Uncontrolled Documentary* (Cambridge, Mass.: M.I.T. Press, 1974)

■ Alan Rosenthal, *The New Documentary in Action* (Berkeley: University of California Press, 1971)

■ For Moholy-Nagy's Bauhaus photography research, see Laszlo Moholy-Nagy, *Vision in Motion* (Chicago: Theobald, 1947).

■ An excellent source on theater-film collaborations is *Tulane Drama Review* 11, no. 1 (Fall 1966), particularly the Michael Kirby essay, "Uses of Film in the New Theater." For reports on film at Expo 67, read Barry Day, "Beyond the Frame," *Sight and Sound* (Spring 1968) and Judith Shotnoff, "Expo 67: A Multiple Vision," *Film Quarterly* (Fall 1967).

NOTES

1. Jim Schaffer, "The Perspective of Frank Zappa," *Down Beat,* September 13, 1973.
2. See John L. Fell, "Mr. Griffith, Meet Winsor McCay," chap. 5 of *Film and the Narrative Tradition* (Norman, Okla.: University of Oklahoma Press, 1974), pp. 88–120.
3. *The Spirit.* Warren Publishing Company, 145 East 32 St., New York, N.Y. 10016.
4. "The Deadly Comic Book," *The Spirit* no. 5 (December 1974).
5. "To Die for Magda," *The House of Mystery* no. 204 (July 1972). National Periodical Publications, P.O. Box 1047, Flushing, N.Y. 11352.
6. *Ibid.*
7. "The Last Battle," *Weird War Tales* no. 9 (December 1972). National Periodical Publications, P.O. Box 1047, Flushing, N.Y. 11352.

Appendix A

A SELECTED LIST OF AMERICAN FILM
REFERENCE PUBLICATIONS

Aaronson, Charles S. *International Motion Picture and Television Almanac*. New York: Quigley Publications, annual. (Production statistics. Personnel, including producers.)

Blum, Daniel. *Screen World*. New York: Greenberg, 1949– . Annual. Year's releases, especially American. Obituaries.)

Cameron, James R., and Joseph S. Cifre. *Cameron's Encyclopedia of Sound Motion Pictures*. Coral Gables, Fla.: Cameron Publishing, 1959.

Cowie, Peter, ed. *International Film Guide*. New York: A. S. Barnes, 1964– . Annual. (Directors of the year, international releases, archives, schools, bookstores, festivals, etc.)

Dimmitt, Richard B. *An Actor's Guide to the Talkies*. 2 vols. Metuchen, N.J.: The Scarecrow Press, 1967. (8000 films by title, copyright date, producer, actors, roles. Until 1964. Vol. 2 lists 30,000 actors.)

———. *A Title Guide to the Talkies*. 2 vols. New York: The Scarecrow Press, 1965. (16,000 features. 1927–1963.)

Film Daily Year Book of Motion Pictures. New York: Film Daily Publishers, 1918– . Annual. (Year's releases, credits, distribution, industry news and statistics, including financial statements and some telephone numbers.)

Gottesman, Ronald, and Harry M. Geduld. *Guidebook to Film*. New York: Holt, Rinehart & Winston, 1972. (Paperback reference with books, periodicals, theses, festivals, awards, museums, archives, distributors, schools, terminology, etc.)

———. *An Illustrated Glossary of Film Terms*. New York: Holt, Rinehart & Winston, 1973. (Nontechnical, sometimes illustrated definitions of acting, critical and production vocabulary.)

Graham, Peter. *A Dictionary of the Cinema*. rev. ed. New York: A. S. Barnes, 1968. (Identification and credits on filmmakers, actors; some essays. Indexed by title.)

Halliwell, Leslie. *The Filmgoer's Companion*. New York: Hill & Wang, 1974. (Directors, producers, mostly actors. Capsule identifications, credits.)

Jordan, Thurston C., Jr. *A Glossary of Film Terms*. Menlo Park, Ca.: Pacific Coast Publishers, 1968. (Definitions of critical and production language.)

Leonard, Harold, ed. *The Film Index: A Bibliography. Vol. 1: The Film as Art*. New York: Arno Press, 1966. (Reprint edition of 1941 annotated bibliography—mostly English—of history, criticism, technique. 8600 entries.)

Limbacher, James A. *A Directory of 16mm Sound Feature Films Available for Rental in the United States*. New York: R. R. Bowker, 1971. (Distributor sources, release dates, actors, director, color or black-and-white, running time, national origin. Distributors shift faster than revised editions, however.)

MacCann, Richard Dyer, and Edward S. Perry. *The New Film Index*. New York: E. P. Dutton, 1974. (Supplement to Leonard, covering 1930–1970. 12,000 citations, 1200 cross-references.)

Maltin, Leonard, ed. *TV Movies*. New York: New American Library, 1973. (Films available to television stations with release dates, capsule synopses, and directors.)

Manvell, Roger, ed. *The International Encyclopedia of Film*. New York: Crown, 1972. (1280 entries, well-illustrated in color and black-and-white. Bibliography. Indexed by personnel and film titles. Excellent essays.)

Michael, Paul. *The American Movies Reference Book: The Sound Era*. Englewood Cliffs, N.J.: Prentice-Hall, 1969. (Actors, some directors, awards, credits of popular films.)

Motion Pictures and Filmstrips. Library of Congress, 1953– . Annual. (Library of Congress entries via printed index cards. Titles thoroughly cross-referenced by subject.)

Munden, Kenneth W., ed. *The American Film Institute Catalog: Feature Films 1921–30*. 2 vols. New York: R. R. Bowker, 1970. (Comprehensive information, eventually on every known American film produced since 1893.)

The New York Times Film Reviews 1913–1968. New York: Arno Press, 1970. (16,000 *Times* reviews plus one-volume index of actors, directors, subject, title. Valuable for credits and synopses.)

Niver, Kemp R. *Motion Pictures from the Library of Congress Paper Print Collection, 1894–1912*. Berkeley: University of California Press, 1967. (Ttitles, credits, footage, dates, synopses. Some 1914–15 material included. Comprehensive indexes.)

Sadoul, Georges. *Dictionary of Films*. Edited by Peter Morris. Berkeley: University of California Press, 1972. (1200 films with credits, descriptions, critical discussion.)

————. *Dictionary of Film Makers*. Edited by Peter Morris. Berkeley: University of California Press, 1972. (International production personnel identified, critical description, major credits.)

Scheuer, Steven H., ed. *Movies on TV*. New York: Bantam, 1969. (Production dates, synopses, but no director credits.)

Smolian, Steven. *A Handbook of Film, Theater, and Television Music on Record, 1948–69*. New York: The Record Undertaker, 1970. (2000 LPs of original cast and American soundtracks. Composers, recording dates, film production dates.)

Spottiswoode, Raymond, et al. *The Focal Encyclopaedia of Film and Television Techniques*. New York: Hastings House, 1969. (Technological, historical, biographical résumés of film technique.)

Note: For more detailed critical descriptions of certain citations, plus foreign-language entries, see John L. Fell, "A Film Student's Guide to the Reference Shelf," *Cinema Journal* 9 (Fall 1969).

Appendix B

A SELECTED LIST OF ENGLISH-LANGUAGE
FILM PERIODICALS

Action. 7950 Sunset Boulevard, Los Angeles, Ca. 90046. (Directors Guild of America publication.)

American Cinematographer. 1728 North Orange Drive, Hollywood, Ca. 90028. (American Society of Cinematographers publication.)

Cinema Journal. Department of TV/Radio/Film, The University of Iowa, Iowa City, Iowa 52240. (Society for Cinema Studies journal.)

Classic Film Collector. 734 Philadelphia Street, Indiana, Pa. 15701.

Film Comment. 100 Walnut Place, Brookline, Mass. 02146.

Film Culture. G.P.O. Box 1449, New York, N.Y. 10001.

Film Heritage. Wright State University, Dayton, Ohio 45431.

The Film Journal. Box 9602, Hollins College, Va. 24020.

Film Library Quarterly. 17 West 60th Street, New York, N.Y. 10023.

Film Quarterly. University of California Press, Fulton Street, Berkeley, Ca. 94720.

Film Society Review. 144 Bleecker Street, New York, N.Y. 10012.

Filmmakers' Newsletter. 80 Wooster Street, New York, N.Y. 10012.

Films and Filming. 75 Victoria Street, London S.W.1.

Films in Review. 31 Union Square, New York, N.Y. 10003.

Hollywood Reporter. 6715 Sunset Boulevard, Hollywood, Ca. 90028.

Journal of Popular Film. Bowling Green, Ohio 43403.

Journal of the Producers Guild of America. 141 El Camino Drive, Beverly Hills, Ca. 90212.

Journal of the University Film Association. 156 West 19th Avenue, Ohio State University, Columbus, Ohio 43210.

Monogram. 63 Old Compton Street, London W.1.

Monthly Film Bulletin. 81 Dean Street, London W.1.

Motion Picture Daily. 1270 6th Avenue, New York, N.Y. 10020.

Movie. 21 Ivor Place, London, N.W.1.

Newsletter. American Film Institute, 1815 H Street N.W., Washington, D.C. 20006.

Screen. 63 Old Compton Street, London W.1.

Screen Actor. 7750 Sunset Boulevard, Hollywood, Ca. 90046. (Screen Actors Guild publication.)

Sight and Sound. 81 Dean Street, London, W.1.

The Silent Picture. First Media Press, 1121 Carney Street, Cincinnati, Ohio 45202.

Take One. Post Office Box 1778, Station B, Montreal.

Today's Film Maker. 250 Fulton Avenue, Hempstead, N.Y. 11550.

Variety. 154 West 46th Street, New York, N.Y. 10036.

Appendix C

FILM STUDY IN THE UNITED STATES

BACHELOR OF ARTS

American University
Antioch College
California State University, San Francisco
Columbia College, Chicago
Columbia College, Los Angeles
Cornell University
Creighton University
Evergreen College
Fordham University
Goddard College
Hampshire College
Harpur College
Humboldt State College
Hunter College
Louisiana State University
Loyola University, New Orleans
Marlboro College
Memphis State University
New Mexico State University
Oberlin College
Pennsylvania State University
Philadelphia College of Art
Pratt Institute
Richmond College

Seton Hall University
Stephens College
Texas Christian University
University of Alabama
University of California, Los Angeles
University of Denver
University of Georgia
University of Iowa
University of Kansas
University of North Carolina
University of South Florida
University of Southern California
University of Texas, Austin
University of West Virginia
University of Wisconsin
Washington State University
Wesleyan University
Xavier University

BACHELOR OF FINE ARTS

California College of Arts and Crafts
California Institute of the Arts
Hunter College
Maryland Institute of Art
New York University
Ohio State University

Ohio University
Rhode Island School of Design
Rochester Institute of Technology
Southern Methodist University

BACHELOR OF SCIENCE

Bob Jones University
Boston University
California State University, San Diego
Emerson College
Ithaca College
Montana State University
Northwestern University
Rochester Institute of Technology
Southern Illinois University, Carbondale
Temple University
Xavier University

MASTER OF ARTS

American University
Bob Jones University
California State University, San Francisco
Columbia College, Chicago
Columbia College, Los Angeles
Cornell University
Humboldt State College
Louisiana State University
Memphis State University
New York University
Northwestern University
Ohio State University
Stanford University
Texas Christian University
University of Alabama
University of Arizona
University of California, Los Angeles
University of Cincinnati
University of Denver
University of Georgia

University of Iowa
University of Kansas
University of North Carolina
University of Oregon
University of Pennsylvania
University of South Florida
University of Southern California
University of Texas, Austin
University of West Virginia
University of Wisconsin

MASTER OF FINE ARTS

California College of Arts and Crafts
California Institute of the Arts
Columbia University
Louisiana State University
New York University
Northwestern University
Ohio University
Rochester Institute of Technology
Southern Methodist University
Temple University
University of California, Los Angeles
University of Oregon
University of Southern California

DOCTOR OF PHILOSOPHY

Claremont School of Theology
Indiana University
New York University
Northwestern University
Ohio State University
Temple University
University of California, Los Angeles
University of Iowa
University of Pennsylvania
University of Southern California
University of Texas
University of Wisconsin

Appendix D

16mm FILM-DISTRIBUTION SOURCES

Films cited in the text are listed in the Index of Film Titles (pp. 263–66), which also designates their distributors where these exist or are known. For general information on distributors and addresses, the following references are suggested.

GENERAL INFORMATION

Audiovisual Market Place. New York: R. R. Bowker, 1973.
Clark, Joan. *A Dictionary of Film Libraries in the USA.* Film Library Information Council, 1971.
Limbacher, James L., ed., *Using Film.* Educational Film Library Association, 1967.
Weiner, Janet. *How to Organize and Run a Film Society.* New York: Collier, 1973.

FILM RENTAL

Artel, Linda. *Film Programmer's Guide to 16mm Rentals.* Reel Research, 1972.
Kone, Grace. *8mm Film Directory.* Comprehensive Service, 1969.
Limbacher, James L. *Feature Films on 8mm and 16mm.* 4th ed. New York: R. R. Bowker, 1974.
NICEM Index to 8mm Motion Cartridges. National Information Center for Educational Media, University of Southern California 1970–   . Published every three years.
NICEM Index to 16mm Educational Films. 1971–   . 3d ed. Published every three years.
NICEM Index to Producers and Distributors. 1971–   . Annual.

RENTALS OF INDEPENDENT FILMS

Canyon Cinema Cooperative. Room 220 Industrial Center Building, Sausalito, Ca. 94965.

Filmmakers' Cooperative. 175 Lexington Avenue, New York, N.Y. 10016.

Note: Several feature film distributors (e.g., Macmillan Audio Brandon, Creative Film Society) also circulate experimental films. For their addresses, consult the directories listed under "Film Rental," above. Sheldon Renan, *An Introduction to the American Underground Film* (New York: E. P. Dutton, 1967), indexes his film citations and indicates distribution sources where known.

ANIMATION

For information on rental of special animation materials, including the annual International Tournée, write; Prescott Wright, 20 Ord Court, San Francisco, Ca. 94114.

Appendix E

DISTRIBUTORS

The abbreviations at the head of each film distributor listed below are used in the Index of Film Titles (pp. 263–66) to identify which films are available for rental through each distributor. Because most distributors work with term leases for rental rights in 16mm, it is always possible that a distributor indicated for a given title may no longer circulate it.

AVC

Avco Embassy Pictures Corporation
1301 Avenue of the Americas
New York, N.Y. 10019

B

Budget Films
4590 Santa Monica Boulevard
Los Angeles, Ca. 90029

BUR

Joseph Burstyn Film Enterprises
250 West 57th Street
New York, N.Y. 10019

CAN

Canyon Cinema Cooperative
Industrial Center Building
Room 220
Sausalito, Ca. 94965

CCC

Cine-Craft Company
709 South West Ankeney
Portland, Ore. 97205

CFS

Creative Film Society
14558 Valerio Street
Van Nuys, Ca. 91405

CHA

Chavard Motion Pictures
2110 East 24th Street
Brooklyn, N.Y. 11229

CIN

Cinema 5
595 Madison Avenue
New York, N.Y. 10022

COL

Columbia Cinematheque
711 Fifth Avenue
New York, N.Y. 10022

CON

Contemporary Films
McGraw-Hill Book Company
Princeton Road
Hightstown, N.J. 08520

CWF

Clem Williams Films
2240 Noblestown Road
Pittsburgh, Pa. 15705

FAC/FACSEA

Society for French-American Cultural
   Services and Educational Aid
972 Fifth Avenue
New York, N.Y. 10021

FCE

Film Classics Exchange
1926 South Vermont Avenue
Los Angeles, Ca. 90007

FMC

Film Makers Coop
175 Lexington Avenue
New York, N.Y. 10016

FNC

Films Incorporated
4420 Oakton Street
Skokie, Ill. 60076

Gen

Generally distributed

GRO

Grove Press Film Division
214 Mercer Street
New York, N.Y. 10012

GW

Mr. George Wehlie
Film Library
University of Southern California
Los Angeles, Ca. 90009

ICS

Institutional Cinema Service
915 Broadway
New York, N.Y. 10010

IDE

Ideal Pictures
34 MacQuesten Parkway South
Mount Vernon, N.Y. 10550

JAN

Janus Films
745 Fifth Avenue
New York, N.Y. 10022

LEA

Leacock-Pennebaker
56 West 45th Street
New York, N.Y. 10036

MAB

Macmillan Audio Brandon Films
34 MacQuesten Parkway South
Mount Vernon, N.Y. 10550

MAY

Harold Mayer Productions
155 West 72d Street
New York, N.Y. 10023

MMA

Film Library
The Museum of Modern Art
11 West 53d Street
New York, N.Y. 10019

MMM

Mass Media Ministries
2116 North Charles Street
Baltimore, Md. 21218

MSP

Modern Sound Pictures
1402 Howard Street
Omaha, Nebraska 68102

NLC

New Line Cinema
121 University Place
New York, N.Y. 10003

NY

New Yorker Films
43 West 61st Street
New York, N.Y. 10023

NYR

New York Review Presentations
250 West 57th Street
New York, N.Y. 10019

P

Pyramid Films
Box 1048
Santa Monica, Ca. 90406

RAD

Radim Films/Film Images
17 West 60th Street
New York, N.Y. 10023

ROA

Roa's Films
1696 North Aster Street
Milwaukee, Wis. 53202

ROB

Peter M. Robeck
Time-Life Films
43 West 16th Street
New York, N.Y. 10011

SGS

Samuel Goldwyn/16mm
1041 North Formosa Avenue
Los Angeles, Ca. 90046

STA

Standard Film Service
14710 West Warren Street
Dearborn, Mich. 48126

SWA

Swank Motion Pictures
201 South Jefferson Avenue
St. Louis, Mo. 63166

T

Twyman Films Incorporated
329 Salem Avenue
Dayton, Ohio 45401

TWF

Trans World Films
322 South Michigan Avenue
Chicago, Ill. 60604

UAS

United Artists 17
729 Seventh Avenue
New York, N.Y. 10019

UNI

Universal 16
221 Park Avenue South
New York, N.Y. 10003

U-W

The Film Center
University of Washington
Seattle, Wash. 98195

WAR

Andy Warhol
33 Union Square West
New York, N.Y. 10003

WHO

Wholesome Film Center
20 Melrose Street
Boston, Mass. 02116

WIL

Willoughby-Peerless
110 West 32d Street
New York, N.Y. 10001

WRS

Walter Reade 16
241 East 34th Street
New York, N.Y. 10016

WSA

Warner Brothers
Non-Theatrical Distribution
4000 Warner Boulevard
Burbank, Ca. 91503

Z

Zipporah Films
54 Lewis Wharf
Boston, Mass. 02110

Index of Film Titles

Dates following titles signify the time of each film's release, which will sometimes fail to coincide with the year of a production's completion. Where the 16mm distribution source of a film is known, this information follows the release date; abbreviations refer to company names and addresses noted in Appendix E, which begins on page 259.

Abbott and Costello Meet the Mummy (1955) CWF, UNI: 119

Adventures of Sherlock Holmes, The (1939) FNC: 117

African Queen, The (1951) Gen, SWA: 158

Algiers (1938) B: 148

All About Eve (1950) FNC: 156

Amazing Dr. Clitterhouse, The (1938) UAS, WIL: 158

American Graffiti (1973): 77

Andromeda Strain, The (1971) T: 245

Angels with Dirty Faces (1938) UAS, WIL: 158

Anna Christie (1930) FNC: 174–75

Antonio das Mortes (1969) GRO: 118

Asphalt Jungle, The (1950) FNC: 76, 156

Ascenseur pour l'Echaufaud. *See* Frantic

Avventura, L' (1960) JAN: x, xii, 76

Barney Oldfield's Race for Life (1913) MAB: 83

Basic Training (1971) Z: 235

Battleship Potemkin, The (1925) Gen, MMA: 64–66, 86–87, 99

Beat the Devil (1953) COL: 137

Becky Sharp (1935) FCE: 100

Beggar's Opera, The (1953) B, WSA: 101

Behind the Green Door (1972): 249

Bellissima (1951): 194

Ben-Hur (1926) FNC: 174–75

Berlin: The Symphony of a Great City (1927) MMA: 45

Bicycle Thief, The (Bicycle Thieves) (1948) BUR, MAB: 153

Big Parade, The (1925) FNC: 174

Birth of a Nation, The (1915) MMA: 61, 153, 178, 191, 221, 236–37

Black Pirate, The (1926) (b&w print) Gen, MMA: 14

Blood of a Poet, The (Le Sang d'un Poète) (1930) B, MAB: 19n, 78

Blow-Up (1966) FNC: 112, 132

Blue Angel, The (1930) B, Gen, MMA: 75, 92, 149–50

Bluebeard (1901): 83

Bonnie and Clyde (1967) B, Gen, WSA: 15, 96, 137–38, 165–67, 215

Borinage (1933): 102

Born Yesterday (1950) B, Gen, MAB: 130

Boston Strangler, The (1968) FNC: 245

Breathless (A Bout de Souffle) (1959) CON: 207

Broadway Melody (1929) FNC: 174–75

Bus Stop (1956) MAB: 156

Butch Cassidy and the Sundance Kid (1969) FNC: 137, 150, 171

Butterfield 8 (1960) FNC: 158

Cabinet of Dr. Caligari, The (1919) B, Gen, MMA: 19n, 110

Cactus Flower (1969) ICS: 130

Carabiniers, Les (1963) FAC, NYR: 16

Casablanca (1942) UAS: 47

Cat People, The (1942) FNC: 93, 119

Catch-22 (1970) FNC: 102

Chair, The (1963) ROB: 233

Chelsea Girls, The (1966) WAR: 242

Cheyenne Autumn (1964) B, Gen, MAB: 210

263

Chien Andalou, Un (An Andalusian Dog) (1928) MMA, P: 190
Chienne, La (1931): 207
Chinatown (1974): 177
Chronicle of a Summer (Chronique d'un Été) (1961) CON: 103, 233
Citizen Kane (1941) JAN, MAB: 18, 69, 108, 111, 119, 150, 169
Cleo from Five to Seven (1961) CON: 73, 80
Cleopatra (1963) FNC: 129
Clockwork Orange, A (1971) WSA: 97, 101
Clowns, The (1970) FNC: 104, 213
Countess from Hong Kong, A (1966) CCC, SWA: 136
Cousins, The (Les Cousins) (1959) SWA: 207
Cries and Whispers (1972) FNC: 101, 112, 115, 231
Crime of Monsieur Lange, The (1935) MAB: 204, 207
Crowd, The (1928) FNC: 174–75

Day of Wrath (1943) CON: 137
Dead End (1937) SGS: 158
Dead Reckoning (1947) B, Gen, ROA: 47
Death of a Salesman (1951) Gen, MAB: 112
Deserter (1933) MMA: 90
Désirée (1954) FNC: 80
Detective, The (1968) Gen, MAB: 121
Devil with Women, A (1930): 158
Diary for Timothy (1945) CON: 78
Diary of a Country Priest (Le Journal d'un Curé de Compagne) (1950) MAB: 93
Dillinger (1973): 215
Dirty Harry (1971) WSA: 121, 215
Discreet Charm of the Bourgeoisie, The (1972): 75
Dishonored (1931) CCC, UNI: 150
Doctor Cyclops (1940) UNI: 170
Dr. Jekyll and Mr. Hyde (1931) FNC: 90, 104–5, 170
Dr. Strangelove or: How I Learned to Stop Worrying and Love the Bomb (1963) COL: 96–97
Don Juan (1926): 92
Don't Look Back (1966) LEA: 233
Dracula (1931) UNI, WHO: 119

Easy Rider (1969) FMC: 118, 229
Eclipse, The (L'Eclisse) (1962) MAB: xii
8½ (1963) MAB: 95, 104, 115, 140, 213
Electra Glide in Blue (1973): 229
Entertainer, The (1960) WRS: 159
Exorcist, The (1973): 41, 135
Experiment in Terror (1962) B, Gen, MAB: 76

Fatal Glass of Beer, The (1931) B, MSP: 170

Fellini Satyricon (1969) UAS: 19, 213
Fièvre (1921) MMA: 59–60
Flesh Gordon (1974): 230
Football (1961): 233
Fort Apache (1948) IDE, MAB: 210
400 Blows, The (Les Quatre Cents Coups) (1959) JAN: 171
Frankenstein (1931) IDE, MAB: 119
Frantic (Ascenseur pour l'Echaufaud) (1957) MAB: 97
French Connection, The (1971) FNC: 19
Frenzy (1972) UNI: 105

Gentlemen Prefer Blondes (1953) FNC: 155
Giant (1956) B, WSA: 19
Gimme Shelter (1970) CIN: 234
Godfather, The (1972): 101–2, 123n, 177
Gone with the Wind (1939): 176
Graduate, The (1967) AVC: 76
Grand Hotel (1932) FNC: 175
Grand Prix (1966): 241, 245
Grapes of Wrath, The (1940) CON, FNC: 210
Great Expectations (1946) CON, UNI: 104
Great Gatsby, The (1974): 177
Great Train Robbery, The (1903) MMA: 83
Greed (1923) FNC: 175, 209
Guernica (1950): 28

Hallelujah the Hills (1963) FMC: 7–8, 237
Happy Days (1974): 230
Hard Day's Night, A (1964) CHA, UAS: 76
Help! (1965) CHA, UAS: 76
High Noon (1952) Gen, MAB: 75, 120
High School (1969) Z: 235
High Sierra (1941) CON, MAB: 158
Horizons West (1952) UNI: 117
Horse Soldiers, The (1959) UAS: 211
Hospital (1969) Z: 235
Hour of the Wolf (1968) UAS: 231
How Green Was My Valley (1941) FNC: 210
How I Won the War (1967) UAS: 76
How the West Was Won (1962) FNC: 210
How to Marry a Millionaire (1953) Gen, MAB: 155
Hunchback of Notre Dame, The (1923) B, Gen: 158

I. F. Stone's Newsletter (1974): 129
I Walked with a Zombie (1943) FNC: 119
I Was a Teenage Frankenstein (1957) B, Gen: 230
In Old Chicago (1938) FNC: 170
Incredible Shrinking Man, The (1953) ROA, SWA: 170
Informer, The (1935) JAN, MAB: 209–11
Intermezzo, a Love Story (1939) IDE, MAB: 9–10, 89

Interpretations and Values (1958) GW: 10
Intolerance (1916) B, Gen, MAB, MMA: 66, 221, 237
Isle of the Dead, The (1945) FNC: 130

Jazz Singer, The (1927) UAS: 92
Jeremiah Johnson (1972): 215
Joe (1970) WSA: 118
John F. Kennedy: Years of Lightning, Day of Drums (1964) AVC: 241
Jules and Jim (1961) JAN: 154, 207
Juliet of the Spirits (1965) MAB: 213
Juvenile Court (1973) Z: 235

King Kong (1933) FNC, JAN: 18
Knack . . . and how to get it, The (1964) CHA, UAS: 76

Lady in the Lake, The (1946) FNC: 107
Lady Sings the Blues (1971) FNC: 191
Last Hurrah, The (1958) B, Gen, MAB: 210
Last Laugh, The (1924) MMA: 108
Last Tango in Paris (1972): 18, 230
Last Year at Marienbad (L'Année Dernière à Marienbad) (1961) MAB: 93, 96, 164, 191, 197–98
Left Handed Gun, The (1958) MAB, WSA: 167
Leopard Man, The (1943) FNC, JAN: 119
Library of Congress Paper Prints (Niver Collection) P: 58
Life and Times of Judge Roy Bean, The (1972): 215
Little Flowers of St. Francis, The (1950): 194
Little Foxes, The (1941) SGS: 197
Long Voyage Home, (1940) B, TWF, WIL: 209–10
Lost Patrol, The (1933) FNC: 209
Lovemaking (1969) CAN: 188
Love Me Tonight (1932) UNI: 90

McCabe and Mrs. Miller (1971) WSA: 102, 137
Magnificent Ambersons, The (1942) JAN: 111, 119, 135, 151
Magnum Force (1973): 21
Maltese Falcon, The (1941) CON, UAS: 6–7, 10, 34–39, 47, 51, 158, 209
Man Escaped, A (Un Condamné à Mort s'Est Échappé) (1956) CON: 93–94
Man Who Shot Liberty Valance, The (1962) FNC: 210–11
Man with a Movie Camera (1929) MAB: 104
Manchurian Candidate, The (1962) CHA, UAS: 245
Marnie (1964) CCC, SWA: 100, 112–13, 169–70
Masculine-Feminine (1965) COL: 132

M*A*S*H (1970) FNC: 137
Medium Cool (1969) FNC: 118
Merry-Go-Round (1923) CFS, RAD: 175
Meshes of the Afternoon (1943) GRO, MMA: 164, 243
Metanomen (1966) MMA: 188
Metropolis (1927) MAB: 111
Mickey One (1965) Gen, MAB: 97
Midnight Cowboy (1969) UAS: 176
Miracle, The (1947) NY: 211
Mischief Makers, The (Les Mistons) (1957) P: 168
Misfits, The (1961) UAS: 156
Moana (1924) MMA: 98
Moby Dick (1955) UAS: 102
Moi un Noir (1958): 233
Monkey Business (1952) FNC: 156
Moon 69 (1969) MMA: 188
Mother (1926) MMA: 108
Moulin Rouge (1953) UAS: 100
Movie, A (1958) MMA: 189
Mummy, The (1933) Gen, UNI: 119
Murmur of the Heart (1971): 96
My Darling Clementine (1946) FNC, MAB: 210
My Life to Live (Vivre Sa Vie) (1962) CON: 157

Naked Night, The (Sawdust and Tinsel) (1953) MAB: 91, 165
Nanook of the North (1921) B, MMA, P: 18–19
Napoleon (1927, 1932): 80, 242
Niagara (1952) FNC: 156
Night and Fog (1955) P: 78–79, 97
Night of the Hunter (1955) UAS: 165
North by Northwest (1959) FNC: 109
Notte, La (1960) CON: 147
N.Y., N.Y. (1958) MMA, P: 241, 243

Occurrence at Owl Creek Bridge, An (Robert Enrico) (1962) CON, P: 78
Odd Man Out (1947) CON, JAN, WHO: 241
Off/On (1967) MMA: 188
Old and New, The (The General Line) (1929) MAB: 100
Open City (Roma, Città Aperta) (1945) CON: 97, 211
Orpheus (1949) JAN: 75, 78

Paisan (1946) NY: 97, 194, 211
Parallax View, The (1974): 177, 230
Passage to Marseille (1944) UAS: 47
Passion of Joan of Arc, The (1928) B, MMA: 64, 137
People of the City (1947): 78
Performance (1970) WSA: 230
Persona (1966) CHA, UAS: 8, 231

Petrified Forest, The (1936) CON, MAB: 158

Pierrot le Fou (1965) CON: 206–7, 223n

Place in the Sun, A (1951) FNC: 91, 165

Place to Stand, A (1967) P: 243

Play It Again, Sam (1972) FNC: 20

Plough and the Stars, The (1936) FNC: 210

Prelude (1961) FMC: 19n

Primary (1960) ROB: 233

Psycho (1960) CCC, CWF, ROA, UNI: 6, 105, 109

Public Enemy, The (1931) CON, MAB, UAS, WIL: 157

Purple Heart, The (1944) FNC: 145

Quiet Man, The (1952) STA: 157, 210

Rage (1973): 177

Rashomon (1950) JAN: 77, 113–14

Red Badge of Courage, The (1951) FNC: 176

Red Desert (1964) MAB: 112, 195

Red River (1948) UAS: 157

Reflections in a Golden Eye (1967) WSA: 172

Rien que les Heures (1926) MMA: 77–78

Rififi (1954): 76

Rio Grande (1950) STA: 157

River of No Return (1954) FNC: 156

Roaring Twenties, The (1939) CON, UAS, WIL: 158

Roma (1972) UNI: 211, 213

Rope (1948): 109

Rules of the Game, The (La Règle du Jeu) (1939) JAN: 71, 194

Saga of Gosta Berling, The (The Story of Gosta Berling) (1923) MMA: 207

Salesman (1969) MAY: 233

San Francisco (1936) FNC: 170

Saragossa Manuscript, The (1964): 74–75

Savage Is Loose, The (1974): 177

Sawdust and Tinsel. See The Naked Night

Seven Year Itch, The (1955) FNC: 156

Seventh Seal, The (1956) JAN: 115

Shadows of Forgotten Ancestors (1965) JAN: 101

Shanghai Express (1932) UNI: 150

She Wore a Yellow Ribbon (1949) IDE, MAB: 157

Shoe Shine (1946): 194

Slaughterhouse-Five (1972) SWA, UNI: xi, 231

Sleep (1964): xii

Sleuth (1972) FNC: 159–60

Smashup (1947): 151

Some Like It Hot (1959) UAS: 136, 156

South Pacific (1958) B: 145

Spy, The (1932) MAB: 78

Stagecoach (1939) B, ROA, STA: 157, 210–11

Strada, La (1954) MAB, MMM: 211–13

Strangers on a Train (1951) WSA: 131–32

Sunday, Bloody Sunday (1971) UAS: 176

Sunset Boulevard (1950) FNC: 132

Tell Them Willy Boy Is Here (1969) CCC, UNI: 172

Ten Days That Shook the World (October) (1928) MAB, MMA: 87–88

La Terra Trema (1948) MAB: 194

That's Entertainment (1974): 100

They Shoot Horses, Don't They? (1967) FNC: 75

Thing, The (1951) FNC: 222n

Three Faces of Eve, The (1957) FNC: 249

Three Little Pigs, The (1933) FNC: 14

Tobacco Road (1941) B, MAB: 210

Tony Rome (1967) FNC: 121

Top Hat (1935) IDE, JAN, MAB: 239–40

Topo, The (1970): 230

Trader Horn (1931) FNC: 175

Tragic Diary of Zero the Fool, The (1969) NLC: 235

Trial, The (1962) MAB: 50

Triumph of the Will (1934) MMA: 108

True Grit (1969) FNC: 158

Tunes of Glory (1960) UAS: 159

200 Motels (1971) UAS: 232

2001: A Space Odyssey (1968) FNC: 97, 164, 230, 245

Two Women (1960) MAB: 95

Umberto D (1952) MAB: 194

Variety (1925) B, MAB: 195

Variety Lights (Luci del Varietà) (1950) CON, MAB: 211

Vertigo (1958): 68

Vitelloni, I (1953) CON, MAB: 211

War and Peace (1956 American) FNC, WRS: 145

War and Peace (1963–67 USSR): 145

Wavelength (1966–67) MMA: 189

Waverly Steps (1948) UW: 78

Weekend (1967) GRO: 81, 207

We're Not Married (1952) FNC: 156

White Heat (1949) UAS, WIL: 157

Who's Afraid of Virginia Woolf? (1966) WSA: 158

Wind from the East (Vent d'Est) (1970) NLC: 81, 104, 191

Woodstock (1970) WSA: 241

Yankee Doodle Dandy (1942) UAS: 157

Young Mr. Lincoln (1939) FNC: 210

General Index

Acting, 152–60; director and, 136; effects of camera on, 138; inadequancies of, 40–41; and intellectual communication, 159; and physical performance, 158; reconstructed through editing, 83; and typage, 153
Adaptations, 31–40, 50
"Against Interpretation" (Sontag), 189
Agee, James, 184, 205
Albertazzi, Giorgio, 164, 197–98
Aldrich, Robert, 203
Allégret, Yves, 201
Allen, Jay Presson, 112
Altman, Robert, 102, 138
American Cinema, 204
American Cinema Editors, 10, 127
Andersson, Harriet, 91, 101, 115
Animation, xi, 69, 94, 132. See also U.P.A.
Anscochrome, 15. See also Color film
Antonioni, Michelangelo, x, xii–xiv, 19, 44, 76, 112, 131–32, 203
Architecture, 49
Arkin, Alan, 102
Arnheim, Rudolf, 12, 15, 44, 99–101, 110, 112, 195–96, 199
Arnold, Matthew, xiv
Arp, Jean, 237
Art of the Moving Picture, The (Lindsay), 183
Articulation, first/second, 220
Aspect ratio, 15, 197. See also Wide screen
Aspects of the Novel (Forster), xii
Astaire, Fred, 119, 158, 239
Astor, Mary, 34–40, 47
Astruc, Alexander, 203
Audience, 227, 229, 231, 247; attendance, x, 140, 247; catharsis, 118; identification, 6, 80–81, 105–6; interest in stars, 155–57
Audion tube, 13

Austerlitz, Frederick. See Astaire, Fred
Autant-Lara, Claude, 201
Auteurism, 39, 200–215, 218–19. See also Director
Autry, Gene, 119

"B" Pictures, 14, 228, 232
Baker, Norma Jean. See Monroe, Marilyn
Balázs, Béla, 193
Balzac, Honoré de, 230, 233
Barr, Charles, 146
Barrymore, John, 92
Barthes, Roland, 220
Bartlett, Scott, 188
Basehart, Richard, 212
Bauhaus, 237
Baum, Vicki, 175
Bazin, André, 6, 28, 31–32, 50–51, 196–97, 199, 201–2, 205, 220
Beatles, The, 76
Beatty, Warren, 137–38, 165, 167
Bechet, Sidney, 97
Becker, Jacques, 201, 203
Beckett, Samuel, 45–46, 235
Belasco, David, 30–31
Belmondo, Jean-Paul, 207
Belson, Jordan, 128
Benedek, Laslo, 112
Benito Cereno (Melville), 100
Benski, 97
Benton, Robert, 138
Bergman, Ingmar, xiii–xiv, 9, 91, 101, 112, 117, 128, 130–31, 189, 203, 209
Bergson, Henri, 4, 191
Bertolucci, Bernardo, 233
Beyle, Marie Henri. See Stendhal
Bierce, Ambrose, xiii, 78
Billboard, 219
Biograph Company, 31

267

Black, Alexander, 82
Black-and-white film, 13, 79; in *The God-father*, 101; as value-inflected, 100. *See also* Emulsion
Black Mask, 34
Blacks: exploitation films for, 118; in *King Solomon's Mines,* 175; treatment of, in films of Griffith, 191; treatment of, in films of Sturges, 80
Blau, Herbert, 238
Blondes, 119. *See also* Hawn, Goldie; Holliday, Judy; Monroe, Marilyn; Rogers, Ginger
Bluestone, George, 34
Boetticher, Budd, 206
Bogart, Humphrey, 6–7, 34–40, 47, 156, 158, 207
Bond, Ward, 209
Brackett, Charles, 131
Brakhage, Stan, 19n
Brando, Marlon, 80
Braque, Georges, 240
Brecht, Bertolt, 80–81, 103, 235–36
Bresson, Robert, 93–94, 203
Brialy, Jean-Claude, 208
Brook, Peter, 101
Brooks, Mel, 247
Brooks, Richard, 131
Brophy, Brigid, 42n, 114
Browning, Robert, 30, 114
Brunelleschi, Filippo, 42
Brussels World's Fair (1958), 239
Buñuel, Luis, 44, 75, 128, 190, 203
Burch, Noël, 190–97
Burks, Robert, 68, 128
Burroughs, William, 4

Cage, John, 45, 235
Cagney, James, 156–57
Cahiers du Cinéma, 4, 200–203, 207, 220
Caine, Michael, 159
Calhern, Louis, 156
California Institute of the Arts, 238
Camera obscura, 5
Campbell-Devon Productions, 177
Cantor, Eddie, 96
Capote, Truman, 138
Capra, Frank, xiii–xiv, 131
Cavalcanti, Alberto, 77–78
Chabrol, Claude, 207
Chandler, Raymond, 107, 131
Chaney, Lon, 158
Chaney, Lon, Jr., 24–27
Chaplin, Charlie, 13, 15, 131, 136, 155, 184, 203
Chapman, Christopher, 243
Character: Freudian view of, 22; Jungian view of, 22, 230; and motive, 74; stock,

32. *See also* Detective films; Hero; Heroine; Villain
Chirico, Georgio di, 44
Cinéma vérité, 103, 230, 232–33. *See also* Documentary
CinemaScope, 12, 14–15. *See also* Wide screen; Aspect ratio
Cinémathèque Française, 201
Cinerama, 243
Clair, René, 201
Clarke, Mae, 157
Clarke, Shirley, 128
Clément, René, 201
Clift, Montgomery, 91, 156
Close-up, 59–61
Cocteau, Jean, 19, 75, 78, 201
Cohan, George M., 157
Cohn, Harry, xi
Collins, Ray, 111
Color film, 13–15, 79, 98–102, 165, 171. *See also* Emulsion
Columbia Pictures, xi
Comedy films, 119. *See also* Genre
Comics, xii, 245–49
Comingore, Dorothy, 69
Composition, 38–39, 41–45; and deep focus, 197; and movement, 39, 43–44, 66–71, 192, 195, 197
Conner, Bruce, 189
Conrad, Joseph, 132
Conventions: in film, 24–27; in narrative, xi, 23–27; in theater, 29–30. *See also* Melodrama
Cook, Elisha, Jr., 37
Cooper, Gary, 120
Coppola, Francis Ford, 101
Cortázar, Julio, 132
Cortez, Stanley, 151, 165
Costume, 134, 174
Coutard, Raoul, 147
Cowan, Jerome, 158
Creative Evolution (Bergson), 4
Criticism, film, 183–87. *See also* *Auteurism*
Crosscutting. *See* Parallel editing
Cubism, 43, 45, 240
Cukor, George, 176
cummings, e. e., 189
Curtis, Tony, 136
Curtiz, Michael, 214

Dagurreotype, 42
Dali, Salvador, 44, 190
Daniels, William, 142, 149–50
Daumier, Honoré, 42
Davis, Bette, 197
Dean, James, 156
Death in Venice (Mann), 21
De Forest, Lee, 13
Degas, Edgar, 42–43

Delannoy, Jean, 201
Delluc, Louis, 59–60
Demy, Jacques, 203
Deren, Maya, 164
Detective films, 6–7, 34–40, 120. *See also*
  Genre
Dialogue: dubbing of, 95–96; recording of,
  94–96, 102; synchronization of, with pic-
  ture, 95–96
Diamond, I. A. L., 131
Diapolyecran, 243
Dickens, Charles, 30, 32, 50
Dietrich, Marlene, 149–50
Dillon, Matt. *See* "Gunsmoke"
Director, 134–41, 162; and actor, 136–37;
  and cameraman, 142; as creative artist,
  138–39; and editor, 140, 161–62; and
  scriptwriter, 128–29, 131, 140; style of,
  140–41. *See also Auteurism*
Director's Guild of America, 127, 138
Disney, Walt, 14, 94, 209
Disney Circle-Vision, 242
Dissolve, 74, 91, 162, 165, 170, 212
Distribution, 231–32
Documentary, 17–21, 51, 78–79, 102–3,
  232–35. *See also Cinéma vérité*
Doniol-Valcroze, Jacques, 201
Dos Passos, John, 77
Dostoevsky, Feodor, 39
Dovzhenko, Alexander, 45
Dreiser, Theodore, 214
Dreyer, Carl, 64, 131, 137, 203
Dubbing, 95–96
Du Pont "World of Chemistry" (1964 New
  York World's Fair), 238, 242
Duchamp, Marcel, 44
Dumas, Alexandre, 157
DuMaurier, George, 5
Dunaway, Faye, 166
Durgnat, Raymond, 51
Dwan, Alan, 66, 138
Dylan, Bob, 233

Eames, Charles, 242
Eastman-Kodak Company, 98, 143
Eastman, George, 42
Eastwood, Clint, 156
Edison, Thomas, ix, 13, 91, 147
Editing, 161–67; and director, 140, 161–62;
  and image-to-sound relationships, 162–
  64, 165–67; mechanics of, 161–62; and
  montage, 89; and time, 78, 84–85; and
  visual relationships, 58, 164–65. *See also*
  American Cinema Editors
Eggeling, Viking, 45
Eindeutig, 230
Eisenstein, Sergei Mikhailovich, 57, 64–66,
  85–88, 100, 153, 163, 192–93, 196, 199,
  216, 237

Eisler, Hans, 97
Eisner, Will, 245
Eldridge, John, 78
Eliot, T. S., 207
Emschwiller, Ed, 237, 239
Emulsion, 142, 232; black-and-white, 13,
  79, 101, 165; color, 98–102; affected in
  lab, 102; orthochromatic, 98–99; pan-
  chromatic, 98–99; in relation to lighting,
  99
Evans, Robert, 177
Evening in Byzantium (Shaw), 178
Experimental films, 46, 51, 231, 235, 238
Expo 67, 242–44
Expressionism, 81, 109–15, 151, 195

Fades, 162, 170
Fairbanks, Douglas, 14
Falconetti, Maria, 64, 137
"Falling in Love Again," 149
Farber, Manny, 184, 186, 205
Faulkner, William, 204
Fellini, Federico, xii–xiv, 19, 44, 104, 115,
  131, 203, 211–13
Ferguson, Otis, 184
Fiction film. *See* Narrative film
Fielding, Henry, 80
Fields, W. C., 170
Figueroa, Gabriel, 128
Film: and ambiguity, 7–12; animation, 69,
  94, 132; and dance, 49; and dreaming,
  4–6, 12, 20–22; and illusion, 15, 19, 85,
  87, 169, 195; and painting, 41–46; and
  prose, 32–40, 58–59, 116; and reality, 51;
  and revolution, 51, 89; silent, 13–14;
  sound, 14–15; study of, 255–56; and tele-
  vision, 4–5, 14, 40–41; and theater, 28–
  32, 58–59, 196–97
Film as Art (Arnheim), 195
Film Comment, 186
Film Culture, 186, 203
Film Quarterly, 186
Film Society Review, 186
Film stock: Anscochrome, 15; Technicolor,
  12, 14, 99–100. *See also* Black-and-white
  film; Color film; Emulsion
Film Technique (Pudovkin), 85
Fine cut, 162
Fitzgerald, F. Scott, 177
Flaherty, Robert, 18–19, 98, 233
Flashforward, 75
Flashback, 32, 74, 239. *See also* Vision
  scenes
Fleischer, Richard, 245
"Flicker" films, 191
Fonda, Henry, 210
A Fool and a Girl (Griffith), 230
Ford, Ford Madox, 32

Ford, John, xii–xiv, 96, 106, 120, 156, 203, 209–11, 218
Forster, E. M., xii, 78
Frankenheimer, John, 245
Free Cinema, 232
Freeze-frame, 33, 171
Fuller, Samuel, 203, 205, 207, 214
Futurism, 43

Gable, Clark, 155, 176
Gaffer. *See* Production unit
Gance, Abel, 80, 242
Gangster film, 12, 89, 118–19. *See also* Genre
Garbo, Greta, 149, 175, 207
Garmes, Lee, 145, 150
Gay, John, 101
Genre, 21, 202, 205, 219; and *auteurism*, 117; conventions, 116; cycles of, 119–21; in melodrama, 116, 118; in myth, 116–17; in prose, 116
Getz, Stan, 97
Gide, André, 204
Gilbert, John, 30
Gilbert, William S., 30
Gilliat, Penelope, 184
Glass shot, 169
"God Bless the Child," 191
Godard, Jean-Luc, 9, 16–17, 19, 63, 80–81, 104, 132, 157, 168, 203, 206–9, 215
Goethe, Johann Wolfgang von, 205, 214
Goya, Francisco de, 131
Grant, Cary, 109, 158
Greenstreet, Sidney, 34–40, 47
Griffith, D. W., 30–31, 57, 61–63, 66, 83–85, 131, 153, 191, 196, 199, 208, 236–37, 245
Groenberg, Ake, 91
Guernica (Picasso), 6, 49
Guinness, Alec, 159
"Gunsmoke" (TV series), 10–12, 24–27
Gustafsson, Greta. *See* Garbo, Greta

Haggard, H. Rider, 175
Haiku, 45
Hall, Conrad, 150
Hammett, Dashiell, 6, 10, 34–40, 50–51, 80, 204
Hammid, Alexander, 243
Hardy, Thomas, 32
Harlow, Jean, 155
Has, Wojciech, 74
Hawks, Howard, 106, 129, 157, 203, 206, 218
Hawn, Goldie, 131
Hayward, Susan, 151
Hedda Gabler (Ibsen), 63
Hedren, Tippi, 113
Hegel, Georg, 85, 87, 219
Heller, Joseph, 102

Hemmings, David, 112
Hepburn, Katharine, 158
Hero, 22, 29, 37, 83–84, 117, 214, 218
Heroine, 29, 83–84
Hill, George Roy, 137, 150
Hitchcock, Alfred, 6, 68, 100, 105, 108–9, 111, 113, 128, 131–32, 137–38, 167, 169, 188, 203, 207–8, 214, 233
Holden, William, 132
Holiday, Billie, 191
Holliday, Judy, 130
Hollywood Quarterly, 186
Holmes, Sherlock, 117, 120
Holt, Tim, 111
Horror films, 111, 119, 241. *See also* Genre
Howe, James Wong, 148
Husserl, Edmund, 220
Huston, John, 34–40, 51, 100, 102, 131, 138

Ibsen, Henrik, 63
Idealism, 194
Iliad (Homer), 63
Image: cinematic quality of, 13–15; composition of, 38–39, 41–45; and film stocks, 98–99, 142, 232; and lens, 143–44; and lighting, 144–45; and words, 47–50
Impressionism, 100, 109–10, 113–14
Ince, Thomas, 206
Intercutting, 84, 221
International Association of Theatrical and Stage Employees (IATSE), 127
Ivens, Joris, 102

Jagger, Mick, 234
Jakobson, Roman, 216
James, Henry, 59, 114
Jazz, 184, 204. *See also* Bechet, Sidney; Getz, Stan; Holiday, Billie; Modern Jazz Quartet; Waller, Fats
Jolson, Al, 92
Journal of Popular Film, xiii–xiv
Joyce, James, 77

Kael, Pauline, 184, 205, 214
Kafka, Franz, 50
Karina, Anna, 207
Kazan, Elia, 131, 203
Kelly, Grace, 120
Kerensky, Alexander, 87
Kinetograph, xi, 13
King Solomon's Mines (Haggard), 175
Kino-Automat, 242–43
Kitses, Jim, 218
Kracauer, Siegfried, 20, 193–97, 199
Kubrick, Stanley, 96–97, 100–101, 131, 230
Kuleshov, Lev, 84, 152, 221
Kurosawa, Akira, 77

Laboratory, film processing, 142, 161–62, 165, 168
Labyrinth (Expo 67), 243–45
Laemmle, Carl, 174
Lamarr, Hedy, 148
Lang, Fritz, 203
Last Tycoon, The (Fitzgerald), 177
Laterna Magika, 239–41
Laughton, Charles, 142
Leacock, Richard, 233
Leigh, Janet, 6, 109
Leigh, Vivien, 176
Lemmon, Jack, 136
Lens, 142; anamorphic, 237; and depth of field, 143–44; diopter, 245; and set, 134; and size of image, 143–44; zoom, 68
Lester, Richard, 76
Lévi-Strauss, Claude, 217–19
Lewis, Jerry, 15, 119, 203–4
Lewton, Val, 93, 119, 131, 176, 205
Library of Congress, 58
Light show, xi
Lighting, 39, 142, 144–45; carbon arc, 92; expressionistic, 151; glamour, 148–50; incandescent, 92; limelight, 30. *See also* Black-and-white film; Color film; Emulsion
Lindsay, Vachel, 183
Linguistics, 216–17
"Livery Stable Blues," 184
London, Jack, 30
Lorre, Peter, 34–40, 47
Losey, Joseph, 203
Lucas, George, 77
Lucas, Hans. *See* Godard, Jean-Luc

McCoy, Horace, 75
MacDonald, Dwight, 184
McLaglen, Victor, 209, 211
McLaren, Norman, 237
MacLeish, Archibald, 93
McLuhan, Marshall, 23, 34, 155, 245
"McMillan and Wife" (TV series), 24–27
McTeague (Norris), 209
Magnani, Anna, 159
Magritte, René, 16, 60, 242
Mailer, Norman, 14, 31, 241
Makeup, 99
Malle, Louis, 96–97
Maltese Falcon, The (Hammett), 34–38
Mamoulian, Rouben, 90, 100, 105, 142
Manet, Édouard, 42
Mann, Thomas, 21
March, Frederic, 112, 157
Markson, Morley, 235
Marlowe, Philip. *See* Detective films
Marsh, Mae, 153
Marshall, Herbert, 197

Marx Brothers, 204
Marx, Groucho, 81
Marxism, 118, 191, 193, 203
Masina, Giulietta, 212–13
Mason, James, 109, 241
Massari, Lea, x
Mastroianni, Marcello, 115, 147, 213
Maupassant, Guy de, 132
Mayer, Louis B., 176–77
Maysles, Albert and David, 233–34
Mekas, Adolfas, 7, 237
Méliès, Georges, 14, 83, 168
Melodrama, 29–30, 76, 97, 111, 118, 121; sensation scenes in, 29–30
Melville, Herman, 100
Melville, Jean Pierre, 140–41
Mendilow, A. A., 73
Meter, Ben Van, 238
Metro-Goldwyn-Mayer (M-G-M), 100, 149, 175–76
Metz, Christian, 4, 203, 220–22, 232, 240
Milestone, Lewis, 145
Milius, John, 215
Miller, Arthur, 111
Miller, Arthur C., 145, 210
Minter, Mary Miles, 148
Miró, Joan, 43
Mise-en-scènes, 213
Mixed media, 235–41
Mixer, 136, 163
Mizoguchi, Kenji, 203
Moby Dick (Melville), 100
Modern Jazz Quartet, 97
Moholy-Nagy, Laszlo, 237
Mohr, Hal, 142–43
Monroe, Marilyn, 136, 155–57
Montage, 89
"Montage of attractions," 85
Montgomery, Robert, 107
Moreau, Jeanne, 147
Morin, Edgar, 103
Morrison, Marion. *See* Wayne, John
Motif, 28, 96; in *The Godfather*, 101
Motion-picture equipment: camera, 142–51; crab dolly, 142; crane, 142; film gauge, 143, 243; sound boom, 142. *See also* Lens
Movies into Film (Simon), 89
Moviola, 167
Mozhukin, Ivan Ilyitch, 85, 221
Mrs. Dalloway (Woolf), 77
Multiple image, 241–47
Munch, Edvard, 110
Murnau, F. W., 69, 90, 196
Music, 45–46, 49, 218; as artifact, 96; in *Bonnie and Clyde*, 97, 167; for films, 41, 97, 163, 239; for theater, 29
Music halls, 184
Musicals, 118–19, 218

Narration, 104
Narrative film, xiii, 35
National Film Board of Canada, 243
Neo-impressionism, 109
Neorealism, 76–77, 194–211
New Wave, 232
New York Times, 185
New York World's Fair (1964), 238, 242–43
New Yorker, 185
Newman, David, 138
Newman, Paul, 137
Newman-Foreman, 177
Nichols, Dudley, 96, 209, 211
Nichols, Mike, 102
Nickelodeon, xiii
Niño, Alex N., 247
Niver, Kemp, 58
Norris, Frank, 63, 209
Novel, 42*n*, 45–47, 77, 80
Novels into Film (Bluestone), 34
Nykvist, Sven, 101

"Occurrence at Owl Creek Bridge, An"
    (Bierce), 78
"Odessa Steps" sequence (*The Battleship
    Potemkin*), 64–66
Odyssey (Homer), 63
O'Hara, Maureen, 209
Olivier, Laurence, 159
Once Again Festival, 239–40
One Man and His World (Expo 67), 242–43
O'Neill, Eugene, 81
Ontario: A Place to Stand (Expo 67), 243
Ophuls, Max, 69, 151, 203
Optical effects, 162. *See also* Special effects
Orphism, 43
Ouspenskaya, Maria, 24–27
Out take, 162

Painting, 41–46, 49, 51, 58, 88, 110
Panassié, Hughes, 204
Panavision, 144
Pangborn, Franklin, 158
Paper prints, 58
Paradjanov, Sergei, 101
Parallax, 67, 105; compared to zoom, 68
Parallel editing, 63–64, 77, 221, 245. *See
    also* Editing
Paramount Pictures, 80, 94, 173, 186, 241
Pasolini, Pier Paolo, 117
Peck, Gregory, 102
Peckinpah, Sam, 230
Penn, Arthur, xiii–xvi, 97, 165, 167
Pennebaker, Don, 233
Perkins, Tony, 109
Peter Ibbetson (Du Maurier), 5
Phonetics, 217
Phonograph, 12, 23, 91, 96
Photography, still, 41–47, 51

Picasso, Pablo, 6, 49, 240
Pickford, Mary, 155
Picture (Ross), 176
Pirandello, Luigi, 104
Pixérécourt, René-Charles Guilbert de, 29
Poetry, 41, 45–46, 51
Point of view, 103–15
Politique des auteurs, la. See Auteurism
Popeye, 189
Pornographic film, 22, 230, 232. *See also*
    Behind the Green Door *in Index of Film
    Titles*
Porter, Edwin S., 83
Positif, 203
Prague Circle of Linguists, 216–17
Preminger, Otto, 203
Printing: contact, 170; mattes, 171, 240;
    optical, 171
Private eye. *See* Detective films
Producer, 135, 154, 173–77
Production unit: assistant director, 135;
    camera operator, 136; chief electrician
    (gaffer), 137; cinematographer, 136, 142–
    51, 165–70; director, 134–41; script girl,
    135–36; unit manager, 135
Programmers. *See* "B" pictures
Properties, 134
Proust, Marcel, 4, 28
Publicity, 186
Pudovkin, Vsevolod, 85, 90, 97, 108
Purvis, Melvin, 215

Quinn, Anthony, 212

Radio, 12, 95, 197
Ragtime, 45
Raw and the Cooked, The (Lévi-Strauss),
    218
Ray, Nicholas, 203, 207
Ray, Satyajit, 77
Réage, Pauline, 239
Realism, 192, 247
Rear-screen projection, 113, 169–70
Redford, Robert, 138
Reinhardt, Gottfried, 176
Renoir, Jean, 37, 69–71, 140–41, 194, 201–3,
    207
Renoir, Pierre Auguste, 42, 202
Resnais, Alain, 19, 28, 78, 93, 164, 191, 197,
    203, 208, 221
Reynolds, Burt, 249
Reynolds, Sir Joshua, 100
Richter, Hans, 45
Riefenstahl, Leni, 108
Ring and the Book, The (Browning), 114
Riskin, Robert, 131
Rivette, Jacques, 203
Rivkin, Allen, 34
RKO Radio Pictures, 119, 151, 168, 239

Robinson, Edward G., 158
Rocha, Glauber, 118
Rogers, Ginger, 119, 158, 239
Rohmer, Eric, 203
Rolling Stones, The, 234
Ross, Diana, 191
Ross, Lillian, 176
Rossellini, Roberto, 97, 203, 208, 211
Rouch, Jean, 103, 203, 233
Rough cut, 162
Rushes, 161
Russian formalism, 216
Ruttmann, Walter, 45

Saint, Eva Marie, 109
Sanctuary (Faulkner), 204
Sanders, George, 155–56
Sarris, Andrew, 203–4
Satie, Erik, 45
Saussure, Ferdinand de, 220
Schary, Dore, 176–77
Schlesinger, John, 176
Schulberg, B. P., 173
Scott, George C., 177
Scott, Lizabeth, 47
Screen, movie: aspect ratio, 15, 197; and composition, 38–39, 41–45. *See also* Wide screen
Screen Actors Guild, 127
Scriptwriting, 129–33, 232; examples, 112–13, 129, 200–201. *See also* Dialogue
Seberg, Jean, 207
Seldes, Gilbert, 184
Selznick, David O., 175–76
Selznick-International, 175
Semiology, 220–23
Semiotics. *See* Semiology
Sennett, Mack, 206
Set design, 134, 174
Seurat, Georges, 110
Seyrig, Delphine, 164, 197–98
Shamroy, Leon, 145
Shaw, Irwin, 176
She (Haggard), 175
Shklovsky, Victor, 216
Shot: angles, 39; close-ups, 59–61; in comics, 245–46; editing conventions of, 24–27; establishing, 60; high-angled, 108; low-angled, 108, 111; movement of, 39, 134; over-the-shoulder, 107; point of view of, 105; reaction, 221; wide-angled, 197
Sica, Vittorio de, 153, 194
Siegel, Don, 121, 206
Silliphant, Stirling, 177
Simile, 87
Simon, John, 89, 184
Simon, Michel, 207
Sinatra, Frank, 121

"Singing in the Rain," 97
Skolimowski, Jerzy, 117
Smith, Henry Nash, 218
Smith, Red, 185
Snow, Michael, 189
Sontag, Susan, 8, 189, 191
Sound, 90–97, 132, 162, 169, 175; aesthetic, 15; amplification of, 13; beginning of, in film, 92; dialogue, 96; dubbing, 95–96; editing, 165; mechanics of recording, 95–96; synchronization of, with picture, 93, 95–96
Sound effects, 162, 166
Space, 33, 49–50, 57–81
Spade, Sam. *See* The Maltese Falcon *in Index of Film Titles*
Spirit, The (Eisner), 247
Steiner, Max, 176
Stendhal, 51
Sternberg, Josef von, 94, 142, 149–50
Stevens, George, 91
Stewart, James, 109
Still cameraman, 136
Stiller, Mauritz, 207
Story of O, The (Réage), 239–40
Strode, Woody, 209
Stroheim, Erich von, 128, 131, 138–39, 153, 175, 196, 209
Structuralism, 217–19
Sturges, Preston, 80, 205, 209
Styles of Radical Will (Sontag), 8
Subtitles, 95–96
Sucksdorff, Arne, 78
Supporting actors, 158–59
Supporting actresses, 158–59
Surrealism, 44, 204
Svoboda, Josef, 239
Swanson, Gloria, 132
Switchback. *See* Parallel editing

Tales of Hoffmann (Hoffmann), 239
Tati, Jacques, 203
Taylor, Elizabeth, 19, 91, 158
Technicolor, 12, 14, 99–100
Telephone, 12, 23
Television: compared to film, 40–41; as competition to film, 14, 145, 227–28, 249; criticism, 185, 187; and film distribution, 120, 231; films for, xii, 164; optical effects of, 241; pace of, 4–5; reporting news on, 232; and space, 61
Thalberg, Irving, 174–75, 177
Theater: canned, 15; collaborations of, with film, 235, 238; compared to film, 28–32, 58–59, 196–97; dramatic structure in, 34; lighting, 14, 30; and melodrama, 29–30; music for, 29; and ritual, 31; and space, 49; and time, 49
Theory of Film (Kracauer), 194

Theory of Film Practice (Burch), 190, 197
They Shoot Horses, Don't They? (McCoy), 75
Thompson, Francis, 241, 243
Threepenny Opera, The (Weill-Brecht), 81, 103
Through the Looking Glass (Carroll), 16
Time, xii, 14, 49, 78, 247; and ellipsis, 84–85, 165; manipulation of, 73–81; and narrative chronology, 33–34, 73–81. See also Flashforward; Flashback
Todd-AO, 15
Toland, Gregg, 69, 150, 210–11
Tom Jones (Fielding), 80
Totter, Audrey, 107
Toulouse-Lautrec, Henri de, 100
Tracy, Spencer, 157
Tri-Ergon, 92
Tristram Shandy (Sterne), 32
Trubetsky, N. S., 216
Truffaut, François, xi, 31, 77, 140–41, 169, 199, 200–204, 214, 232
Trumball, Douglas, 245
"Try a Little Tenderness," 96
Twentieth Century-Fox, 94, 155
Twenty Years After (Dumas), 157
Two Weeks in Another Town (Shaw), 178
Typage, 153

UFA Studios, 111
Ulysses (Joyce), 77
Unions, 136
United Artists, 186
Universal Pictures, 143, 174
Unmarked Interchange (Once Again Festival, Ann Arbor), 239–40
U.P.A., 94
U.S.A. (Dos Passos), 77

Valentino, Rudolph, 157
Van Gogh, Vincent, 102
Vanity Fair (Thackeray), 100
Varda, Agnès, 73, 80, 203
Vertov, Dziga, 104, 203
Vicomte Lepic et ses deux filles, Le (Degas), 43
Videotape, xii, 228, 232
Village Voice, 204
Villain, 22, 29, 35, 37, 84, 117, 119, 121, 218
Virgin Land, The (Smith), 218

Visconti, Luchino, 194, 203, 209, 218
Vision scenes, 30. See also Flashbacks
Vitaphone, 92
Vitascope, xi
Vitti, Monica, x, 112
Vogelsang, Judith, 102
Vonnegut, Kurt, Jr., xi
Vorkapich, Slavko, 89

Wagner, Richard, 28
Waller, Fats, 186
Walsh, Raoul, 157
War and Peace (Tolstoy), 32
Warhol, Andy, xi, 236, 242
Warner, Jack, 34, 148
Warner Brothers, 34, 37, 91–92, 158, 177
Wayne, John, 106, 157, 158, 209, 211, 219
We Are Young (Expo 67), 243
Weill, Kurt, 97
Welch, Raquel, 249
Welles, Orson, 12, 50, 59, 95, 111, 119, 140, 142, 203, 208
Western, 119–20, 210. See also Genre
What Is Cinema? (Bazin), 6
Whiteman, Paul, 184
Whitney, John, 128
Wide screen, 99, 145–47, 196–98, 214. See also Aspect ratio
Wiene, Robert, 110
Wilder, Billy, 131
Wills, Chill, 159
Wilmington, Michael, 202
Wilson, Edmund, 184
Winters, Shelley, 91
Wise, Robert, 245
Wiseman, Frederick, 234
Wollen, Peter, 218
Woodward, Joanne, 249
Woolf, Virginia, 59, 77
Wordsworth, William, 77
Workprint, 161–62
Writers Guild of America, 127; strike by, 131
Wyler, William, 129, 197

Yablans, Frank, 177

Zappa, Frank, 232
Zavattini, Cesare, 76–77, 153
Zola, Émile, 28, 77, 230